TAIWAN CONNECTIONS: FOND MEMORIES

By Faye Pearson

www.xulonpress.com

Table of Contents

Dedication:

I lovingly dedicate this book to missionary children (MKs) who went with their missionary parents to East Asia. They endured hardships, struggles, victories and challenges alongside their parents. Most of them, never once, questioned their parents' call, that brought them to a strange place they learned to love and call "home." They blessed our lives abundantly with their smiles, hugs, laughs, jokes, winsome personalities, adventuresome spirits, and their love for the Lord Jesus and for life.

Acknowledgments:

M any thanks to the thirty missionaries who were willing to share their journeys of faith with me. Without their taking the time to share their stories, journals, articles and notes, there would be no book.

A big thank you to my brother, Harold; a dear friend, Ms. Ruby Lee Knight; and missionary colleagues, Patsy and Hunter Hammett, for their valuable insights and to Karen McFetridge for assisting me with her excellent computer skills. Each one made the 'impossible" task easier.

A large thank you to Michelle Levigne for her encouraging and gentle spirit and the endless hours spent on editing. What would this book look like without Michelle?

A special thank you to Judy Gibbons and the Xulon Press staff, who made the process seem so simple and finally made it happen.

And, with a heart filled with gratitude and praise to our gracious and loving God, who called us to serve Him through loving and sharing His amazing love with Chinese people.

FOREWORD

A t the age of twelve, God called me to be a missionary. He used various experiences, schools, churches, ministries, family and friends to equip me for missionary service.

Sixteen years later, I was appointed as a missionary to Taiwan. I saw myself as an ordinary person, however, I became part of a mission family whom I saw as extraordinary—gifted, talented, highly qualified and richly experienced in music, theological education, church education, evangelism, church planting, etc. How blessed I was to work alongside these missionaries.

From 1999-2004, I taught at the Nanjing Theological Seminary in China. In the fall of 2004, I returned to the Taiwan Baptist Theological Seminary in Taipei to assist the Seminary in writing the curriculum for a newly established missions department, and direct the ministry of the World Mission Center.

I was surprised and thrilled to see the emphasis being given to global missions. The students and faculty were interested in missions. Faculty was placing more emphasis on contextual Christianity and encouraging students to participate in short-term mission trips. Students came to my office asking, "How does one know God is calling him or her into missionary service? How could God use someone with limited experience, a non-Christian background? How does one confront parents when they are strongly opposed to their children serving as missionaries? How does one become willing for their children to grow up in a foreign country?" These and other questions created the desire within my heart to use stories of missionaries who came to Taiwan to encourage our students in their seeking to know and follow God's plan for their lives.

The book, *A Link In God's Chain*, was published in Chinese, October 2008.

Approximately 270 Baptist missionaries were appointed or transferred from other countries to Taiwan between 1949-1997. I have chosen to tell the stories of thirty of these missionaries who were appointed to Taiwan between 1952-1976. These are the stories of ordinary men and women from the cities and rural communities of America. They met, fell in love, married, and started families. All of them wanted to be involved in church-related ministries, and most of them wanted to be used in the major cities and large churches in America until God opened their eyes to see a world where people lived without having heard the name of Jesus. They experienced the call of a Holy God to a far-away, undeveloped country filled with breath-taking beauty, exotic smells, strange sights and a charming, inspiring people – Formosa – Beautiful Island – Taiwan, Republic of China.

The experiences these missionaries have shared, gathered into this book, occurred during war and peace, victory and defeat, disappointment and excitement, as these couples sought to live out their response to God's call in a strange land. These are stories of fear and calmness, of loss and gain, of failure and success, of hurt and blessings, of faith and doubt. These are stories of tears and of laughter, sickness and health, and how they learned to depend on the faithfulness of their powerful, awesome God.

The stories now come to you in English. It is my hope that those who read this book will catch a new vision and develop a deeper passion to share "The Old, Old Story of Jesus and His Love" with those near and far.

Charles and Dona Culpepper
A Couple for the Chinese

Life's Start

Genetics, role models, influence, talents, education, circumstances, and culture are the ingredients that become in His hands stuff of divine process. The author sees all of these in the lives of two called Charles and Dona.

The twentieth century was only 20 years old when Charles Culpepper, Jr., entered the world, in the famous cowboy town of Fort Worth, TX, which housed the well-known Southwestern Baptist Theological Seminary, where his parents were students.

Little Charles was very young during his first stay at Southwestern, but the influence of Texas remained with him for a lifetime. His parents graduated from Southwestern Seminary, and pastored small, rural churches. They were, however, committed to leave Texas for missionary service to China.

Bound for China

Charles was only three years old when he sailed with his parents to far-away China. He was an active little guy who entertained his parents, other missionaries, and total strangers on the ship. About the fifth day out, a tidal wave caused by a monstrous earthquake in Japan rocked their ship, and most of the passengers were terribly seasick. Charles, though he was a toddler, took it upon himself to pat the sick adults and try to entertain them, expressing words of sympathy and encouragement. The jokes and entertainment became a part of him.

When they reached Japan, they couldn't disembark, due to the total destruction caused by the earthquake. The missionary families studied the terrible destruction from the ship. Houses were still burning and human bodies floated in the bay. After this experience, landing in China was a relief. However, all these new and shocking experiences must have been hard on such a young boy.

The first year, 1923, his parents studied Mandarin Chinese in Beijing, and spent many hours in language school away from home. Charles was surrounded by people who looked different and spoke a different language, so his first memories as a three-year-old were of a strange land and feeling lonely.

His family moved to Shandong Province in north China. His father served in orphanages and worked with rural churches. Later, his father taught in theological education. But when Charles was young, his father was known for riding a horse to the churches in the province, since many roads were merely paths impassable for motorized vehicles.

The Kid at Boarding School

There were no international schools for the missionary kids to attend, so the children were home schooled or sent away to boarding school. Charles was eight years old when he went to Chifu to attend the school for the children of missionaries, established and operated by the China Inland Mission. The children who attended the school were from England and Scotland, and ten children were from the U.S. The educational system was British, so not only was Charles educated in the British system, he also spoke English with a British accent.

The dorm rooms were small, but they still housed three or four boys in one room. He and the others were typical boys, ready to enjoy life and adventure. There was emphasis on academia and sports. Charles liked sports. They played soccer and football, since most of the students were from the two countries where these sports were emphasized. Charles liked recess times the best, because the boys could swim in the Pacific Ocean.

Charles missed home. His father came to Chifu once a month to purchase groceries and other supplies. He always took Charles to lunch, and Charles drank his first Coca-Cola on one of these visits, when they saw colas in one of the stores.

He went home for two weeks during Easter holidays and two months during Christmas and Chinese New Year. He also had summer vacation. These were hard days for a young boy away from home. Boarding school was difficult on missionary children. Many children carried the pain all of their lives. Charles had already retired and returned to Taiwan to teach one semester at the Taiwan Baptist Seminary when he and the author were on the same flight to Hong Kong. He shared experiences from his childhood growing up in Shandong Province. He said with a cracking voice and tears in his eyes, "I still remember how lonely I was the day my father left me at the Boarding School in Chifu. I was just a little boy. As I grew older, I made the decision that I would never send my children to boarding school until they were in high school, and only then, if they wanted to go."

During the time Charles was away at boarding school, his baby sister, Carolyn died of dysentery. Carolyn was only four years old when she died of this ravaging illness, however, her short life had a great impact on many people. It could even be said that she once had saved many lives.

In those times, warlords, government forces, and bandits were constantly at war. Little Carolyn was on a bus with her father, Charles Culpepper, Sr., when angry soldiers stopped the bus. It was pretty clear that they planned to kill everyone on the bus by rolling it down a hill. Her father had hidden Carolyn behind a curtain on the bus, hoping to protect her. But the angry leader of the militia yanked the curtain back, only to see a little "foreign devil girl" with ringlets, who very politely said in flawless Chinese, "Honorable sir, how are you?" The soldier was speechless for a minute or two, and then could not help the smile that spread over his face over the incongruity of this beautiful white girl's politeness. Finally, he began to laugh, and eventually waved the bus on. All of the people on the bus were thankful for the little "foreign devil" who saved their lives.

Charles' command of the Chinese language was also amazing, and at school he was exposed to other languages, too. One boy came from a Russian family, and he and Charles decided to confront each other's wrestling skills. They wrestled all afternoon, but he could never pin Charles to the floor, so Charles was declared the winner. The award was for the boy to teach Charles a few words of Russian. The phrase the boy taught him was probably total gobble-dygook, but it sounded intense, so it became a popular word in the Culpepper household for the second, third and fourth generations. It might be pointed out that Charles never knew the meaning of the "Russian phrase," but this may have been the beginning of Charles' interest in languages.

Charles' Spiritual Growth

The missionary teachers from England had the souls of their students on their hearts. When Charles was about eight years old, one of the teachers told the story about the three men in the fiery furnace and how they were saved by Christ's presence. When she asked if they planned on being alone in their troubles without Jesus, she noticed that Charles had tears in his eyes. She told him that if he still wanted to think about the question that night, he could come to her to talk. He did, he went, and he gave his life to the Lord.

Charles was privileged to grow up in the Shandong Revival era. The revival began with the spirit of conviction among the missionaries. The missionaries felt the need to seek cleansing from sin, and they also were aware that James 5:16-17 speaks of confession of sins as a part of physical healing. Ola Culpepper, Charles' mother, was going blind, and there was nothing the doctors could do. The missionaries had gathered for a prayer session to seek God and to confess sins, and then to pray for the healing of Ola's eyes. The missionaries confessed their sins, asking forgiveness from God and confessing their jealousy, etc., to each other. They all were in prayer and brokenness, seeking the Lord. The Holy Spirit took over the meeting and miraculous healings of emotional and spiritual wounds occurred.

A few hours later, they remembered they had not prayed for God to heal Mrs. Culpepper's eyes. She, also, had forgotten they were gathered to pray for her healing. She then realized that her eyes had been healed! (She didn't wear glasses again until a few years before she died at age 90.) This was the beginning of the great Shandong Revival for Baptist missionaries in China.

Soon, the power of the Holy Spirit that flowed from the Shandong Province began to change even the children. Mary, Charles' sister who had been born two years after Carolyn died, was very touched by God's convicting Holy Spirit. She was a tomboy, always pulling some stunt or antic. At night as she lay in bed, she would remember sins she had committed that day, and she felt compelled to wake up her parents and confess. She later said that she had been spared one confession because she had actually been caught at that particular one!

Charles, who was in his preteen years, was also influenced by the prayer and spirit of those days. He wrote later, "I was truly revived. That was the beginning of five great years of growth at school. I led my first person to Christ and was active in spiritual growth."

The Man and His Dogs

There were many things to like about Charles. However, one had to like his dogs if one wanted to spend time with him. His love for dogs started early in life. Sister Mary writes, "It seems he inherited this love for animals and particularly for dogs from father. We spent endless hours training the family's dogs and teaching them tricks. They never had any of those little fluffy dogs people pamper today and keep in the house. They were usually German shepherds or hunting dogs which stayed outside and were treasured friends and very obedient."

An important dog in Charles' life was Wolfe. He got him when he was 15 years old, while still living in Chifu. He and his father purchased him from a missionary family in Jinan City for five yuan. Wolfe had weak bones, but he was very alert and a very good watch dog. He was Charles' best friend and his companion as he explored the countryside on his bicycle during summer holidays. Once, when Charles' bike was stolen, Wolfe traced the path the thief had taken by tracking the scent, and Charles was able to find the bike in a neighboring town! Wolfe stayed with the family after Charles returned to the U.S. for college.

Wolfe was with Charles' father when he was interned by the Japanese. Wolfe wouldn't leave Charles senior. The Japanese soldiers wouldn't give Wolfe any food, so he starved to death. He was a friend to the end, loving and caring for his best friend's father.

College for a 17-Year-Old

Charles graduated from high school in 1937, three weeks after the Japanese had invaded the capital city of Beijing. He had received 23 credits in the ten years it took for him to graduate from high school, whereas the U.S. system required only 16 credits and gave a student twelve years to complete the work. With a British accent and a background rooted in north China's soil, an all-grown-up 17-year-old arrived at Baylor University in Waco, TX. Charles majored in philosophy and explored the new field of girls. He had never dated a girl alone. They had "double-dating" or what the boys called "gang dating" in North China. His first date at Baylor was with a girl with whom he talked about Algeria all evening. Needless to say, she did not want another date with the missionary kid from China. Charles reported that he dated lots of girls, but girls were not standing in line asking for a free ticket to Tibet, where Charles wanted to go as a missionary.

Charles' years at Baylor were filled with socializing with friends; dogs, studying, girls, sports, and participating in the missions activities on and off campus, and what he called a "quarter-time preacher." This meant that he preached at a church every 4th Sunday. It was a common practice for small rural churches that didn't have the resources to pay the salary for a full-time preacher. He received $25U.S. per month, but after the first year at one of the churches, the chairman of deacons told him, "We can find better preaching for less money, so we are going to let you go." Little did that rural Texas church realize they were "letting go" a young man who would assist in training hundreds of young Chinese men and women for worldwide ministry.

Seminary Hill and God's Surprise

It was natural for Charles to plan to attend Southwestern Baptist Theological Seminary, because he had been born there 20 years before. He and his roommate, Ralph Reasor were serious students. Studies and grades were top priority for the young seminarians, and they didn't have much time for extra-curricular activities. By this time, Charles knew Tibet was closed to mission work, but he was definitely committed to serve overseas.

History Changes Lives

Charles didn't realize then that a young woman with a Swedish heritage would change his life. Her grandpa, Nels Wendell, came from Sweden to the United States in the 1800s. It took hard work and determination to survive life in Nebraska, where he and his wife (also from Sweden) home-steaded. They arrived in their new land in midwinter and had to hack out blocks of frozen dirt to build the sod house that got them through their first year. As farmers, they needed a son to farm the land, but God blessed them with only daugh-ters. There were eight of them, and Dona's mother was the seventh daughter, Lillian Wendell. Lillian grew up and left a teaching career for life in the city of Omaha, NE. She enjoyed her job in a large real estate company, learned to drive, and owned a car with her sister. It was during this time, that she met "B.B." Jones.

Bernard B. Jones had graduated from college in Iowa and became an expert in developing farming as an industry. He met, dated and married Lillian, and after seven married years in Wisconsin, they had a baby girl. They had planned for a boy, and they had already embroidered many of the baby items with "Donald"! So when a girl arrived instead, they unraveled just the last "d" in the baby things she had embroidered and named her "Donal." After they married, Charles renamed her "Dona," and that seemed to take.

B.B. Jones' world was turned upside down when Lillian died two years later, but after about two years, he met and married Helen Bonebreak. The family moved to New Orleans, where B.B. became a developer for the city.

Dona became a Christian at an early age, and after graduating from Louisiana State University with a major in pipe organ, she entered Southwestern Baptist Theological Seminary to work towards a Master's degree in religious education. She wanted so much to glorify and honor the Lord by serving in church work. She didn't know it at the time, but years later, when asked why she went to the seminary, she would say, "I was there to answer Ola Culpepper's prayers. For you see, she started praying for Charles' wife when he was four years old."

Back to Seminary Hill

Back to Charles and Southwestern: Charles met a young, attractive freshman girl who worked in the library. Her name was Dona Jones from New Orleans, LA. Their first encounter could have simply been called a failure. Charles always liked challenges, and he knew this girl was going to be a challenge!

Dona worked in the library stacks in the evening. Charles had come to the library to study, and had managed to sneak his pet Chihuahua in. He was very well trained, and would sit for hours under Charles' chair while Charles studied. Dona, the night librarian, noticed students were laughing and pointing at the little dog, and she went to talk to this student about causing a disturbance in the library, to say nothing about the rule that pets couldn't be there to begin with! Dona informed the missionary kid from China that canine friends, regardless of how polite they were, were not allowed in the library. As they discussed the situation, she eventually agreed to let things be, but he had definitely taken notice of the young woman from New Orleans.

Dona was a popular young woman on campus, and Charles had to stand in line for his turn to date her. The first time he asked Dona out on a date, she refused, stating that she didn't know him well enough. He finally reached his goal of getting a date with Dona. It was March 17, 1942. He had learned by this time not to talk about Algeria on the first date, but he tried to hold her hand and she demurred. Dona had many young pursuers. She was dating a young medical student when she had made the decision to enter Southwestern Seminary. He had wanted her to make a commitment to marry him before she left for Fort Worth, but she surprised herself when she answered him, "I can't. I'm going to be a missionary to China." She declares, "To this day I don't know where this statement came from, because I had no such plans!"

Charles never minded competition, and he surely didn't when it came to pursuing a relationship with Dona. A short time into their courtship, she was involved in a minor car accident. Dona stayed in the hospital for a few days. One morning, the physician looked out the window and said, "Here comes Henry with a few red roses," and then he said, "Oh, here comes Charles with a dozen red roses!" She received several proposals, but she didn't accept any of them for some unknown reason. Charles realized this was the woman whom he wanted to take on the mission field. He knew she had the makings of a good wife, mother, missionary and colleague. She was beautiful, charming, talented, had a good sense of humor, and he was in love. How could he help her to realize "her calling" to be his wife?

The decision wasn't as easy for Dona, because Charles was going to be a missionary and she didn't have a call from the Lord to serve on the foreign mission field. She was growing more in love with the young man from China, but she couldn't agree to marry him.

Missionary Service

The Foreign Mission Board (now International Mission Board) was anxious to have a large number of missionaries appointed and ready to go to China when the war was over. Dr. Baker James Cauthen set up a meeting to talk with Charles and Dona. They had to face the question of whether or not she was called to be a missionary. She clearly stated that she had not received a call from God to be a missionary. Dr. Cauthen then asked her, "Do you feel called to be Charles' wife?" and she could answer a very strong, affirmative "yes."

The Foreign Mission board was anxious for Charles and Dona to be appointed, so they were appointed as two single missionaries for missionary service to China in April of 1944. They were married on July 14, 1944 in New Orleans.

They were ready to depart for China, but the dark days of World War II prevented their departure for the land of Charles' childhood. Charles pastored First Baptist Church in Eagle Lake, TX. Tom, their first child, was born while they were there.

Back to the Middle Kingdom

The Foreign Mission Board had a large number of missionaries under appointment for Japan and China. They were waiting on the west coast for ships with soldiers coming home from World War II to arrive in San Francisco. As the service men disembarked, the missionaries of various denominations would board these ships that would transport them across the Pacific to lands that war had destroyed. These ships returning to Asia were filled to capacity with missionaries. Male and female were separated into two holds: one for men and the other one for women and children. They slept on hammocks. Tom was a little guy, approximately two years old. Dona chained his bed (a laundry basket) to her hammock to keep him from rolling away from her as the ship rocked on the waves.

In early 1946, Charles, Dona and little Tom arrived in Beijing. Charles still remembered and used his Shandong language. Charles and Dona studied Mandarin in Beijing. And, much to Charles' frustration, Dona made better grades than he did, because the teachers spent the year trying to eliminate his Shandong dialect and accent.

This China wasn't the China that Charles had left some ten years earlier. Everything was damaged or destroyed by World War II, and the Communists were fast claiming the country. Dona and Charles had been appointed to do evangelism work and plant churches in Zhejiang Province, in the city of Yangchou. Yangchou is one of China's most beautiful cities, surrounded by rivers, lakes, and traditional architecture. Dona went to work on setting up the house, hanging curtains, unpacking wedding gifts, making a quiet, restful place for her husband and son. They planned to stay a lifetime. Within a month, the Communist armies were bombing outside the city as they advanced on the Nationalist Chinese armies. The U.S. Counsel told Charles and Dona to leave that night. They had time to pack only family pictures and their toothbrushes before fleeing to Shanghai to stay with Charles' parents. Charles Culpepper, Sr. was the president at the All China Theological Seminary in Shanghai at that time. During this time in Shanghai, Dona gave birth to Tom's baby sister, Carolyn, in 1948.

However, the country was in disarray and the U.S. Embassy soon informed the missionaries it was time to leave the country. Dona and Charles discussed and prayed about their future. They continued to work – preaching, feeding the hungry, finding transportation for the refugees, and encouraging the believers. However, it was getting more and more difficult to do this. They were not only in danger themselves, but in some ways they put Chinese believers in danger by their presence.

The Mission Board made plans for the missionaries to continue language studies in the Philippines. Charles and Dona left China for the Philippines, feeling somewhat a failure. They had been there less than two years. There were so many people, so many needs, and they were being told to leave. Would they ever return?

After a year of continued Chinese language study in the Philippines, Charles felt the pull to return to China, to see if he could work under the Communist system. Dr. Cliff and Ann Harris and Charles went to Kweilin to help and support the churches and the many refugees who were coming from North China. Soon after arriving, Charles was involved in various ministries including medical ministry, assisting missionaries, and Chinese brothers and sisters. Needs were overwhelming and needed resources were in short supply. Charles was often called in to help with surgeries, usually administering the ether anesthesia (for which he had no training) due to the shortage of medical workers.

They were confronted by dangerous experiences every day. During Charles' stay in Kweilin, he wore rural Chinese clothing. The Communist soldiers, who considered Americans their enemies, would ask the local people if Charles were Chinese. They would tell the soldiers to go ask him. When they did, he would speak Shandong dialect, and this would confuse the soldiers even more. Some of them never figured out that he was a foreigner.

When it finally became too dangerous for the Chinese Christians for the Americans to be there, they knew they had to leave. The trains leaving China for Hong Kong were totally packed with people desperate to get to a safer place. Charles and Dr. and Mrs. Harris managed to get seats on one of these southbound trains. However, even though they had seats, the train was so crammed with people that there was no room to sit down. There were even people stuffed in the luggage racks above the seats! All the people were hungry, frustrated, scared, homeless and confused. Charles and the Harrises ate their last can of peaches, and then they had to use the can for bathroom facilities, since no one could move in any direction on the train because there were so many people!

On the second day of the journey, the train was stopped because the Nationalist soldiers and the Communists were in battle on the train tracks. Many people left the train because they didn't want to be in the crossfire. When Nationalist planes started flying over to bomb the train and the Communist army, the engine driven by the conductor took off! They were stuck in the middle of a war! Miraculously, no one was hurt, and the conductor eventually returned after the battling armies moved on. Charles always laughed as he related how he and the Harrises had stayed on the train. It was Ann Harris' birthday, so he felt people in America were praying for Ann's safety. He stayed in her shadow throughout the day because he hoped some of the prayers being said for Ann would cover him as well!

Meanwhile, Dona remained in the Philippines to continue her studies. The Mission administrator for Asia encouraged wives with small children to return to America. Dona had discovered that she was pregnant with her third child, and even though she was torn about returning to the U.S., she knew it would be a burden on the other missionaries in the Philippines to take care of her, a newborn and her other two children. Again, she dealt with disappointment, fears for Charles, and loneliness as she and her two small children boarded the ship for America. She finally docked in San Francisco and made her way to New Orleans, where her parents were living.

Charles Leaves China

The remaining missionaries were being forced to leave China. Charles left China with a sad heart, wondering what the future held for the land he had called home for so many years. However, he had a family in New Orleans and he could hardly wait to be reunited with them. He arrived barely in time for the birth of their third child and second son, Richard. The year was 1950. The city of New Orleans holds many good memories for the family: a new baby joined the family, Tom started school in the French city, and Charles finished his Th.D. at New Orleans Baptist Theological Seminary.

Taiwan Bound

Charles' parents had gone to Taiwan, where Dr. Culpepper, Sr. was involved in church planting and the theological seminary there. Charles and Dona heard about the exciting things happening in Taiwan. Oz and Mary Quick (former missionaries in China) had transferred to Taiwan to join the Culpeppers and six single ladies who were working in student ministries. Charles and Dona felt a sense of rightness to pursue transferring to Taiwan, but the Mission Board didn't encourage this decision because of the Board's policy that parents and children shouldn't serve in the same country.

The island was green and covered with mountains, and refugees were flooding into the island from China. The Nationalist Government had established the Republic of China in Taipei. The needs were great. Theological education was needed to provide leaders for the newly started churches and for the discipling of new believers.

The need for pastors and the response to the Gospel won out over the Mission Board's policy. Another reason for allowing the Culpeppers, Jr. to transfer to Taiwan was Charles' ability to speak Mandarin. He was prepared for the challenges of a land filled with people who needed to hear the Good News. They had been in America for several years – too long – they were ready for Taiwan.

Charles and Dona, along with their three children: Tom, 6; Carolyn, 4, and Richard, 2, joined the newly established Taiwan Baptist Mission, the organization of Southern Baptist missionaries serving in Taiwan, in 1953. They moved to Hsinchu where he pastored the Hsinchu Baptist Church. They later moved to the Seminary campus in Taipei, where they lived until their retirement in 1985.

Charles taught Bible, Systematic Theology, Philosophy, Ethics, etc., at the Taiwan Baptist Seminary for approximately 30 years, and served in various positions as the needs arose: Acting President, VP, Treasurer, Business Manager, Dean of Students, Academic Dean, etc., on more than one occasion.

Students enjoyed his classes. He required lots of reading and research. He wasn't the traditional or typical seminary professor. One would often walk by his classroom and see him sitting on the desk, telling some stories. The students wondered where he was taking their discussion, but he always made his point and the students were able to understand his meaning. He was very practical, and expressed complex theological issues in simple terms that others could understand.

He often used Chinese proverbs, sayings, and humor in teaching and in preaching. He was never for the new approach of Theological Education by Extension. He thought this was against Chinese thought and traditional education. He expressed his opinions very strongly, yet he always respected missionaries who wanted to pursue this approach to theological training.

Charles worked on various convention committees. He preached in churches, started churches, ordained pastors, taught at the Seminary, spoke at retreats and conferences, married the young, visited the sick, comforted the grieving and buried the dead for the next 30 years. He was also the pastor's pastor, translator and negotiator for many Chinese pastors and church leaders.

Dona headed up the work in Christian Literature ministries. One bookstore was started in Taipei. There were eight Baptist bookstores across the island when she left for retirement. She was active in strengthening newly planted churches. Her strategy was to go to a new church when they returned from furlough and she would serve in this church for four to five years (until the next furlough), teaching English classes, Sunday school, and music classes to various age groups in the church. The results were outstanding and she was able to assist in training and discipling many new believers, as well as using English as an evangelistic tool to touch non-believers.

Dona taught organ and piano to music majors at the Taiwan Baptist Seminary. She also taught seminary wives to play three hymns: one praise hymn, one invitation hymn, and one children's hymn. This was a tremendous help to the churches, because the churches had only small pump organs, but often there were no church members who could play them.

Charles and Dona served on numerous mission committees. Some of them were: church planting and evangelism, missionary housing, missionary education, publication and literature, and church music. Charles supervised the building of many church buildings and other physical facilities to house the Baptist work. He was also a board member for Morrison Academy (begun during their early years in Taiwan), with the purpose of educating missionary children. He was often asked to serve as a chairperson on committees because he was able to achieve agreements and cooperation from many differing personalities.

Culpepper's Household

Charles and Dona were actively involved missionaries, but they gave what they could to their children. The fourth and last child, Cathy, was born in 1955.

In their home they had an antique Chinese board bed with traditional canopy, usually associated with a newly married couple. They installed it in the old Chinese farmhouse on the campus and lived there during their last term. Along with other antiques they had collected, it was quite an attraction for the missionaries. The old antique bed was the dinner conversation during many visits in their home. Traveling American church leaders enjoyed learning about Chinese culture and history when they stayed in their home.

On their annual summer vacations, Charles and Dona left their work to have a family experience. The Culpeppers went mountain climbing, swimming in the ocean, hiking across the island, taking a bicycle ride to Taichung; spending summer vacations at Sun-Moon Lake, and visiting O Lan Bi, and other coastal villages. The children remember their father nurturing bonsai trees, carving walking canes, and finding him in any crowd because he would usually be wearing a Chinese jacket and a Texas Stetson hat. Charles was never worried about causing a scene, and never seemed to be embarrassed. The family attended sports, school events, concerts and mission activities as well as the Chinese church services. The children were later allowed to attend the English speaking church services. When the Culpepper kids were young, Charles would let them know when to come in for dinner or bedtime by blowing on a large water buffalo horn to which he had attached a trumpet mouthpiece. Later, when they were grown adults and able to return to Taiwan to visit their parents, he would bring the huge water buffalo horn to the airport and blow it for them as they were trying to clear Customs. Needless to say, the airport authorities thought this was very strange! Richard brought his new wife to Taiwan to meet his parents for the first time, and her first impression of her father-in-law was of him causing a scene in the Taipei airport, blowing the water buffalo horn while wearing his trademark Stetson. The family get-togethers were always marked by lots of laughter. Dona says, "I wasn't a model mother, but I was a happy mother. The children have discussed the happy times we had together as a family."

The Man and His Wit

Charles was humorous and it seems to have started early in his life. His comments often had a theological twist, even from childhood. His mother was giving him a bath one evening when they were discussing Joshua marching around Jericho and the great town in rubble. Charles gave a ministerial pound on the tub and declared, "I doubt it!"

Another time, while taking a test at the British Boarding School his answer to Paul's thorn in the flesh was, "Though the Bible doesn't say clearly, I think it must have been he had a little sister." While others in the family thought this to be funny, sister Mary could never find the humor in his answer.

Because Charles had grown up in North China, he had a good command of several Chinese dialects. At the Seminary parties and fun nights, he sometimes dressed in the outfit of an elderly Chinese woman, and walked around while holding a fan and reciting a monologue in the Shandong dialect that would bring peals of laugher from the students and faculty.

The Culpeppers and Their Mission Family

Although Charles was not tall, he had quite a large presence in the mission. Herb Barker said, "I have several memories of Charles and Dona that bring smiles to my face. Charles had a sharp wit and could use it to enliven a situation or to cut one down to size if the situation called for it."

Charles often served as mission chairman, and in that position often moderated during mission meetings. At times he carried two small stuffed animals with him, and when someone did something or reported something commendable, he would toss the person "a warm fuzzy" – something to affirm him or her. On the other hand, if someone stated something very negative or out of order, he would throw to that person a stuffed toy of the devil, which had printed on it, "The devil made me do it!" This would often lighten otherwise tense discussions.

Charles and Dona were of different personalities, and often expressed different opinions, even in public. During mission meetings, they sometimes took different sides, although not to the point of disrupting proceedings. At one session, Dona asked the chairman, Charles, to rule on a particular motion, but he took the opposite position. She again questioned the ruling. He replied, "I know your position, but I am just going to let my superior wisdom rule!" Dona and everyone else burst into laughter!

Many have a picture of Charles sitting in a mission meeting or some committee meeting with his head down, whittling on a stick of some kind. He was not asleep; he was intently listening and engaged in the discussion, and sometimes he would raise his head to add some bit of wisdom or a joke.

On one occasion, when a missionary lady arrived late for a meeting that was in progress, she explained that she had been out seeing about getting a carved chest. Charles looked up and quipped, "Did it hurt?"

Retirement

Charles and Dona retired in 1985 and returned to San Antonio, TX. They spent several years taking care of Charles' parents (Dona's parents had already died). He often said, "I want to retire so I can spend time with my parents because

I lost those years in North China. I want time with my children and grandchildren so they can have memories."

He had a few short years with his parents before their fruitful lives came to a close. Charles, Sr. died in 1987, and that same year, Mary, Charles' sister, and her husband Bill Walker retired after 40 years of mission work in Japan. Mary and Bill then took over the care of Mother Culpepper. Charles and Dona bought land north of San Antonio, outside the little town of Blanco. Charles was able to fulfill a lifetime dream to have a "grandchildren ranch." They had a horse, a dog, a swimming hole, and many other wonderful animals and equipment for the grandchildren. The grandchildren have happy memories of visiting with them and camping, chasing dogs, riding in the back of Grampy's truck, swimming, hunting deer, and hearing more than 70 years of Chinese stories. The gravel road filled with deep potholes that led to their farmhouse was a road that the children and grandchildren always looked forward to traveling, because they knew there would always be an adventure there!

Charles was diagnosed with Progressive Supranuclear Palsy in 1995. This is a rare, incurable, degenerative brain disease in which physical movement becomes more and more limited, but the brain is still somewhat active. Charles, the erudite professor, became unable to move and talk, and even to have facial expressions. However, even in this, he and Dona maintained their upbeat and cheerful approach to life.

On his 80th birthday, his family gathered to celebrate with him, and he was able to hold his great-granddaughter. What a gift! His father had told his grandchildren that he prayed there would always be one of his descendants serving on the mission field until the day the Lord returned. Both of his living children, Charles and Mary, served their entire lives in Asia, and Mary's son, Bill Walker, was appointed to

Japan. Who will be the person for the next generation and the next one?

Charles' sister, Mary said, "We returned to the U.S. during World War II, and I was a 15-year-old trying to understand a new world and society from the sheltered, very conservative life in a British Boarding School. My brother, Charles, was my refuge and advisor in many situations – from geometry to dating. He had a patient, thoughtful approach to everything and explained things in a way that I accepted and didn't feel "bossed," but made to feel more confident. He was my true friend, hero and brother."

And many missionaries also felt Charles was their true friend, hero and advisor. Those of us who knew Charles well remember a humble man, a humorous man, a wise man, a sensitive man, a quiet man, a man who understood Chinese culture and language and appreciated both; and a man with a purpose. We remember a unique man who lived and worked among strong personalities, but who was always his own person, finding his place and "doing his job" with dignity.

On August 28th, 2004, family and friends gathered at First Baptist Church in Blanco, TX, to remember, honor, and celebrate the life and ministry of Charles Culpepper, Jr. He was a scholar, a preacher, a teacher, a counselor, an administrator, a missionary, a husband, a father, a grandfather, and a friend.

Charles was buried in his Chinese gown and with his Chinese Bible in his hands. Rightly so, for it had been 80 years since the little guy sailed with his parents to China. He wore his Stetson hat to many gatherings and meetings, but he always had a Chinese heart.

Dona lives on their "grandchildren's ranch," enjoying the children and the grandchildren, who come often to eat and remember their Taiwan roots. What a contribution the lady made to the Kingdom, even though, as she will tell you today, she never had a call to missionary service. Of course, few believe her!!

Dona's cancer returned a few months ago, and as the book goes to the publisher, she is resting peacefully as the children take turns caring for her and writing her dictated notes. She still has her sense of humor and looks forward to joining Charles around the throne as they praise the One who saved them and called them to the Chinese world.

Charles and Dona Culpepper

Jeanette and Carl Hunker
Living a Life of Faith

How often God has given Carl a special hymn that becomes a part of his life story! In recent days, singing through his heart is **"All the Way My Savior Leads Me, what have I to ask beside? For I know what e'er befall me, Jesus doeth all things well."** That hymn is also the story of Abraham, leaving a secure life and taking his family and all their possessions to a new land of which he had little knowledge. His journey was a tremendous *turning point*, not only for him, but also for the journey of all people who are followers of Jehovah God. Through Abraham's life, early in life God spoke to Carl, then guided him through many *turning points* in life.

As a young man prior, to the Civil War in the 1860s, Carl's grandfather immigrated from Germany to America, following two brothers who had come earlier. He worked for others before buying and working on his own farm in central Missouri. At age 27, he married a young German lady of 15. Every two years, they gave birth to a child until there were eleven. Carl's father was number eight.

Hard and hot work on the farm caused his father to dream of venturing to the far west. He went as a young man to Montana, and later moved to Lakeview, OR. As a single man, he ate his meals at the home of the Bosworth family, who had four daughters and later had three sons. The oldest of the Bosworth girls was Louise, who taught in a school about two hours away. She traveled to and from the school by horse. She came home every few months.

A turning point! As a rural school teacher of 16 students in several different grades, Louise could only return occasionally for home visits. One day at lunch, Carl's father saw the young lady standing in the kitchen door in her home. He told the story, and his heart said, "I want her to be my wife." As they worshiped together on Sundays, friendship grew into romantic love, and they married on Easter, March 23, 1913. The wedding was held in the Bosworth's home, following Sunday morning worship. Their wedding dinner was the special Sunday dinner and the announcement of their wedding was made that night at the Sunday evening youth gathering. There was no honeymoon. They went back to their regular work on Monday. The marriage was good and strong, lasting over 60 years before their deaths in 1974.

A turning point! Their first child, Leonard, was born July 4, 1914, and their second child, Carl, was born April 24, 1916. Both sons were born during World War I. A most heart-breaking change came in the summer of 1916, when his father's laundry was completely destroyed by fire. There was no insurance and no other way, but for them to return to the farm in Missouri. As a family of four, they lived in a small one-room house for hired workers on the Hunker place. However, when Carl was two, they moved to a small house in Marshall, MO where his father worked in a laundry.

A *turning point!* When Carl was four, his mother developed tuberculosis. The treatment was dry climate, lots of sunshine, rest, and nourishing food. So the family moved from Missouri to Canon City, CO in December 1920. His parents bought a small farm with 100 various kinds of fruit trees. It was located at the very edge of the snow-covered Rocky Mountains. This is still Carl's heart-home today. Financially, life was very difficult for the family, due partly to the Great Depression of 1927-1934. His family tried many, many ways to make a living. They raised over 2,000 laying hens, but the cost of grain caused them to earn no profit from eggs. This caused a financial crisis. His father worked in the coal mines, and later traveled into the high mountains to abandoned gold mines looking for rich veins of gold. Carl's mama worked as a nurse in a home for the elderly, working long hours from 7 a.m. to 7 p.m. Therefore, home responsibilities were divided between Carl and his brother. Leonard worked on the farm and Carl was the housekeeper – cleaning the house, washing, ironing, and baking cakes for school lunches.

Sundays were happy days. The family went to Sunday school and worship in the mornings, youth meetings and evening worship in the evenings. Carl's parents sang in the choir and guided Leonard and Carl with their eyes as the boys sat on the second bench. The boys played with other farm boys in the neighborhood on Sunday afternoon.

A turning point! Carl walked to Harrison Elementary School for his elementary grades. He and his brother rode their bicycles to Roosevelt Junior High, and later to Canon City High School. Carl was a good student and ranked second in his graduating class. This honor gave him an academic scholarship to any of the six universities in Colorado. However, the hardships of the Great Depression meant there were no additional funds for college expenses.

A turning point! God in His love gave Carl a home in which God was honored, worshiped, and obeyed. They had family worship in the evening before going to bed. When he accepted Jesus as Savior, he did not experience a great change in lifestyle because, Carl said, "I never knew what it meant not to obey God." He was baptized at age 12 as a confirmation of his personal salvation in Jesus. In his mid-teens, he attended a revival meeting. It took great courage, but he went to the front and knelt for prayer and confession.

As he rode his bicycle home later that evening, he felt great peace and joy in knowing Christ was in control of his life. Carl taught Sunday school, participated in youth activities, and sang in the choir. He decided early that he wanted to be in church work of some kind. He said, "I did not have a struggle of resistance, but a deep love and joy in doing God's work." At that time, the only kind of church work Carl knew was being a pastor. Each year, his Northern Baptist church had a missions emphasis, which was well-done, but Carl did not feel a life calling for missions.

A *turning point!* After graduation from high school in 1934, Carl had no work or study opportunity, so he enrolled in President Roosevelt's program for the youth of disadvantaged families, the Civilian Conservation Corps. This program involved various projects of environmental improvements. This was a wonderful opportunity for Carl and his family. The youth were paid $1.00 per day and were allowed to keep $5.00 each month. The balance was sent to the young person's family. Carl was sent to a camp in the high mountains about 100 miles from his home. He encountered a lifestyle so different from his own. The adjustment was hard. His parents didn't use the earnings he sent home, but deposited them in the bank, saving these funds for his college education. Carl resigned after sixteen months to begin his college education at William Jewell College, Liberty, MO. He was able to obtain a scholarship, which paid half-tuition for ministerial students.

Before leaving for Liberty, the young people in the various churches of Canon City arranged a farewell worship service and asked Carl to preach. How Carl struggled, being back in this environment and preaching to such a large group of young people. His message focused on the hymn, **Jesus is all the World to Me,** a true commitment of his heart for a life-long ministry. In August 1936, Carl traveled by bus for 11 hours to Kansas City and then on to Liberty, MO – the home of William Jewell College. He faced a tremendous challenge of faith for his future.

A *turning point!* College, for Carl, was one of the most enjoyable periods of his life. After his two years in a work environment, he was intellectually hungry for study. There were 750 students on campus. There were 125 of these students going into church-related ministry, so Carl enjoyed both these fellow students and the professors. His major was Greek, with minors in history and psychology. Carl found the religious activities helpful – chapel, evangelistic services where he learned to witness, all-night prayer meetings, devotional times, and prayer partners.

Money was a problem. In his freshman year, he worked on campus, climbing and trimming tree branches. In his sophomore year, he was called as pastor to a half-time church, receiving $5.00 each trip. His junior and senior years, he was a full-time pastor of a rural church west of Kansas City.

Carl was able to pay off his college debts before leaving for Seminary in August 1940. He had a full academic scholarship, worked as a teaching assistant in the religion department, received salary from the rural churches he pastored, worked in the fields during harvest times, and worked one summer for an electric company.

A *turning point!* In the fall of 1940, Carl began studies at the Southern Baptist Theological Seminary in Louisville, KY. This was a major decision for him, as his background in Colorado was with the Northern Baptist Convention. He had also been a member of the Wolcott Baptist Church in Kansas, a Northern Baptist Convention church, during his college days. Carl liked the evangelism and missions emphasis of the Southern Baptist Convention churches. He sought the Lord in prayer about the decision to become a Southern Baptist, and believes today it was the right decision. Carl loved seminary life and studying was a joy to him.

Finances again became a major challenge for him. He did not have financial support from any church, therefore, work was necessary. He worked in the dining hall for three years. He had an evening ministry among youth in a depressed area of Louisville. This was a neighborhood of people with a lifestyle of broken homes and moral problems. On Saturday nights, Carl worked with a team of students doing street preaching in difficult areas of the city. He realized more than ever humanity's need for the salvation of the Lord Jesus.

A *turning point!* In the spring of his third year of Th.M. study, Carl represented the seminary students in a joint project with the women of the WMU Training School, to have city-wide youth revivals led by the youth. They had more than 60 churches participate. It was called "Eight Great Days" of local church revivals. The program was inspiring and blessed the churches and their young people. This project also gave the seminary students opportunity to grow in evangelism. This meant many planning committee meetings. Prayer chairperson for the women of the Training School was Jeanette Roebuck from Texarkana, AR. Carl and Jeanette met often for prayer and planning for the city-wide crusade. At the close of the crusade, they continued meeting, praying and sharing God's call for ministry. This led to a deeper and deeper love for each other, and a growing sense of the Lord's leadership for a life together in the Lord's service.

When Jeanette was two years old, she fell in the children's room at her church and injured her spine, which developed into tuberculosis of the spine. The weakness of her spine meant a brace on her back from waist to shoulders to strengthen her back. Each year, the brace was lengthened, until at age twelve, surgery was done by taking a sliver of bone from her leg and grafting it to her spine. This also meant that she would not grow taller, never reaching five feet. For her, the pain did not cause bitterness. Instead, she became a loving person, with a sweet personality and a strong commitment to a life of service to our Lord.

Often, Carl and Jeanette walked in Cherokee Park near the seminary and shared their commitment to the Lord's service. In the spring of 1943, Carl gave Jeanette an engagement ring just before their seminary graduation. A fall wedding was planned.

They were married on October 2, 1943 in Texarkana, TX. The wedding was far different from their plans and dreams. Carl had started his Ph.D. studies, majoring in missions, and pastored two half-time churches. The week before the wedding, he developed a high fever and was placed in the seminary infirmary. His fever went down by Thursday, and he was able to leave on Friday by train for Texarkana. He did not arrive in time for the rehearsal, but they had a beautiful wedding and a commitment that lasted for more than 40 years. The following Saturday, they returned to Louisville.

A turning point! The summer of 1943, two rural churches in Kentucky invited Carl to serve as their pastor. The churches were located about 125 miles from Southern Seminary. Carl did not have a car, so they had to hitchhike to the churches. Carl and Jeanette went to one church on the first and second weekend of the month, and the other church on the third and fourth weekend. They walked to the homes of church members for visitation. They learned much about pastoral ministry in these two churches.

A turning point! The hurt and loss of World War II deeply moved the hearts of the seminary students. They conducted weekly prayer meetings and prayed for those suffering from the war, and they also sought the Lord's will for their future. Some students left the seminary and entered the war as chaplains. Carl began to feel that one way to bring world peace was to share the Gospel with the nations of the world. One night, as he tried to prepare his teaching plans to teach the next day, he was unable to prepare the material. He wanted to know God's will for himself and his family in life-service. Finally, he put his books aside and began writing on a small piece of notepaper all the reasons he ought to give his total life to missions. On the reverse side of the notepaper, he listed the reasons he should serve at home.

Carl said, "As I looked at both sides of the notepaper, it became so obvious that reasons on one side were basically selfish and sinful. The reasons on the other side were the spirit of Jesus, who came and gave His life for my salvation and of all humanity. Leaning my head on my books, I prayed and verbally committed my life to foreign missions. A great peace flowed over my entire being. Back to my preparation, I felt set free and was able to complete my preparation within an hour." Since Jeanette was asleep, Carl did not wake her.

As Carl walked to the campus the next morning, he felt a burden had been lifted. To test his decision, he did not share with Jeanette or with his prayer group for more than a week. One evening, when he returned to their apartment, he looked at Jeanette as she was preparing supper and said, "Jeanette, how would you feel if God called us to be foreign missionaries?"

It would be wonderful, Carl. I gave my life to Jesus to be a foreign missionary when I was seventeen. I have been praying for you to respond." This was the spirit of their marriage – one in the Spirit, one in heart and commitment to the Lord.

A turning point! David was born May 5, 1945 only 11 months before Carl completed his Ph.D. On Monday morning, April 5, 1946 Carl finished all requirements for his Ph.D., and at noon, leaving David with friends, he and Jeanette traveled by train to Richmond, VA. In four days they completed all requirements for missionary appointment and on Friday, April 9, 1946, with 44 others, were appointed for missionary service. The summer was spent buying equipment – stove, bed, refrigerator, clothing and shoes for David for five years, and three bicycles. Carl and his father built crates, and packed and sent the freight to San Francisco. Due to a labor strike, their ship did not depart for six months. Carl's parents drove from Colorado to San Francisco to send the little family to China. On a cloudy dismal Sunday, Carl, Jeanette, and two-year-old David boarded the *Marine Lynx* for Shanghai. It was December 15, 1946. Their emotions were out of control – so excited to go, so sad to leave family for their first term – five years.

The ship was a troop ship, just back from the war in the Pacific, which meant no private rooms. Carl was in a sleeping compartment of 40 men. Jeanette and David were in a women's compartment of more than 200.

Carl said, "I am unable to describe my emotions as the ship pulled out of the harbor on the way to China." There were 950 passengers, of whom 675 were missionaries of various mission boards. Sixteen days after leaving San Franciso, December 31, 1946, they pulled into the wharf in Shanghai. And, for the first time in Carl's life, he saw a Chinese person. The man was waiting for passengers to depart the ship. Carl greeted him, "I am from America, I have come to tell you about Jesus." His response showed that he did not understand one word of English.

A turning point! A senior missionary, H.H. McMillan, met the Hunkers and took them by train, a two-hour trip, to Soochow, a walled city of 500,000 population. They thought it would be their home for the next 40 years. There were seven Southern Baptist missionaries living in Soochow and they were of help and encouragement to the young couple. Carl and Jeanette soon started studying the Soochow dialect. Carl played basketball with the boys at the Yates Boys Academy, and taught English to grades 11 and 12. They worshiped in the church on Yates Academy campus, not understanding any of the language. One of the memories of Soochow was welcoming a baby girl, Joyce Lynn, to the family. Joyce

Lynn was born May 3, 1948. These were fulfilling days and days of frustration and doubt.

After two years of study, Carl preached his first sermon in the Soochow dialect, December 1948. Carl, like all missionaries, felt sorry for those who patiently listened. After lunch, Carl received a call from Dr. Cauthen, Secretary for the Orient, requesting him to go to Shanghai to talk about evacuation. He resisted, saying, "I am ready now to begin what God has called me to do." But the Communist armies from the north were within a few miles of Soochow, and all the Baptist missionaries in north and central China were being evacuated. More than 25 missionaries met in the Cauthen's home in Shanghai for an update on the war situation. Plans were being made to send the young missionaries and their families to the Philippines. Carl felt like a blanket of darkness was over his head. He prayed for understanding as he sat on the floor during the meeting, and looked to God for an answer. The Holy Spirit spoke to his heart through the words of a hymn Mrs. Cauthen sang, *Great is thy Faithfulness.* The Lord comforted his heart with His word, Trust in the Lord and He will give you the desires of your heart, trust and wait upon Him (Psalm 37).

Back in Soochow Carl taught his boys' English class. After teaching the class, he told the class, "Boys, this is my last lesson, because my family is having to leave. But we will be back within a few weeks." He did not realize that it would be 39 years before he would see Soochow again. He visited Soochow in 1987, the year after he retired from Taiwan.

Within three days, Jeanette and Carl had packed two trunks and were at the train station to depart for Shanghai. They were not prepared for the tremendous crowd at the station, people fleeing from the north on the way to Shanghai. They were thankful for the students and church friends who came to see them off. Carl, Jeanette and David, who was three, were finally pushed on the train. They suddenly realized that Joyce Lynn, only six months old, was being held by a friend who was not on the train. The students wrapped her in a blanket and passed her through the crowd until she was in Jeanette's arms.

The city of Shanghai was a tragic mob of desperate people seeking refuge. Carl and others felt helpless. They could do little. The Hunkers flew to Manila, where after several days, they joined other missionary families in Baguio, located in the northern Philippines, for a "temporary" stay. The days lengthened into weeks. Dr. Cauthen arranged for the transfer of four Chinese language teachers from Peking to Baguio, to set up a language program for the 25 or more missionaries who came out of China. This meant that Jeanette and Carl had spent two years learning the "Wu" dialect, which is the Soochow dialect. They would have to change to Mandarin. Carl said, "The doors of China were closed. We could not return. I suffered through great discouragement, trying to reconcile my situation with that strong call during seminary days of being a missionary to China for 40 years. These were dark, dark days."

A turning point! In 1951, the Hunkers completed their first term of missionary service. The family lived in Texarkana with Jeanette's parents. Carl and Jeanette did extensive travel in deputation work all over America.

In the spring of 1952, Dr. Cauthen gave the family an option of returning to the Philippines to work among Chinese, or to go to Taiwan. They transferred to Taiwan and lived in Taichung for the first year. Carl taught in the seminary and did evangelism and church planting. Because nearly three million from the mainland had gone with Pres. Chiang Kai-shek and his government to Taiwan, the people were open and seeking comfort and security for their future. Their hearts were open to the Gospel of comfort in Jesus. These years were some of the most fruitful of all his missionary service

– evangelism, discipleship, beginning new mission points, and training believers in the formation of mission points and churches. Carl remembers in great joy, "In 1957, I baptized 222 in five different churches and chapels." Missionaries felt that within 10 years, at least, 30 percent of Taiwan's people would be baptized believers.

A turning point! Along with evangelism, the academic program of the Taiwan Baptist Theological Seminary, begun in 1952, equipped church leaders. After one year in Taichung, the Hunker family transferred to Taipei, where Carl and Jeanette taught at the newly organized seminary.

The next period of service for Carl was the "golden years" the evangelistic response. It continued through the 1950s, into the early 1960s; Lingtou Baptist Assembly was started; land was purchased in major cities on the west side of Taiwan for new churches, such as valuable property bordering Taiwan University for Grace Baptist church in Taipei; Baptist Book Stores were opened in six population centers on the west coast of the island; a radio ministry was begun in Taipei; local growth ministries included churches reaching out to begin new mission points; student centers built near university campuses; special training weeks for discipleship and evangelism; new curriculum written; women's ministries (WMU) and Brotherhoods were established.

Jeanette not only taught in seminary and helped in churches, she was an energetic worker in local and district WMU, which took her all over Taiwan. Her commitment and enthusiasm working with both women and youth groups carried over into her seminary teaching.

In 1954, Carl and other missionaries worked with a Chinese committee in the forming of a Chinese Baptist Convention. There was great excitement, but due to local financial needs, the convention grew slowly. The Mission wanted the churches to be self-supporting. Carl knew this was the right philosophy, but it was hurtful to watch many young pastors, who were his former students, struggle to meet these objectives. It was exciting to watch the Convention send Chinese home missionaries to Hualien and to Green Island. A year or two later, Chinese missionaries were sent to Thailand and to Korea.

In 1962, the Seminary cooperated with six other Baptist seminaries in east and southeast Asia in forming The Asia Baptist Graduate Theological Seminary, to provide advanced degree study for future seminary professors or church leaders. As president of ABGTS, Carl had the privilege of visiting the branch seminaries, including the Vietnam Seminary during the troubling, unstable months before Saigon fell.

A high point in life of the Hunker family was the annual Missionary Summer Retreat in July at the Sun-Moon Lake. Later Mission Meetings were held at Morrison Christian Academy and other places. The Taiwan Missionary Fellowship, composed of many denominations, blessed and strengthened their lives through many years.

A turning point! The school education process of their children is always a challenge for parents. Carl and Jeanette lived in a Japanese house in Taichung. Their house had a little covered walkway to a separate room, so they purchased furniture and made a one-room schoolhouse. Jeanette taught David in the first grade. Joyce Lynn insisted on going to school, so Jeanette arranged a study activity for her. In spring of 1953, when they moved to Taipei, they shared a Jeep and driver with five other missionaries, who provided a vehicle to transport the children to school. Beginning with the eighth grade, David and Joyce Lynn attended Morrison Academy in Taichung. They came home twice a month. Separation was very difficult for Jeanette and Carl, so they made the weekend visits very special family times.

In 1963, David left Taiwan and enrolled in William Jewell College. Three years later, Joyce Lynn also went to William Jewell. At the Taipei airport, it was so difficult for

Carl and Jeanette to watch them walk the short distance on the runway, turn in the doorway and wave for the last time before the door closed. Jeanette and Carl found it difficult to talk as they drove back to the Seminary, but now they had to give their children to the love and guidance of God.

A turning point! In 1977, America recognized Beijing as the official government of China. Gloom and disappointment covered Taiwan. Chinese co-workers called for a special prayer meeting for co-workers and missionaries in the Taipei area in Culpepper Chapel. There was open grief as the co-workers shared and comforted the missionaries, assuring the missionaries not to be afraid of what might occur.

The meeting closed by making a huge circle of Chinese and missionaries praying aloud with great emotion. However, this event help Carl to realize more than ever that it was time for a Chinese to be seminary president. This crisis led Carl to resign in 1980 as president of the Taiwan Baptist Theological Seminary. In 1982, after two years of searching for the right person, Dr. Chang Chen-kwang was elected and installed as president. Carl and Jeanette continued to serve as faculty members.

A turning point! Carl led a mission retreat for the Thailand Mission in 1982. When he returned home, Jeanette shared her doctor's report that probably there was pressure on her vertebrae, which caused great pain, and this would require surgery. Within two weeks, she had surgery at the Chang Gang Hospital in Taoywan, near Taipei. Carl and Jeanette were blessed and encouraged by the prayer, love and care of the faculty, students and missionaries, but so disappointed when the back surgery did not solve her problem. The pain in both feet was so intense that she could hardly walk. In the summer of 1982, Carl and Jeanette flew to Houston, TX, and doctors there found the pain was due to a malignant tumor putting pressure on her pancreas. She was given 24 radiation treatments, which reduced the pain somewhat. They were granted doctor's permission, with Jeanette's insistence, to return to Taiwan. She taught several classes in the living room of their home, but beginning in February 1983, she grew weaker, and by spring had to be admitted to the hospital.

In April of that year, David and Joyce Lynn came to Taiwan for several days. The family had a blessed time together. Carl's teaching schedule was heavy, and he went to the hospital every morning, noon, and evening. They realized it was time to prepare for leaving Taiwan and return to Kansas City, MO, but Jeanette insisted Carl finish the school year before they returned to the U.S.

However, on the Wednesday morning of the last week of school, Carl went to the hospital for his early morning visit. He met Jeanette's two doctors as they left her room. Carl said, "They told me Jeanette probably would live three days before leaving me. In her room, she and I talked and prayed, both of us realizing she would soon meet our Savior face-to-face." Seminary graduation was the following Monday evening at 7:30 p.m. She died on Monday evening, May 30th, approximately one hour after seminary graduation. Her wish was for Carl to finish the school year, which he did.

The following Friday, Carl had a cremation service, followed by a Memorial Service three weeks later in the Culpepper Chapel on the Taiwan Baptist Seminary campus. Carl spent the following weeks packing out their house, attending farewell dinners, and preaching in churches. He returned to the U.S. in July, carrying Jeanette's urn with him. It is buried in a small, well-kept rural cemetery close to the ancestral Hunker home in Missouri. Service for their Lord had come from thankful hearts for the mercy of the Lord – beyond a five-year term, past 36 years, to a full 40 years for Carl as missionary to the Chinese.

A turning point! Returning to the States in 1983, Carl said, "How I grieved in my loneliness, but then discovered a secret of healing: singing as I drove to appointments and listening to wonderful music of praise." Within nine months, he began to feel he wanted to serve the Lord more. The IMB invited him to teach in the Malaysia Baptist Seminary. He later did pastoral training in several places in India. He finally went back to Taiwan in 1986 to direct the planning and conduct the celebration of 150 years of Baptist work in China, 1836-1986. Carl's prayer was that this history of courageous Christian witness for 150 years would challenge Chinese Christians and missionaries to renewed zeal in witnessing in their generation.

After Carl returned to America in 1986, he taught at William Jewell College for two years. He was a part of discovering more than 6,000 Chinese in greater Kansas City, so he worked with others in establishing the Emmanuel Chinese Baptist church in the late 1980s. Today, the church has a staff of five, and annually gives 24 percent of its budget to missions. The church began a new mission point in October 2007 in the greater Kansas City area, plus a Christian Fellowship for Chinese students at University of Missouri at Kansas City.

There have been many 'turning points' in Carl's life; he has been found faithful in each opportunity. His spirit compels him to sing with a thankful heart "*All the Way My Saviour Leads Me.*"

Carl and Jeanette Hunker

Harry and Frances Raley
The First Ones

The father was a farmer and the mother was a simple country housewife, in the beautiful South Carolina farmlands. This is the type of family into which Harry Raley was born in 1925, the last of four children, and the only son.

The family attended a rural church. The church was unusual in the rural south because they had a large church building with a two-floor educational building. The family walked to church each Sunday because they had no car.

Harry attended Sunbeams and heard stories about far away China and about boys and girls who didn't have the privilege to attend church with their families. He had a good singing voice as a child. The pastor stood him in a chair at the front of the church and he often sang for worship and other church events.

Martha Berry College is located in the beautiful foothills of North Georgia, near the city of Rome. The school, well known throughout the south, was established by a wealthy lady named Martha Berry. She had a love for students who didn't have the financial means to attend high school or college. Martha Berry School was located on a large farm. All the students were required to work on the farm during their time at the school.

57

Harry was 12 when his father died. His mother reared her four children, but life was difficult financially. Harry's three sisters attended Berry College, and it was understood that this was the place Harry would also study.

World War II brought dark clouds across the world, and Harry was among the young men who felt they had a responsibility to protect their homes and their country. After completing two years of college, Harry joined the U.S. Navy. He was stationed on a ship that sailed the Pacific, calling at many ports, delivering cargo. The ship was in the area during the Battle of Okinawa, one of the turning points in the war. It was during his years on the ship that he sensed God's call for ministry.

He returned to South Carolina after the war and entered Furman University to prepare for the ministry. He had many opportunities to sing and preach as a young minister at the university. He entered Southwestern Baptist Theological Seminary in 1948 to prepare to pastor churches in the southern United States, and had the surprise of his life there. He knew he would find quality education and lasting friendships, and to his joy, he found the love of his life, which has lasted for more than 50 years.

Harry was a third-year student at Southwestern in 1951, when Frances Bibb entered Southwestern Seminary. Frances grew up in the Mississippi Delta near Drew, MS. She says, "I grew up in the cotton fields of the Mississippi Delta and enjoyed life with six brothers and sisters." She explains their family was poor, but her parents were so good at working with the children that they didn't realize how poor they were. Her family was also active Baptist church members. Frances became a Christian at the age of nine. As she grew up, a major influence in her life was her mother. She taught the adult Sunday school class, and was a faithful officer and member in the WMU of 5-8 members. The WMU met weekly at their little church. Frances learned about giving for missions as she watched her mom joyfully give to foreign missions a portion of the money from the sale of eggs. Two foreign missionaries and a pastor came from this home.

Frances went to a local junior college for two years, and then entered Mississippi College, owned and operated by Mississippi Baptists. Frances loved Bible classes and other courses taught at Mississippi College. She was very popular on campus and was a gifted pianist. She served as a summer missionary in Hawaii and had the privilege of working with Chinese, Japanese, Koreans, and Polynesians. She gave her heart to those Asians that summer. Lots of friends assumed she would go as a missionary after her summer in Hawaii, but she simply replied, "No, not unless God clearly calls me, and He hasn't done that yet."

After graduation, she worked at Calvary Baptist Church in Kansas City, MO, as a secretary and youth director. Her pastor was a member of the Foreign Mission Board. He went to the bi-annual Board Meetings and returned to his church and reported on the progress, struggles and victories of the Mission Board. One Sunday night in church, as her pastor talked of the recent testimonies of the newly appointed missionaries, she said in her heart, "Lord, I know now, for sure, that this is what you want me to do." Frances arrived at Southwestern Seminary with a heart eager to learn how to prepare for missionary service.

Harry and Frances met at a welcome party for the new students in September 1950. The students stood around the piano and sang long after the party was over. Little did the two young adults know, but in the next 50-plus years, they and their children would spend lots of time around the piano.

Harry and Frances spent time together. They learned they had similar roots, interests, goals and vision. Music and missions pulled them toward each other. By April 1951, Frances had said yes to Harry, and they were married nine months later; August 21, 1951. Harry graduated from Southwestern Seminary and they decided it was time to move on to what God had in store for them. They moved to South Carolina from Fort Worth, TX. They lived in North and South Carolina for four years and served in two churches. Harry and Frances enjoyed working with people in these churches, but their vision for lands and peoples who had never heard the Gospel was ever before them.

Frances always thought if she were to go as a missionary, she would be appointed to Japan because she had served in Hawaii as a summer missionary and her experience had been positive. Harry always thought of going to Guatemala, since hearing a missionary from there speak in seminary chapel.

In December 1953, Frances taught the mission study for WMU, and it was on Taiwan. She shared the content of the mission study with Harry. Well, it was 1954, and there were many names for the little island in the Pacific. One name was Formosa, which means 'Beautiful Island,' given by the Portuguese. The most recent one was the Republic of China, where the Nationalist government had set up their new government a few years earlier. In 1949, Mainland China had fallen to the Communists. Those who could afford to leave and could find transportation were leaving China. People were going to various Asian countries, but especially to Hong Kong, Macao, and Taiwan. The island was flooded with approximately two million newly arrived refugees from China, who had left possessions and many family members behind to find protection and safety.

All Southern Baptist missionaries who had served in China were out of China by 1951. Six single missionaries – Bertha Smith, Lila Watson, Ola Lea, Josephine Ward, Inabelle Coleman, and Olive Lawton – transferred from China to Taiwan. The land was ripe unto harvest, and these women were winning many people to Jesus Christ and starting churches. Of course, being Baptists, these ladies could not baptize anyone. Four missionary couples transferred to Taiwan from China: Hunkers, Quicks, Culpeppers, Sr., and Culpeppers, Jr.

However, these were not enough workers to reap the harvest taking place. It was not uncommon for people to knock on the missionaries' door and ask how to be saved. The small group of missionaries requested and even begged the Mission Board to send missionary couples to Taiwan. They prayed and sought the Lord's guidance to their place of ministry. After much prayer and communication, the Raleys turned out to be one of the couples God had prepared for Taiwan. They were appointed as the first Southern Baptist missionaries to Taiwan in December 1954.

The Taiwan Mission family received the news that a new couple was coming to Taiwan with great excitement. They were gifted musically, were strong on relationships, and were deeply committed to Jesus Christ. They were sure of their mission call and were hard workers. The Mission family was ready and waiting for the new couple and their baby son, Lynn.

Frances and Harry sold furniture and purchased needed supplies for a five-year term. They said their good-byes and sailed on the *U.S.S. President Cleveland* on March 18, 1955, and arrived in Taiwan early April 1955, with two-year-old Lynn.

Harry and Frances Raley walked into the arms of the Old China transfers. They had prayed for the Raleys. They loved them already and would teach them how to love and relate to the Chinese.

Harry and Frances studied Mandarin for one year in Taipei, the capital city of Taiwan. This was a busy year, but they were able to learn how to relate to their Chinese co-workers by observing the missionaries who had come from the mainland. Lynn adjusted to life there very quickly. The language was much easier for him than for his parents.

Harry also had many opportunities to sing for weddings, worship services, and funerals. The little boy who stood on a chair and sang in the country church was now singing in another language and blessing others as he was blessed.

They moved to Tainan, a city in the southern part of Taiwan, where Harry served as a general evangelist. Frances was busy learning to keep house in the new culture, teach Bible classes, participate in women's work, play the piano for worship services, and deal with two older single missionaries who had the answers to all of life, especially how to take care of Lynn. Lynn found great joy in attending Chinese kindergarten. The family found time to welcome their second son, Bruce, to the family. The year was 1956.

In 1961, the family moved to Taipei, where Harry held several different jobs. They spent the next 25 years in Taipei. Harry was Treasurer, Business Manager and Chairperson of the Taiwan Baptist Mission. Harry also served as manager of the Baptist Literature Centers for six years. He pastored different churches for short periods of time, with the goal of raising up Chinese pastors to be indigenous leaders of their churches.

Harry served his Mission family with understanding, patience, and wisdom. He was always helpful and tried to assist missionary and Chinese believers and non-believers when the need arose. He became known as someone who was always ready and available to share his faith with friends and strangers on the street, in the shop, on the train, in church, at the ballgame, or on the bus.

Frances had a missionary calling that took her to Taiwan. She had a calling to be Mrs. Harry Raley, and she had a sacred calling to be the mother of four adorable children. Son, David, joined the family in 1958. The three little boys waited and planned for a baby sister. When Beth arrived in 1964, she was a welcomed and loved addition to the Raley household.

There were adjustments to having a girl in the family. The boys taught her how to enjoy life and keep up with them, and they have always treasured their little sister. Taiwan people were kind and friendly, but they were very curious about western children with blond hair, blue eyes, and glasses. People often touched or spoke about Lynn, Bruce, David and Beth. It was sometimes frustrating for them, and they reacted as most children would react. All of them learned Chinese to various degrees and enjoy using it even today. They have great appreciation for their Taiwan roots and are proudly informed about events in Taiwan.

Frances was a gracious hostess and super cook, and many friends – Chinese, business people and missionaries – enjoyed delicious food and fellowship around the Raley table. One such memory was the evening a new missionary sat next to a Hong Kong missionary who was visiting the Raley family. Of course, there was conversation between the new missionary and the older Hong Kong missionary, who had recently lost his wife. Much to the surprise of the new missionary and the Raleys, the Hong Kong missionary appeared at the missionary's door the next day with a box of chocolates and a marriage proposal. The proposal was not accepted, but this was a good example that most anything could happen around the Raley's dining table!

Frances and Harry lived at Lingtou Baptist Assembly for five years. Harry worked at the Mission office, and Frances served as hostess for the camp. This was a super place for the children to roam the grassy hills, play with the dogs, dance with the Chinese children on the grounds, and fight with the missionary kids up the hill.

Frances directed the work of the Baptist media center for a number of years. This ministry was a significant part of evangelism, as the missionaries used films in both rural, urban and student evangelism. She was very active in nation-wide Woman's Missionary Union ministries, and was able to travel with the women to many of the Asian Women's Meetings. She met and worked with women from all over Asia. These were significant experiences for Frances and the many women in Taiwan churches.

One of the highlights of Frances' ministry was teaching English to women in the churches where they served. She was able to make friends with women in all walks of life, education levels, and religious backgrounds. She cried with them in their struggles and laughed with them in their victories. She became active in Taipei Christian Women's Club, and often her English class women would attend with her.

Frances and Harry wanted their children to have precious memories of growing up in Taiwan. The family spent many evenings around the table playing table games, because they did not have TV for a long time. Sports were important to the boys, and Beth loved cheering them on. Each of the children took piano lessons, and some played other musical instruments, because music was a significant part of their family life.

The children attended Bethany Christian School and then the Taipei American School. The Raleys knew, like all missionaries called to follow God to foreign lands and take their children, that one day their children would graduate from high school and return to their native land to continue their education. The day came when Lynn graduated from Taipei American School, and the date was set for him and another missionary son to catch a flight to America. Many of the missionaries and co-workers prayed for the Raley family, and made their way to the Taipei Airport to comfort and support them in their difficult task of sending their first-born off to America. Everyone watched as the family tried to be strong. As everyone tried to comfort Frances through her tears, she laughingly said, "Oh, don't cry for me. I have had 16 years to prepare for this day and I have cried every day in anticipating this day." Those who surrounded them on that rainy afternoon did cry with her and prayed for Harry and her in the weeks ahead. They sent three other children off from Taipei's airports to return to America, continue their education, and start their own lives apart from being a missionary child.

The Raleys, like other missionaries, realized they were not only raising children, they were raising adults. They realized their children would make mistakes, but they prayed as they left the land of their roots that they were grounded in God's love and their love, and somehow God's grace would see both child and parents through the separation.

Harry was a missionary who placed strong emphasis on relationships. He spent scores of hours listening to and encouraging co-workers. He was never too busy to listen and support the fellow missionary and co-worker. He believed and lived out his faith in his relationships, and he believed he should share his faith. He never missed an opportunity to give a tract or a Bible, and tell someone the story of Jesus. He worked with the National Brotherhood for years in their street evangelism. The men in the Taipei churches met at different churches on Saturday morning, and invited people walking around the church to come in for only three minutes. The men would share with the outsider for three minutes, and then they were free to leave. However, most of the time the outsider would not leave. The person would stay and continue to ask questions about faith, God, Jesus, and the church. Several decisions were made in these weekly activities. Harry also told taxi drivers, new friends on the buses, waiters and waitresses, policemen, government officials, teachers, and students about the Christ who loves them and came to Earth to change their lives and set them free. One Chinese co-worker said, "Pastor Raley is one of the best seed planters I know. It is his nature to tell people about Jesus."

Harry and Frances continued to be actively involved in the lives of their fellow missionaries through encouragement, prayer support and sharing the mission's story in the churches. The Raley children had finished their education, married and started their families, and pursued their careers. Suddenly, they realized the time had come for retirement. Were they ready to leave Taiwan? No, Taiwan was home.

Taiwan had changed since 1955. There were superhighways, the Taipei World Trade Center, a strong economy, a higher cost of living, longer lines of traffic that moved without the sounds of car horns. Churches also had changes: beautiful buildings, larger memberships, ministers who were equipped and qualified to carry the load, larger seminary enrollment, and a larger mission family. They knew it was time to go, but the percentage of believers in Taiwan was still very, very low. Many had yet to hear the Story.

Frances and Harry left Taiwan in 1990. They reside in a lovely home not far from Mississippi College, Frances' alma mater, which is a Baptist college with a strong emphasis on missions. They retired from the International Mission Board, but not from missionary service. They returned to Grace Baptist Church in Taipei and worked as English language pastor for six months; served with the Chinese Church in Fairbanks, AK for two summers; and now work with the Chinese Baptist Church in Jackson, MS. Harry directs the prayer ministry for Mississippi Baptists.

Chinese traditions and values are very much a part of the Raley family. When the children visit and share a meal around their parents' table, memories of growing up in Taiwan quickly become a part of the conversation – riding on the bus with their dad and watching him share the love of Jesus with a stranger, having their mother drive them and other missionary cousins to Sunday night services, shouting in Chinese to a taxi driver, 'you have a flat tire!', eating dumplings at a sidewalk restaurant, visiting an orphanage, developing friendships with classmates from around the world, vacationing in Hong Kong, swimming at O Lan Bi, playing in a piano concert, eating popcorn and playing table games by candlelight during typhoons, singing in Chinese worship services, long flights to and from America, and listening to their parents praying for the lost of Taiwan.

The Raley children know they missed some things by not growing up in their homeland, but they also know they gained many things: International travel at an early age, a global view, love for people of all races and colors, an international education, and parents who were willing to follow God, whatever the cost. The values they learned from their parents, they are passing on to their children and grandchildren.

Frances and Harry arrived in Taiwan in 1954. They had excellent role models in those men and women who had served in Mainland China and transferred to Taiwan. They, too, were excellent role models for the missionaries who followed them. They were always available, taking a new missionary to the market, inviting a hurting couple to dinner, praying for a sick child, keeping a baby while the parents needed a few hours of free time, transporting MKs to the English language church, fixing a flat tire or changing the oil in the car for a single missionary, changing air tickets for a missionary child, accompanying the policeman when a missionary's car was stolen, participating in convention meetings, retreats, seminars, and attending Chinese worship services, encouraging a Chinese co-worker, visiting a sick pastor, witnessing to a lost person, preaching at funerals, and singing at weddings.

Their lives have changed since 1954, and so has Taiwan, but they continue to love Chinese people and pray for the peoples of Taiwan that someday, His church will cover the land, for in Christ there is no east or west. The Raleys gave their lives, their dreams, their time, and their talents to that beautiful island, and they continue to give their 'hearts' to Taiwan. To God be the Glory!

Harry and Frances Raley

Bynum and Sybil Akins
Changing Roads

They lived in a small farming community in northwest Texas. There were the old chores – canning, quilting and washboard laundering. The 15 children helped with the chores and made life enjoyable for this large family. Mr. Akins liked sports, so his children had many opportunities to join in various sports – basketball and baseball teams. The year was 1923. Luther Bynum Akins was the 11th child born into this family. He had an older brother, nine sisters, three younger brothers and one younger sister.

The family was unusually large, but they loved each other. They also loved the Lord. The Akins family was a Baptist family. Sunday worship and Sunday school were a part of their weekends. Bynum trusted the Lord as a nine-year-old boy in a summer revival. He was baptized and became very active in the little Baptist church. He was a Sunday school teacher even in his later teens.

Three of the children graduated from seminary, five became teachers and one a nurse. Bynum finished high school and soon entered the Navy in 1942. It was the days of World War II. While serving in the Navy, he had the opportunity to visit the Caribbean and South America. He visited with missionaries in the areas. It was a way of life different from his northwest Texas upbringing. Bynum had felt the

Lord's call to preach as a teenager, but had not responded. As he saw the needs of the Gospel in other places and other cultures, he came under strong conviction about his own response to the call of God upon his life. As a young Navy sailor, he responded to God's call to preach and to serve overseas.

After his discharge from the Navy in 1946, he enrolled in Howard Payne College to prepare for the ministry and to serve in cross-cultural ministries. The first week of school, in the library, Bynum noticed a tall, beautiful young lady. Her name was Sybil Lea Means. She had been in his English class. He asked her to help him with English, since he had been out of school for a while. She took note of the newly returned Navy man. Bynum and Sybil spent time together studying English. Bynum needed to learn more about this young woman.

Who is Sybil Lea Means? She was the second in a family of four children. The family lived on a farm when Sybil was little, but moved into a small town in south Texas when Sybil was school age. Sybil's mother was a Christian but not very active after the children came, probably because Sybil's father was not a believer. Sybil didn't have an interest in church; here again, probably because her mother didn't go to church, but sent the children. The family had a car, but Mrs. Means did not drive. Mr. Means spent Sundays at the farm, so the children had to walk to church. Sybil didn't like being late, walking the dusty road and having no friends when she arrived at church.

One day a neighbor invited the children to go with her. What was good about this invitation? The lady had a car and she could drive it. The church people were friendly. It was in this church that Sybil heard about God's love. She says, "Although Jesus knew all about me, He still loved me and wanted to be my best friend." Sybil believed this promise and took it seriously. She accepted Jesus as her Savior and

He became her best friend. She was 12 years old. She says, "I grew in my love for the Lord through the help of the church, but mostly through a personal relationship with the Lord Jesus."

When Sybil was 16, a lady came to her church and started mission organizations. It was in these organizations that Sybil learned about missions and missionaries. She discovered God's world through the need to take the Good News to the ends of the earth. Sybil wanted to serve the Lord. She thought it would be a privilege to serve the Lord in full-time ministry. When she was seventeen, she participated in a summer camp and committed her life to His service, saying, "Anywhere, Lord, I am ready to go."

She enrolled in Howard Payne College in 1946 to prepare for ministry – anywhere. Sybil participated in the Mission Volunteer Service Group. She helped Bynum with his English course. And, she took note that Luther Bynum Akins was also active in the Mission Volunteer Service Group. They had similar interests and were both preparing for missionary service. The Missions Volunteer Ministry used drama as an avenue to introduce missions to the churches. Bynum and Sybil were on the same drama team. It was the natural thing to do – play together, study together, and do ministry together. It wasn't long before Bynum and Sybil started dating. They enjoyed studying, playing, and serving together, and they soon declared their respect, their commitment and their love for each other. They made plans to marry after graduation, in the summer of 1949. Bynum had applied and was accepted at Southwestern Baptist Theological Seminary in Fort Worth, TX. He had been called as pastor of a small church near Fort Worth.

These were good years for the young couple, but there were challenges, too. Bynum was a full-time student and a full-time pastor, as well as being a husband and father. Sybil taught school for two years before their first child, Barbara, was born in 1950. Sybil found time to take seminary classes, be a mother to a new baby, be the wife of a young seminary student, and serve as a pastor's wife. And before Bynum's graduation in 1953, another baby joined the family. This time they had a boy and named him Lee.

Bynum received his Bachelor of Divinity in 1953, and they were ready for ministry in Texas churches. In fact, Bynum had already pastored three churches before seminary graduation. It had been four years since they entered Southwestern Seminary. They had good experiences in the Texas churches, so they came to feel it would be easier and better to stay in America. Their missions call had gotten lost in the busy and good schedule. Church life was good and family life was good. But God had other plans!

An Associational meeting in December 1953 was held in their church. Bynum was busy with the meeting and ended up sitting across the aisle from Sybil. During the invitation, Sybil wanted to go forward to recommit her life for missionary service. She looked over and saw Bynum, and knew he was moved, too. That night after they had gone to bed, he simply said, "I'm writing the Foreign Mission Board tomorrow." This was the right thing to do, as far as Sybil was concerned. She knew they were called to serve God overseas.

After the applications, physicals, and interviews, the process moved quickly. They were appointed in 1956 to Taiwan, commonly called "Formosa" where there was "an open field," according to Dr. C. L. Culpepper, Sr., who had been a speaker in their church that year. Harry and Frances Raley had been the first couple appointed to Taiwan, in 1954. Bynum and Sybil Akins proudly took their place as the second missionary couple appointed to Taiwan, Republic of China.

Bynum and Sybil prepared their church for their departure, prepared their four pre-school children – Barbara, four-

and-a-half years old; Lee, almost three years old; John, 18 months old; and the new baby, Carol, six months old – for a new land. They shopped to supply a five-year term, packed their freight, and prepared their family members and friends for the five-year separation. When they arrived in San Francisco, Sybil and two of the children had a strep throat infection, but they were able to board the ship. Oh, how God provided for the young couple. They were thrilled to have Dr. and Mrs. Culpepper, Sr. on the ship, as well as other Baptist missionaries going to the other newly opened fields across Asia.

Sybil and Bynum had their arms full of caring for baby Carol, and their legs were tired from running after the three active pre-schoolers. Mrs. Culpepper was available to hold Carol, answer questions, and encourage the young missionary mother. One of the highlights of the voyage was a Bible study Dr. Culpepper conducted each day for the young missionaries, while the children were in daycare activities. The days on the ship were enriching and enabled the young couple to prepare their hearts for the challenges ahead. How blessed they were when the ship docked in Keelung harbor. They looked out and were shocked to see the missionaries and Chinese Christians who had come to welcome the Culpeppers and the Akins family to their new home.

Their first year of language learning was with a private teacher in Taipei. It was quite a year! The children were sick a lot, they had no car, and the rains were the worst on record that winter. The trunks of the 26 trees in the front yard even turned green. They did have a phone, and Mrs. Culpepper was so faithful to call each week to laugh with Sybil, encourage her, and at times, cry with her. Challenges are part of life on the mission field. One of the privileges of the first year was the weekly prayer meeting on Saturday, with other missionaries. They listened to each other, lifted each other up in prayer, and hugged each other. The struggle between Taiwan and Mainland China was very real in those days. Missionaries were advised to keep luggage packed at all times, in case of emergency, with the understanding that Sybil and the children would leave first, followed by Bynum at some unknown date. This was another adjustment for the young couple, but they felt in their hearts that God had called them and He would direct their paths.

With a year of language and cultural learning behind them, the family was happy to move to sunny Chiayi the next summer. Bynum supervised the building of three churches in south Taiwan, and also the building of a missionary house for his family. Sybil taught freshman English in a Chinese high school. Under God's grace, they were able to start a church. Sybil stayed busy with supervising four children – trips to the open market, stopping by the rice shop and flower shop on the way home. The children rode their bicycles down the dusty, unpaved streets in front of the house, went fishing, played basketball in the yard, played marbles with the Chinese children, and walked in the open rice fields. Bynum continued full-time language learning and Sybil studied three hours per day – part-time by Missions requirements but "full-time" for a young mother with four children.

Many American military people were stationed in Chiayi. Barbara and Lee were allowed to attend the American Military School. John attended a small Overseas Missionary Fellowship school – one teacher and two first-graders. Fellowship with meals, conversation, prayer and encouragement was something that Bynum and Sybil looked forward to with missionaries from various denominations living in Chiayi.

During one of the summer mission meetings, Bynum and Sybil planned for the family to spend an additional week at Sun-Moon Lake. They were aware this was typhoon season. As they drove up the winding mountainous road to

Sun-Moon Lake, a typhoon blew in. The wind and rain were blinding, so it took an extra two hours for the trip.

As they drove up the mountain, they could only see a short distance ahead, the deep gully on one side of the road and wooded cliffs on the other side. When they reached the village nestled beside the lake, they could see an open space where they could see for miles across the lake to the seemingly low hills on the other side. There was an island in the middle of the lake and a stairway of a thousand steps leading to a shrine at the top of the hill, just beyond the island. It was truly beautiful to Sybil.

The first few days, they were busy in the meeting and did not mind the typhoon's wind and rain. Then the electricity went off, and their two rooms became dark, musty caves. The water in the bathrooms was turned off due to problems with the septic tanks.

Before the second week was over, another typhoon struck the island, almost on the heels of the first one. The rains were unusually heavy, and the family listened intently to the radio as they learned of extensive damage the rains brought to the mountain roads.

The children had to return to school, so the decision was made for them to walk down the mountain. The roads were muddy and slick. Everyone wore plastic tablecloths as raincoats. The miles grew longer and longer, the muddy shoes heavier and harder to pick up. The day wore on, and they were all hungry, wet and tired. John, the second son, lost one of his shoes in the mucky clay. He began to cry, but there was no way to find the shoe.

They saw bus stops, but no busses. They saw a taxi, and two missionary ladies went to bargain for the taxi. "The taxi is already spoken for by a man and his son," said the taxi driver. However, a few minutes later, the driver told the women he would take them down the mountain. The car was old, dented, rusted, but it looked wonderful to the ten who piled in with the driver.

Someone asked the driver, "Why didn't the man and his son take the taxi?"

"Oh, they are in the trunk," he said. "They are getting a free ride." That meant there were thirteen people in that car!

Bynum and Sybil were able to complete their language requirements during this time. At the end of five years, exhausted and happy, they returned to the U.S. for their first furlough, and of course, they shared their trip down the mountain with friends, family, and in the churches where they spoke.

They lived in Texas. The children had to adjust to relatives, the school system, American churches, and no high walls to protect the family when their father was away on speaking engagements. They also missed the noisy sounds and delicious Chinese food. Barbara came home from school one day, deeply concerned about American children.

"Mother," she said, "I feel so sorry for American children. They have never been overseas."

Bynum and Sybil had many opportunities to tell the Taiwan story across Texas. The first furlough was over before it started and they were back in Taiwan at the end of 1962.

On returning to Taiwan they moved to Tainan. The Barkers had moved to Chiayi, and the Spurgeons in Tainan were due a furlough. The Mission felt it was a good thing for the Akins to move to Tainan. Here again, Bynum spent much time doing what he did best – counseling, encouraging, praying with young men in the ministry, and visiting churches. Sybil worked with women. She was blessed by the faith of these women. One year later, the Spurgeons returned from furlough and wanted to stay in Tainan. It was time for the Akins to pick up family and belongings and move again.

Sybil never complained about moving. They were following God to new places, new needs, new opportunities.

Where did the family move? To Kaoshiung. Why Kaoshiung? Because two of the single ladies were retiring. Sybil taught English to women and attended the women's meetings. Some of the women were looking for places to serve, some wanted to study the Bible, some wanted Christian fellowship, and there were those who needed Sybil to encourage them in their marriages, take them to the doctor and carry food to them. Sybil found fulfillment in working with these women.

These were rewarding years for the children. They attended the American Military School in Tsoying and played with the Morris children. It was difficult for them when the time came for another move.

These places had special needs. Bynum was called the "fireman." He had the personality, gifts, and skills to help start churches. He also had the experience to help organized churches with church struggles and help churches and pastors with relational and communication problems.

Bynum worked with rural churches; mainly four mountain churches. Here again, he did what he did best – encourage, assist, and pray with young pastors in the ministry. Many of them were not young in years, but they were young in their faith and in the ministry.

The Akins were happy as a family and in ministry in Kaoshiung, but the Mission requested the Akins move to Hsinchu because of personnel issues. There were many new challenges in Hsinchu, but the major one was no international school or American military school. It became Sybil's responsibility to teach the children until they finished the ninth grade. Barbara went to Morrison Academy in the ninth grade. She enjoyed living at the boarding school. It was approximately an hour's train ride from Hsinchu. There were trains filled with pigs, chickens, bags of rice, and crying children. However, Sybil and Bynum made it possible for their little girl to ride one of the better trains, because she made these trips alone until her brother, Lee, entered Morrison Academy one year later.

It was here in Hsinchu that Sybil and Bynum learned more about God's grace. There are often struggles for the missionary to know how to deal with family needs and meet responsibilities in the ministry. One morning, Sybil and Bynum were preparing for their day, which was already full, when a call came from Carol. She had finished her medication and needed more medicine. Within a few minutes, a missionary, who was a nurse, called and told them that Lee had fallen over a 20-foot waterfall and they could not stop the bleeding from his ear. The decision had been made to put Lee on the train for Taipei, where he would be taken to a hospital there. The nurse told Sybil and Bynum they were to get on Lee's train when the train stopped in Hsinchu and go with him to Taipei. Well, what were the other issues?

Bynum had a funeral scheduled in the afternoon. Sybil had a Bible study that afternoon. There was no time or way to cancel the Bible study, and how does one cancel a funeral? They looked at their watches and realized they could do everything that needed to be done!

There was time to pack a small bag for an overnight stay. Sybil went to her Bible study. Bynum conducted the funeral. Then tickets were purchased for Taipei and Taichung. Sybil boarded the train Lee was on, going north. Bynum boarded the train going south to take Carol's medicine to her. Sybil said, "We learned to be calm and that God's gives peace in decision-making."

One of the memories Sybil recalls of their Hsinchu days was having the wrong name.

"Are you sure your name is not Wey?" the young Chinese undercover agent kept asking. "We are looking for an American named Wey."

"Oh, how I wished my husband were home! What kind of trouble are we in?" Sybil remembers thinking. "Our amah had answered the gate bell and led these two well-dressed, English-speaking Chinese men into our living room. They had asked for a Mr. Wey Chwan Ih. They seemed puzzled and sounded like they doubted me when I said there was no one living here by that name. Our Chinese name was Ai. The only American named Wey we knew lived in Taichung, two hours drive from Hsinchu.

"I nervously dug around in my husband's desk drawer to bring out our passports and residence certificates to prove we were named Ai and not Wey. The older man seemed to believe me, but he was still puzzled. I asked what the problem was. The other man said President Chiang Kai Shek and other officials of the National Parliament had received threatening letters written in English from a Mr. Wey Chwan Ih, and the return address on the letters was our address.

"Oh my," Sybil remembers thinking. "We could be in trouble if this isn't straightened out. Here we were foreign missionaries to the Chinese and in trouble with their government! We were not there to be involved in political affairs, but to present the Gospel in word and deed.

"Then I remembered a Mr. Wey who lived in Hsinchu, although he was not American. About a year before this, a strange little Chinese man, who insisted on speaking English to us, had visited us. He was very troubled about what his family was doing to him. Wey Chwan Ih believed they were involved in underground activities against the government and thought he might report them.

"We suspected Wey was mentally disturbed and so did not pay much attention to his fears. His visits were frequent for a while, always with the same complaints. Then he stopped coming for several months. One day the gate bell rang and there was Mr. Wey again. He pushed in past me and ran into the house, continuing to look back as if he feared someone were chasing him. In his hand was a package wrapped in newspaper. 'My step-father has kept me tied to my bed and would not give me anything to eat for a week. He threatened to kill me!' Wey hurriedly whispered.

"He showed us the rope burns on his wrists, ankles, and neck. Someone had tied him up! He told us of his plans to leave Hsinchu before his step-father found him. 'These are my books, the most precious things I have,' he said with a sad look on his face. 'Would you keep them for me?' We readily agreed, gave him some money for food, and he left. That had been about eight months ago. Our Mr. Wey must be the man the government agents were looking for. Did he write the threatening letters? Or did his step-father try to incriminate him by writing them and signing Wey Chwan Ih's name? How would the step-father have gotten our address? Was there a step-father? Maybe the whole story was Wey Chwan Ih's imagination, but what of the rope burns?

"After I recalled the story to the agents and gave them the package of books, they nodded their heads. Mr. Wey's name and address was on the package, and it was different from ours. 'Thank you. You won't have to worry about this anymore,' the two men assured me as they left."

About a month later, a formal letter came from the office of the President, thanking the Akins for their cooperation, stating Mr. Wey had been found and they had taken care of the matter. Bynum and Sybil wondered what that meant. They never saw Mr. Wey Chwan Ih again.

Bynum served as Chairman of the Mission at times, meaning he traveled to Taipei several days a week. The Akins left for their second furlough in 1967. Barbara graduated from high school during the three years the family was in the U.S., and started university studies. This was a very difficult time for the Akins to return to Taiwan, because Sybil felt she would not see her daughter again. She said, "The Lord had to speak directly to me, telling me that He would take care of my child if I would let go."

They returned to Taiwan for their third term. Lee, John and Carol attended Morrison Academy. Here again, Bynum and Sybil did what they did best – work with struggling churches and encouraging pastors. They say today, "This type of work is not always romantic, but it is needed and brings lasting results."

Barbara came for the summer, with the funding for travel provided by the Foreign Mission Board, and Lee graduated from Morrison Academy and returned to the U.S. with Barbara, to attend Howard Payne College.

Carol had problems with the new Morrison facilities, which caused her to have seizures. About the time Carol's problems started, the Mission asked Bynum to return to Taipei and work in the Mission office full-time. Sybil and Bynum saw God's hand in this move, which met two needs. Carol entered and later graduated from Taipei American School while living at home. Bynum was able to meet the Mission's need. John graduated the next year and returned to Texas Tech for college, where relatives were living. The Akins felt this was an important factor for missionary parents to consider when their children return to their homeland alone.

Bynum worked full-time at the Mission office and pastored Mei Ren Li Church. He preached once a month, but the major responsibility was starting a new church in a needy part of the city. It was a very rewarding time for the Akins and three believers, who lived in that area, to meet for prayer and encouragement, and to watch God answer their prayers. He provided the location and facility, a congregation came together, and a young seminary graduate was called as pastor.

Carol graduated from Taipei American School in 1975. Bynum and Sybil prepared for their fourth furlough, which was now three years instead of five years.

This furlough was relating to the General Convention of Texas, which had asked for furloughing missionaries to live in different sections of the state and promote missions through stewardship emphasis. The Akins lived in Midland, TX. Carol enrolled in Texas Tech, the same school as John. Lee had moved to Dayton Art Institute, with a special interest in art and a young lady who was in school in Ohio. He had dated Susan Wilson, the daughter of the Wilsons who served in Taiwan, during his senior year in high school at Morrison Academy. They graduated from their different schools and married in Midland, TX, just before Bynum and Sybil left for their fifth term of missionary service. Barbara was now at Southwestern Seminary in Fort Worth, TX, preparing for missionary service. This was no surprise to her parents or siblings, because at the age of sixteen, attending a Foreign Missions Week at Glorietta Baptist Assembly in Santa Fe, NM, Barbara had committed her life to missionary service.

When Bynum and Sybil returned to Taiwan, they moved to Chongli and lived near the Chong Yuan University. Carol had a difficult time in the university. This was not easy for her parents, but they claimed God's promises each day. Carol later returned to Taiwan and lived with her parents for one year. Lee and Susan returned to Taiwan to teach at Morrison Academy; Lee taught art, and Susan served as school nurse. John returned and worked at the Baptist Mass Communication Center for one year. How good it was to have three of their four children back "home" in Taiwan.

Bynum again did what he did best – counseling, encouraging and helping local pastors and starting new congregations. Sybil and Bynum both taught English at the two universities in Chongli. These classes opened many opportunities for them to develop relationships and share their faith.

They returned to Texas for their fourth furlough in 1978, with the understanding they would stay in the U.S. with Carol until she finished college. Carol graduated from college and found work, so Bynum and Sybil thought it was time to return to Taiwan. However, the Baptist General Convention of Texas invited Bynum to serve as the Chinese Consultant for Texas Baptists.

For seven years, they traveled all over Texas, starting and encouraging Chinese churches or Bible studies near colleges and universities. These were rewarding years for this couple who had been called to work with Chinese people, and they now could minister to Chinese in their own homeland.

During this time, Barbara graduated from Southwestern Baptist Theological Seminary, and served for six years in Washington State before being appointed in 1982 as a missionary to Japan. Lee and Susan were living in Dallas, TX. Lee taught art in the public school system and Susan was a nurse at Baylor Hospital.

In 1993, Bynum and Sybil retired to Denton, TX. They pastored a medium-size church on the edge of the city. However, God had other plans. They received a call from the pastor of Grace Baptist Church in Taipei, asking if Bynum would serve as pastor of the English-speaking congregation of that church. It had been 15 years since they left Taiwan, 1978. Taiwan had changed in those 15 years, but they still loved Taiwan and her people. They were overjoyed. They could hardly wait to return to Taipei.

Sybil taught English classes at Grace Baptist Church. She assisted in writing a book on "The Use of Puppets in the Church" for the seminary's media class. She felt privileged to teach an English class at the seminary. She remembered one of her morning walks to the Seminary – fall was in the air, the street filled with yellow jackets on sleepy children;

a mother with a third-grader on a motorcycle on the way to school; an old man with a broom sweeping in front of his door; a chubby boy, huffing; sister and brother walking together, she holds his hand; singing caged birds; the hump man who always had a smile; blooming trees, pink with huge blossoms; and a sense of His rightness in being in Taiwan.

Bynum worked with the English Congregation – preaching on Sunday at the two English speaking services, leading Wednesday night prayer services, working with a young married group in their homes, attending youth meetings, visiting people in the international community and counseling those who were attempting to adjust to living overseas. There were many Chinese students and those who had been saved in western churches who wanted to worship in an English-speaking church. These were good years back in Taiwan. They were thrilled. It was the finishing touch to their ministry.

They recall during a scheduled baptismal service, there was a strong typhoon pounding Taipei. They baptized 14 that evening. Two of them were from the English congregation. During another scheduled baptismal service, another typhoon pounded Taipei, but five from the English congregation were baptized.

Their children's lives are richer because they spent their formative years in Taiwan. Their Chinese cultural experience helped them to have a more global view, and has influenced their success in their chosen professions.

Carol and her husband spent more than three years working with a new university in Hong Kong. John and his wife have a daughter who has felt God's call to missions. Lee studied with a Chinese art teacher when he was a teenager, and this experience has affected his style of art. Barbara served as a missionary to Japan for 25 years. She was well received and loved by Japanese Christians and non-Christians. Their children have seen their parents love and relate to Chinese people. They had shown them by their lives that God loves all people – red, yellow, black and white.

Sybil and Bynum sum up their missionary journey: "The Lord planted a love in our hearts for all people. We were called to express that love in word and in deed in everyday experiences. He sent us to live out that love among Chinese, but it is the same wherever His children live, always open to opportunities. Always ready to tell of the hope that is within us and which is open to all who will receive."

The Akins went to Taiwan 52 years ago. The journey has taken many roads, highways, expressways, alleys, lanes and paths, but God was faithful beyond their dreams. Sybil and Bynum are officially retired, living in Garland, TX with their daughter, Barbara, who has returned from Japan. And every day, Bynum and Sybil remember their Taiwan roads with thankful hearts!

Bynum and Sybil Akins
Barbara, Lee, John and
baby Carol

Harlan and Joann Spurgeon
What A Journey!

Harlan was born June 30, 1931, at home in Bolivar, MO, in a small house occupied by his parents and five older siblings. His father was a rural mail carrier and his mother was a busy homemaker. His father, Hobart, had served in the Navy in World War I and had only become a Christian after marriage. Clara, and her mother before her, both were devout Christians. Harlan's mother told him some years later that she had dedicated him to the ministry before he was born, and on the day of his birth felt that the Lord had answered her prayer when the county health nurse presented her with her son saying, "Here is your preacher." She asked why she had said such a thing and the nurse replied, "He looks like a preacher to me."

Harlan was reared in church from his earliest childhood, and at age nine he received Christ and was baptized in his home church, the First Baptist Church of Bolivar, MO. He grew up in Sunbeams. His intermediate Sunday school teacher gave him his first job in his Ben Franklin Dime Store, and remained an encourager for Harlan all of his life.

When Harlan was 15 years old, his sister just older than he eloped with her boyfriend to Kansas. They were both too young to get married without parental consent. After reconciliation, the young married couple wanted her younger brother, "Buddy Boy," to come spend the summer with them. His parents consented and upon arriving in Eureka, KS, Harlan started looking for a church and a job. He found a job in a local grocery store. He first found the Nazarene church, but found that he knew few of their hymns. By the following week, he had found a small American Baptist church. Harlan formed a close friendship with the 24-year-old pastor, Rev. Bob Huston, and spent most of his free time doing pastoral visits and youth work with the pastor. In August, near to the time when he was to return home, he experienced a profound sense of call to the ministry. Rev. Huston wanted him to stay on and live with them and finish high school in Eureka while serving the church as minister of youth. Harlan's parents felt it wise for him to return home, which he did. Bob was a graduate of Moody Bible Institute and wanted Harlan to begin his education for the ministry there. Harlan's home pastor, Knox Lambert, encouraged him to attend Southwest Baptist College, the local two-year college.

The summer of 1950, before his second year at Southwest Baptist College (now SBU), Harlan was called as pastor of the Pleasant Hill Baptist Church in neighboring Dade County. In August of that year, Harlan returned to college one week early as a member of the school's BSU Council. The Council planned campus recreational and spiritual activities for the coming year. At that meeting, he noticed a lovely, brown-eyed brunette, and through one of his friends inquired about her availability. The word came back that the boy she returned to school with was like a brother. Harlan sent her word that he was not looking for a sister, since he had four at home. Thereafter the students loved to torment the two of them by singing, "O My Loving Brother." Harlan was ordained by his home church that same year, December 1950.

The young, lovely, brown-eyed brunette was available, and Harlan had time to get to know her. Joann Long was born in Indianapolis, IN. Her birth-mother, Thelma, was a Christian Scientist. Joann's birth was attended by a Christian Science Practitioner. Her father, Roy Long, was a salesman out in the rural areas. When he returned, he saw that his wife was very ill. He demanded that the people related to her religion leave the house immediately, and he called a physician. It was too late, and Joann's mother died as a result of infection one week after Joann's birth.

Joann lived with her father's sister for the first two years of her life, at which time her father married a wonderful Christian and Baptist lady named Ruth Sigman. Ruth is the only mother Joann remembers. They had a lovely relationship until Ruth's death. The family moved to south St. Louis, MO, and later two brothers were added to the family. The family was active in the Kings Highway Baptist Church. Joann accepted Christ when she was nine years old. She loved her church, and across the years was active in Sunbeams, missions organizations, Sunday school and choir.

Harlan and Joann married September 1, 1951, and moved to Liberty, MO, where, with Joann's assistance, Harlan completed his last two years of college at William Jewell. He first served as pastor of churches in Missouri and Kansas during this time. Joann worked at the snack bar at the college and later at Farmer's Insurance Company in Kansas City. Their first child, a son, was born on Christmas Day 1953. After graduation, Harlan taught in a rural school in Kansas for one year, in an attempt to get financially prepared for seminary.

The summer of 1954 found Harlan, Joann and six-month-old Tim starting out for Louisville, KY, where Harlan would attend Southern Seminary. They drove their 1949 Ford as far as St. Louis, where they visited Joann's parents. Joann's father, Roy, sold auto parts for NAPA. Noting the condition of the used Ford's engine, he suggested that they let some reputable mechanics that he knew take a look at the car. A complete engine overhaul was performed on the car while they were there. On the next leg of their journey, the car started heating up at Vincenes, IN. The radiator was unable to keep up with the tightly overhauled engine. Stopping at a garage, they were told that it would take a complete overhaul of the radiator before they could continue. All the money that Harlan and Joann had saved over the year of preparation for seminary was now gone, and it was necessary for them to make a collect call to Joann's parents to obtain more money to continue the journey to Louisville. They spent the night in a cheap hotel, so scared that they could hardly sleep. Harlan and Joann learned an important lesson about trusting God instead of making their own plans.

Soon after arriving at Southern Seminary, Harlan was introduced to a small rural church. After preaching both services at the Poplar Grove Baptist Church, Harlan, Joann and their son, Tim, were asked to wait for just a minute in the car. After about five minutes, a deacon came out and announced that they had just called Harlan to serve as their pastor for $25 a week. Harlan knew that the distance made such a financial arrangement impossible, and apologetically told him that the least he could accept was $35. The deacon asked them to wait again, and he returned after a brief while to say that Harlan had been called for $35 a week. This was the beginning of a wonderful relationship with rural Kentucky folks. The Spurgeons continued to serve there until they left for Taiwan three-and-a-half years later.

Seminary was a time when the call to missions became clear to Harlan. Joann had already dedicated her life to missions as a G.A. When Harlan had proposed marriage, he had assured her that if it was God's will for her to go to the mission field, God would call him also. He might not have been completely honest at that time, but God made an honest man out of him. In the introductory course to missions, the professor emphasized that God's plan of redemption for all the world's people was the theme of the entire Bible. He required that every student read the entire Bible during the semester. This caught Harlan's interest, and he proceeded to take advanced classes in missions.

In the late spring of 1957, Dr. James Sturtz came to the seminary campus with other representatives of the Foreign Mission Board for missions week. Harlan and Joann talked to the Mission personnel. He wanted them to make a decision in the service. Joanna was unable to be there because she was working. Harlan did make a public decision for missions.

A student friend later told Harlan that he had told the Lord in that service that if Harlan went forward for missionary service, that it was God's sign that he should go forward also. He thought Harlan was the least likely person present to make a commitment to serve the Lord overseas. This student kept his promise, did go forward and spent many years in Africa.

Dr. Sturtz told Harlan that if he and Joann would send their life histories to him in a few short weeks, they could be included in the missionary orientation to be held at Baylor in June. The year was 1957. At that time, only two orientation conferences were being held for new missionaries each year, each lasting one week. Harlan wrote his life history first during final examinations, and then watched Tim, age three and Twila, age one, while Joann closeted herself in the tiny church office and wrote her life history. The documents arrived in time, and Harlan and Joann were able to attend the orientation.

Harlan and Joann, after much prayer and conversation, felt led to the island of Taiwan. It was a very difficult decision, as Harlan felt that his experience with Biblical languages had not been particularly stellar, and he was concerned about learning the Chinese language. The promise of preaching to people who had never heard the Gospel, leading them to the

Lord and to discipleship, and bringing them together into churches, presented a great attraction to him.

Harlan's father and mother attended his seminary graduation in May 1957. After the ceremony, Harlan's father told him that he and his mother were anxious for them to return to Missouri so that they could come frequently to hear him preach. Harlan shared with them concerning their call to missions and that they would be going to Taiwan, if appointed. His father was very disappointed and said, "Formosa, Ambrosia, where in the world is that?" His father later told Harlan that when he returned to Bolivar, he proudly shared with his fellow postal workers the fact that his son was going as a missionary. An agnostic in the group said, "Take your boy to a psychiatrist; he has gone crazy." His father became a strong defender of his son's decision from that day.

Harlan and Joann were appointed missionaries to Taiwan in December of that year, 1957.

The Spurgeons said their good-byes to the little Kentucky church in January 1958 and made their way to St. Louis, where Joann's parents were living, and Bolivar, where Harlan's parents were living. Joann suffered a miscarriage while the family was in Bolivar, and First Baptist Church ministered to their loss. With crates filled and preparations complete, they left for San Francisco in a 1956 Chevrolet that they had purchased for the Foreign Mission Board. Harlan's dad went to work early that morning to avoid saying "goodbye." Harlan felt that he could not leave that way, so he went to the Post Office for a brief visit. They sailed in March on the *President Cleveland* to Yokahama. They flew to Taipei from Yokahama, and arrived on April 1, 1958.

The Baptist missionaries living in the Taipei area met the Spurgeons at the airport when they arrived. Dr. Charles and Ola Culpepper took them to their home to spend the first few days, while arrangements for housing and furniture were made. The first night in the Culpepper's Japanese-style house was memorable.

Harlan and Joann began the study of the Chinese language at the Taipei Language Institute, located in the Ren Ai Baptist Church. After a few months, it became obvious that Tim and Twila required more time with their mother, so Joann started studying at home. After a few months, an apartment became available at the Grace Church compound, and the Spurgeons were asked to move there.

Tim, age four, and Twila, age two, attended the preschool at Grace Baptist Church. That year, Tim won the "Hau Bau Bau Award" for memorizing the most Chinese Bible verses. His Chinese language acquisition proceeded rapidly as he played with the Chinese boys. While Harlan and Joann could barely speak, Tim knew the names of bugs and birds and spoke fluently. One day, Miss Lillian Lu, a student worker at Grace Baptist Church, came to see Harlan and Joann. They sat down with her and she told them that Tim had learned how to use bad words in Chinese. Harlan and Joann were very embarrassed, and cautioned Tim to watch his speech when playing with the other children.

While continuing language study, Dr. Hunker invited Harlan to preach in the evening service at Amoy St. Baptist Church, on the importance of Christians receiving training. It was Harlan's first experience preaching with the use of an interpreter. Harlan found it confusing and difficult to have an even flow in presenting his message. After the service, Harlan ducked out the side door and went to the car. When he arrived home, he wept as he prayed to the Lord, begging for fluency in the Chinese language. He told the Lord, "If I can't learn this language, there is no reason for us to remain here. Please, Lord, help me." Harlan dedicated himself to the study of Chinese, spending many hours in language classes each morning, and an equal number of hours each afternoon in preparation for the next day.

In the summer of 1959, Harlan and Joann were asked at a mission meeting to move to Taichung and take the place of Oz and Mary Quick while the Quicks were on furlough. Language teachers, were found and the Spurgeons continued full-time language learning. There were four small churches and chapels in the area where Harlan was asked to preach each month and observe the Lord's Supper. This became a vital part of Harlan's language learning, as he prepared one message each month in Chinese and preached it each week in one of the churches and conducted the Lord's Supper and baptism. Joann co-taught a Sunday school class of small Chinese children and participated in WMU at the Taichung Baptist Church.

In August after their arrival in April, word came that Harlan's father had undergone colon surgery and that he had advanced cancer. He had kept this secret to himself so that Harlan and Joann could leave for the mission field without this concern. While in Taichung, word came from Harlan's home pastor and friend, Dr. Earnest White, that his dad's cancer had returned and that he could not live many months.

He recommended that Harlan return home to see his dad, rather than trying to come home for the funeral. Harlan sent a cable to Dr. Baker James Cauthen, president of the Foreign Mission Board, asking for permission to return at his own expense. His request was granted. It was hard to leave Joann, Tim and Twila. It was also hard to borrow $1,100 for the plane ticket from the mission. Harlan flew to St. Louis, was met by Joann's parents, and preached that Sunday in Joann's home church, Kings Highway Baptist Church. He went on to Springfield, MO, where his father had just undergone his second surgery. As he walked into his dad's hospital room, his father looked up and said, "Son, I knew you would come. I had prayed to that end and God had assured me that you were on your way." Harlan and his father had three wonderful weeks together, searching scripture and praying before Harlan had to return to Taiwan. Harlan also preached at his home church and they received an offering, which, along with the checks given to Harlan at Joann's home church, came to exactly $1,100. Harlan and Joann knew this was another demonstration of God's loving care.

The Mission asked Harlan and Joann to move to Tainan. Harlan would serve as a general evangelist and church planter. At the time, Tainan was the third largest city in Taiwan. That fall, a cable came announcing the death of Harlan's dad. Dr. White, a Christian counselor as well as pastor of Harlan's home church, sent a tape of the funeral so that their little family in Tainan could experience the funeral and begin processing their grief. The Spurgeons learned death and grief are a part of the missionary journey.

In Tainan, Harlan and Joann worked initially with a church in Gang Shan and a mission point at Er Gau. They also worked with the pastor at the downtown church and conducted a monthly fellowship meeting for Americans living in Tainan. Harlan worked with a new seminary graduate to begin a church on Health Road. God blessed the joint efforts between the young missionary and the young pastor. Today, Health Road Church is a strong, healthy church. Joann became advisor for women's work in the Tainan area churches, and often rode the local bus to Er Gau and Gang Shan. She also served as Mission treasurer for the area.

Harlan conferred with Rev. Roland Chang to find still another location in Tainan to begin new work. They went to a poor area of the city, where retired military families lived. The tiny houses were situated on government land. Harlan was able to rent two small storefront buildings on the main road, with a total area of about 12 by 24 feet. Pastor Chang found a young man to be the custodian. Thomas Sywen was a Christian, a young single retired Chinese air force officer, and active in the downtown church. He was a gentle person who was deeply committed to Christ. He very quickly became invaluable to Harlan, visiting in the homes with Harlan and serving as a Sunday school teacher. Starting a new work in such an area proved to be difficult. Since the land was government owned, there were no churches in the area.

A question arose early as to what the Baptists had to offer. Catholics often brought food products that were given by the United States A.I.D. agency. Other denominations gave clothes. They were told that the Baptist mission gave the grace of God freely. Mrs. Tswei, an outstanding co-worker, often took soup to the sick and prayed with them. She was discerning regarding those who really needed help. Harlan worked with the men to help them find employment. The work grew and converts increased, along with the need to prepare the new believers for baptism. It was a joyful occasion when Harlan baptized 14 at the baptism service.

Tim and Twila enjoyed life in Tainan. They attended Wainwright School, the U. S. military dependents school in Tainan. They were actively involved in sports and had friends in both the Chinese and international community.

The fellowship with Baptists among the military population filled a great need, giving the Spurgeon children an outlet with English-speaking children. One evening after Bible study and prayer, one of the fellowship groups mentioned that they should start a congregation and build a church on the road to the air base, as a witness for all to see. They said that Americans should be remembered for their faith, and not for immoral activities. They wanted the building to house both an English and a Chinese congregation. The group started meeting on Sunday evenings at the En Tsz Tang student center, and the congregation grew.

In 1961, Joann was expecting. Harlan took her to the Tainan Air Base Hospital for a check up. The commander of the hospital was a Christian and offered to deliver the baby at the hospital. Ruth Ann was born soon after midnight on November 15, 1961. The doctor had Joann spend one night in the hospital, and then released mother and daughter the next evening, which cost a total of $44. The doctor showed up the next day with diapers, baby formula, and other necessary items and presented them as a gift. Harlan and Joann were deeply impressed by his kindness.

The congregation grew at North Gate Mission. The congregation was moved to fervent prayer that somehow land could be purchased and a building built. Harlan invited Dr. Chen Wei Ping to preach a revival. Dr. Chen was the son of the first ordained Methodist minister on the Chinese mainland. He had served large churches on the mainland, and had served as Counsel General for the Chinese government in Australia. On Taiwan, he had served for a time as preacher at the President's church, as Mandarin teacher for Madam Chiang, and as spiritual leader for her prayer group. He was a small man with a gray mustache. He had a great voice, beautiful and clear Mandarin, and was humble and very spiritual. He spoke flawless English, as he had a doctorate from an American university.

Dr. Chen stayed in the Spurgeon home during the revival. Since he was advanced in years, Joann asked what she could serve him at meals. His response was, "Prepare whatever you do for your children and it will be just fine for me." One Sunday morning, while Dr. Chen was staying with the Spurgeons, the family started down the lane near their home with the children holding his hands on each side. An American child living in the community asked Tim and Twila if Dr. Chen was their grandfather. The children looked up at Dr. Chen, in his long, flowing Chinese gown, and with a wide smile on their faces said, "Yes, this is our grandfather." It made Dr. Chen and the entire family feel very proud.

Many were saved in the revival. A piece of land was soon purchased for a new church building. The Spurgeons:

Harlan, Joann, Tim, Twila, and Ruth Ann went on a one-year furlough in 1963. They hated to leave Tainan, but Byrum and Sybil Akins moved to Tainan for the year. For six months, the Spurgeons lived in St. Louis, MO to be near Joann's mother and father. It was a good experience to be near Joann's parents and her home church. The church could connect them with their friends.

During the last half of their furlough, the Spurgeons moved to Harlan's hometown to be close to his mother and other family. His mother moved into an apartment and allowed her son and family to live in her home. Harlan preached a revival at his home church, the First Baptist Church of Bolivar, as well as represented missions throughout Missouri and the surrounding states.

The work at North Gate Road had continued to grow. The time had come to build on the property purchased in the area. A chapel and a small pastor's residence were built with Lottie Moon Offering funds. The people were so grateful for God's blessing that they planted flowers throughout and called it "the Garden of Eden."

A new mission house was constructed while the Spurgeons were on furlough. The family enjoyed living in the new house. There was a storage facility that Harlan turned into an office. There, he continued studying the Chinese language and preparing sermons. On one occasion, one of the children was asked at school what their father did. Other fathers went to work. She answered that her father didn't do anything. He just went outside to his office. This caused Harlan to be more diligent about letting his children know what he was doing.

Joann was expecting their fourth child in 1964. The commander of the base hospital had changed and it was not possible to use those facilities for the delivery. As the time drew near, Harlan took Joann to Chiayi to await the birth and to utilize the Christian hospital there. She stayed with Miss Marie Connor. It was difficult for her to be away from the family and for the family to be separated from her. Debbie came on September 5, 1964.

A couple of days later, mother and baby were released and Harlan traveled to Chiayi, about one hour away, and brought them home. Her siblings were overjoyed. That afternoon, Joann complained of a pain under her shoulder blade. Since Joann's mother had died of infection following Joann's birth, Harlan and Joann were concerned. Harlan took Joann to the base hospital so that the American doctors could check her out. By that time, the pain had spread and she had a fever. The doctor diagnosed infection and began massive doses of antibiotics. The doctor took a culture, but told the Spurgeons that by the time the culture returned, Joann would either be healed or deceased. They sent Joann home, but told her that she could not breast feed Debbie because of the high level of antibiotics in her system. The medication worked perfectly and Joann was soon back to normal. Many friends, Chinese, missionaries and the international community, prayed for Joann. They rejoiced in answered prayer.

The English work at the Kind Chapel grew. The time had arrived to pursue the dream of the American Air Force Baptists who wanted to build a sanctuary on the base road. It was not possible for the American congregation to legally purchase land in Taiwan, so the Baptist Mission agreed to allow the land to be purchased in their name, with the understanding that when the Americans left the land, the buildings would belong to the Chinese congregation. Land was purchased on Ta Tung Road, and the building constructed. The congregation was organized into the Trinity Baptist Church on March 20, 1966. Very soon thereafter, a Chinese congregation and an English pre-school program were started in the building.

In his second term, Harlan was elected chairman of the mission. This involved chairing the Annual Mission Meeting of the Southern Baptist missionaries on Taiwan. During his year-long term as chairman, Harlan also convened the Executive Committee that met between annual meetings. This was Harlan's first experience of administering a larger organization.

As their second term drew to a close in 1968, Harlan and Joann felt uneasy in their spirits, as if the Lord might be changing the direction of their ministry. They did not know what this meant. The work on Taiwan had grown. Whereas in the past there were very few ordained pastors leading the churches, now almost all of the ministers had been ordained. The role of the missionary was changing.

Harlan was asked to become the Executive Director of the Taiwan Evangelistic Crusade, scheduled for 1970 following furlough. Returning to the States, the Spurgeons settled in the missionary home across the street from First Baptist Church in Bolivar. Harlan was again asked to preach a revival at his home church, which he considered a great honor. Joann learned to drive during this furlough, and became the children's driver for all the school activities.

As the end of the furlough drew near, Dr. Marshall invited Harlan to stay on with the Personnel Department as a field representative with an office in St. Louis. Harlan went so far as to look for office space in the St. Louis area, but his heart was not at peace about the change. One Sunday morning, Harlan asked Joann and the children to go across the street to Sunday school and morning worship, so that he could have a time of prayer at home alone. When they returned from church, Harlan shared with them that he knew the Lord wanted them to return to Taiwan.

Back in Taiwan, the mission asked the Spurgeons to live in Taipei in a new duplex that had been built on the back of the Grace Baptist Church compound, in order to do his work as Executive Director of the Taiwan Evangelistic Crusade. The work was very demanding. There were 500,000 copies of the Gospel of John printed for distribution through the churches.

Choirs and musicians were invited, and writers such as O.K. Armstrong were invited to speak on university campuses. These well-known individuals opened many doors for the missionaries and Chinese Christians to share the Gospel.

The evangelistic meetings of the crusade were scheduled so that members of the Executive Committee of the Baptist World Alliance could serve as evangelists. Working out special meetings in the churches and chapels, as well as accommodations and travel schedules for the speakers, was a monumental job. God blessed and many heard the Gospel. Harlan was exhausted when it was over, and nodules were found on his thyroid. The nodules turned out to be stress-related.

Following the crusade in 1970, the Spurgeon family was asked to move to Kaohsiung, the port city in southern Taiwan. There, they would serve as church planters. The Spurgeons had a productive experience in Kaohsiung, but less than one year later, they were asked to move back to Taipei where Harlan served as Mission chairperson and as interim pastor of the Calvary Baptist Church. The family moved to the pastor's house near the church on Grass Mountain. The scenery around the house and church was beautiful. The children rode a school bus to Taipei American School. Joann would often ride a public bus down the mountain to buy groceries and attend meetings.

In the spring of 1971, the Spurgeons received a letter from a friend at First Baptist Church in Bolivar, saying that the pastor had resigned. The church had formed a pastor search committee. The committee member informed the Spurgeons that the committee had done a survey on the kind of pastor the church wanted. The committee and the Spurgeons were shocked that several people wrote in Harlan's name. Harlan and Joann were happy in Taiwan and found fulfillment in ministry.

Throughout the summer and fall, this friend continued to write saying that the committee was progressing with its work. She indicated that the congregation was a strong mission-minded church and filled with college students. This, too, was a mission field worthy of consideration. Joann and Harlan felt that this pressure was wearing them down. They wished to be left alone, but in their heart of hearts, they knew that they would have to do what the Lord wanted, not what they wanted.

In early December, Harlan and Joann decided they needed to settle the matter once and for all. They prayed that if the Lord was in this matter, they hear from the committee no later than the first Monday in January 1972. It would be possible to return to the states on a short furlough and settle the matter in person. Both Harlan and Joann felt at peace with this decision. From that point, the matter was dropped and the busy schedule continued.

On the first Monday in January 1972, Harlan went to the Mission Office to prepare for the Executive Committee that was meeting there that day. He checked the mail. There was no letter from America, so Harlan breathed a sigh of relief, feeling that the matter of his home church was settled. About five minutes into the meeting, the phone rang in the conference room. It was a routine matter, so Harlan instructed the secretary not to allow the meeting to be interrupted. A few minutes later, the phone rang again. Executive Committee member Bob Hunt said he would answer the phone and make sure no other calls were allowed. When Bob answered, he looked puzzled. He said, "Harlan, it's a call for you from the United States." At that time, international calls were not frequently made. Harlan took the call in another room.

The voice on the line said, "I am John Playter, chairman of the pastor search committee of First Baptist Church in

Bolivar, MO. All the committee members are in the room. We voted to invite you to preach in view of a call at FBC, Bolivar." The chairman of committee explained he felt he could not wait to write a letter. Harlan knew why. He and Joann had prayed. They did not want to return to America, but in view of the way this had happened, he now believed that God was in it and that they had to take a serious look at First Baptist Church, Bolivar.

The Spurgeon family arrived back in Bolivar in early February 1972. After repeated meetings with the pastor search committee and after much prayer, Harlan and Joann knew it was God's will for Harlan's name to be presented to the church in view of a call to become pastor. In early March, Harlan and Joann were visiting Joann's parents in Farmington, NM, where they had moved in retirement. A phone call confirmed that Harlan had been called as pastor.

The Spurgeons had hardly settled into the parsonage when a phone call came saying that Joann's mother had died suddenly from a stroke, and one week later at about the same hour, her father passed away in his sleep from a heart attack.

The four Spurgeon children settled into the local public schools. Having the advantage of English-speaking schools in Taiwan helped greatly in their adjustment. However, life on the mission field had its share of struggles, and now being children of the local pastor was no less challenging.

Harlan considered it a great honor to serve as pastor of a church where his first and second grade teachers were members, along with several of his high school teachers and superintendent of schools. Also in the congregation were classmates who had gone from first grade through high school with him.

The years at FBC, Bolivar proved a joy and challenge. They built new church facilities. The existing building was constructed in 1927. Plans were made to build a sanctuary that would hold up to 1,200, along with church offices, choir suite, and a recreational building. Harlan and Joann served the congregation with great joy. Harlan also completed a doctorate at Midwestern Seminary while serving the busy pastorate.

After serving First Baptist Church for over seven-and-a-half years, an unexpected opportunity came to Harlan and Joann. Southwest Baptist College invited Harlan to become president of the two-year college. About this time, they were given an opportunity to exchange pulpits with a pastor friend in London, England, and Harlan and Joann saw this as an opportunity to get away and sort things out. Tim and Twila were both married by this time, so they took Ruth Ann and Debbie with them.

Long walks gave Harlan an opportunity for solitude and prayer. Harlan and Joann returned one month later, not knowing why, but firmly believing that it was the Lord's will to walk by faith and accept this position at the college. Both the call to First Baptist Church and the call to Christian education were quite confusing to them. They both still felt that their primary calling was to the world mission of the church.

It was difficult to move from Harlan's home church to the college across town. They knew many of the faculty who had been members of his church. Harlan had been honored by his alma mater with a Life Service Award in 1963, and an honorary doctorate in 1976. Both he and Joann had a great appreciation for the college where they met and courted.

Although he did not know it at the time, the college experience provided Harlan with valuable administrative experience. As a local boy who grew up in Bolivar, Harlan was able to tie in local people by establishing a Polk County Community Scholarship Fund. This made it possible for more local young people to attend. He also helped the institution move to university status. Attendance was further enhanced by starting a football program. But Harlan felt that his most important work was in the spiritual lives of the young people. During this period, Joann received the Life Service Award and completed her college education.

While serving at the college, a partnership between the Missouri Baptist Convention and the Taiwan Baptist Convention was established. Harlan was asked by the Executive Director of Missouri Baptists to serve as consultant for the state staff. During one visit, he had the opportunity to present an honorary doctorate from SBU to Pastor Paul Hsieh, whom Harlan regarded as one of the most outstanding pastors he had ever known.

Three years into the college experience, Harlan and Joann began to feel that it was time to return to their first calling. They attended Foreign Mission Week at Glorietta, NM and talked with Dr. George Hays, Area Director for East Asia. George counseled them that it would be difficult to return to Taiwan after more than ten years. So they returned to Southwest Baptist University to continue their work there.

In December 1982, a call came to Harlan from Dr. Keith Parks. Dr. Parks said that Dr. Bill Marshall, Vice President for Human Resources at the Foreign Mission Board, had resigned and he was looking for his replacement. He was looking for someone with significant missionary experience, pastoral experience, and administrative experience, and that several people, including Dr. George Hays, had mentioned Harlan's name. Now Harlan and Joann knew why God had led them in such a roundabout path.

Harlan met Dr. Parks in St. Louis in early 1983, in a motel near the airport. They talked missions all day and into the evening. Harlan was elected at the spring Board Meeting and appointment service in Indianapolis, IN. He began his work at the Foreign Mission Board on June 1, 1983.

Harlan considered the opportunity to serve at the Foreign Mission Board God's grace and a great honor. He participated in the creation of plans and direction of the Foreign Mission Board worldwide. It was an exciting time to be at the FMB, as Bold Mission Thrust looked forward to having 5,000 missionaries on the field by the year 2000. The "conservative resurgence" changed the direction and course of the IMB. Dr. Parks announced his retirement effective on his birthday in October 1992. Harlan retired from the Foreign Mission Board on his 62nd birthday, June 30, 1993 after 25 years of mission-related service.

After retirement, Harlan worked for three years with Dr. Parks at the Cooperative Baptist Fellowship Global Missions office in Atlanta, GA, starting a new missionary enterprise. This assignment gave Harlan great satisfaction, as it meant hands-on work with one part-time secretary, trying to do the work he had done at the Foreign Mission Board with 113 full-time staff. Before retiring at age 65 in 1996, Harlan and the Global Missions staff had processed 120 career missionaries for service, primarily going to countries where the Gospel has never been heard.

Harlan and Joann are grateful for the unusual pilgrimage they believe God chose for them. However, their love and admiration for the Taiwan Mission family and his fellow missionaries, continued to grow over the years. It was their prayer that they be found faithful, whatever the Lord led them to do.

Harlan and Joann retired to Springfield, MO, to be near family and friends. Since retirement, they have participated in five interim pastorates in Missouri and two interim pastorates in Mirfield, England. Their four children have meaningful marriages and are active in their local churches. The Spurgeon children all profess that the experience of growing up in a missionary family in Taiwan was a wonderful education in itself. Their five grandchildren are a blessing, as they find their place on this journey of faith.

Harlan and Joann still hold dear the scripture verse given to them by Dr. Carl Hunker before they departed for Taiwan in 1958. "Have I not commanded you? Be strong and courageous. Do not be terrified; do not be discouraged, for the Lord your God will be with you wherever you go." Joshua 1:9

This has been true in the Spurgeons' journey of faith, wherever He led them!

Harlan and Joann Spurgeon

Richard and Tena Morris
A Family for Taiwan

I n the western plains of the southern state of Tennessee, about 35 miles from Memphis, there is a small rural town, Somerville, a farming community where the U.S. south was lived out on a daily basis in the 1940s. It was the place where much of this story begins. The Morris family moved around during the 1940s. Mr. Morris was an entrepreneur. He chose to follow the military and set up restaurants near military bases. He was a country man with strong family values, including hard work. His eldest son, Richard, often went to the cafe at 4 a.m. because the cook had shown up drunk. Richard's job was to mix the pancakes. Time made Mr. Morris long for his home and he returned his family to their southern roots in Somerville, TN. Here, he purchased an old barn at the edge of town and built a construction company, naming it Grady Morris and Son Lumber Company. He had great dreams for the number one son, Richard, to join him in the family construction company. Of course, this was not to be, but Bobby, the second son did eventually join their father in the family business.

So it was that the Morris family lived in various places during Richard's younger years and returned to Somerville when he was a sophomore in high school. He immediately became popular with his many friends, became captain of the high school football team, and was the life of the party. He loved to play musical instruments, was popular with the girls in school, enjoyed sports of all kinds, and had a pleasing, enjoyable personality. He danced and entertained the young women on Saturday night and served as Sunday school director on Sunday morning. He was a Christian, but not a serious one.

It was during this time that he met a petite, dark-haired, beautiful, charming young lady by the name of Tena Simmons. Tena, too, was a product of Somerville. Her father was a postman and her mother was a homemaker. Her mother loved the piano, and Sunday afternoons were usually spent with her playing with Tena, and her sister, Freda June singing.

Tena was serious about her faith. During a week-long revival, on the closing night, a Saturday night, she went forward. Her mother, who was playing the piano, whispered, "Wait until we are able to talk together." The reason her mother was concerned was because Tena was only six years old, her sister had made a profession of faith earlier in the week, and she thought Tena might be going forward because Freda June had gone forward. Years later, her sister doubted her faith and her salvation experience, but Tena never one moment doubted what happened that Saturday night, when a little six-year-old girl walked down the aisle and gave her heart to the Lord Jesus. In the years to come, Tena was an honor student and popular among her classmates. They elected her as a high school cheerleader.

Tena had met Richard Morris because they attended the same church. However, she wouldn't date him because she felt he wasn't serious about his faith and she was very serious about her commitment to Jesus Christ. Richard moved on to Duke University, a North Carolina university, to study pre-med. He was on a Navy ROTC scholarship. He was popular on the college campus, too, but soon discovered he was failing in studies, relationships, and life in general.

Surprising news was to bring great changes! Richard's mother worked with the young women's missions' organization called Young Women's Auxiliary. So, it was through his mother that Tena heard Richard was coming home from Duke and felt he was ready to make some changes and really live for His Lord. That got Tena's attention! Richard and Tena had their first date on Easter Sunday night, 1948, when Tena was a senior in high school and Richard was studying architectural design in Memphis.

That summer, 1948, Tena went to Ridgecrest Baptist Assembly in the breath-taking North Carolina mountains. She, like hundreds of other young women of her time, heard and was deeply touched by the message of Baker James Cauthen, executive director of the Foreign Mission Board. Tena had grown up hearing about the needs of a lost world. She was confronted that week with, "How should I respond to those needs?" Her mother worked with Sunbeams, so Tena went to Sunbeams as a child. She sat in a small chair and listened to her mother tell missionary stories. God had prepared the soil and it was easy for Tena that evening at Ridgecrest to write in her Bible, "I am ready to follow you. I will go anywhere you send me."

When she returned from Ridgecrest, Richard told Tena about an encounter he had had with the Lord. Richard had felt a sense of call to preach the Gospel, and she told him what had happened to her at Ridgecrest. They were on the same page. Their dreams were going in the same direction. They wanted to follow their Lord!!

At this time, Richard's father was upset to think his oldest son had made a decision to go into the ministry, rather than continue in business. After all, Richard was training as an architectural draftsman at William R. Moore School of Technology in Memphis, TN, and from all reports was an outstanding student. His father tried to talk Richard out of his new decision and even asked the pastor to talk Richard out of it. Richard's mother was thrilled and was very supportive.

Richard proposed to Tena on the day her daddy died. They had been dating and he simply offered to take care of her from then on. That was November 11, 1949. They were married on June 6, 1950 at First Baptist Church, Somerville, TN. Tena was 18 and Richard was 21. This was a relationship, a partnership, a love affair that was to last 34 years. They shared the best and the worst of times.

They moved to Jackson, TN, where they started their first home and went to Union University. Tena became pregnant with their first child, a little girl whom they named Marilyn, born in 1951. Tena dropped out of school before Marilyn was born, but this didn't keep her from being involved in the various activities that Richard participated in. He was on the tennis team, played the trumpet in the band, attended sports activities, and preached in small churches on Sunday. Tena and Marilyn were always there to support him.

Richard graduated from Union University in the summer of 1952 with a major in Biology. The young couple was sincere, and anticipated serving the Lord in Tennessee churches. However, they knew theological training was necessary. They packed their few possessions and headed for Southwestern Baptist Theological Seminary in Fort Worth, TX, to prepare themselves for effective ministry in America. Tena had thought of serving cross-culturally, but at this time, this was not a part of Richard's plans.

They entered Seminary in the fall of 1952. Seminary life was hard work and they lived on a small budget, but they still had fun. Marilyn was happy to welcome a baby sister, Rozanne, in 1953, and another sister, Melanie, in 1955. The Morris family was growing. Southwestern Seminary was a wonderful place for little girls to grow up. Marilyn attended kindergarten while her parents prepared for the ministry.

Even as small children, the girls were being taught that it was a family ministry.

One ordinary day, Tena was home ironing clothes, unaware that Richard was attending one of Southwestern's famous Missions Days. Missionaries and mission executives had been invited to speak in classes and in chapel. These speakers "brought the world" into these places, and through the workings of the Holy Spirit students, were able to see a lost world through the eyes of Jesus. Richard came home from school that day and walked over to the ironing board where Tena was ironing. He gave her a big hug and her response was, "Where are we going?" He told her what had happened during the morning's chapel service.

Baker James Cauthen spoke in chapel that morning. He closed his message with the words, "When God called you to preach, did He call you to a little church in Tennessee, Mississippi, or Texas, or did he call you to the world"? Dr. Cauthen then challenged the students to consider foreign missions. Richard knew in his inner being that he was called to serve God overseas and he simply said, "Yes, I will go." Tena had made that commitment at Ridgecrest years before when she had written in her Bible, "Lord, I will go anywhere you send me." God had prepared her heart through Sunbeams when she heard about children in far away China.

They contacted the Foreign Mission Board and started the appointment process. Seminary graduation provided an opportunity to move to a church in the small town of Iron City, TN. Richard needed to complete pastoral experience required for missionary appointment. The Board encouraged Tena to finish her college education. Tena had never been one to run from challenges, so she enrolled in what was then called Florence State University in Florence, AL. She boarded a bus each morning at 6:00 a.m. with a group of laborers, to travel across the state line to Florence where they worked, and she studied at Florence State. In the evening, she and the same group of tired men boarded the bus back to Iron City. She often walked in the house to smell burnt food cooking and see three tired little girls. These were not easy days, but Richard never complained. Tena and Richard had a clear vision of God's call to the nations.

It wasn't long before a trip to the doctor revealed that they were expecting baby number four. It wasn't easy, but she and the kicking little one inside her boarded the bus at 6:00 a.m. for Florence State five days each week, and they returned on the same bus at 6:00 p.m. As she grew larger and more exhausted, Richard, Marilyn, Rozanne, and Melanie would meet their student/wife/mother at school and drive her home. They happily welcomed daughter number four, Beverly, in 1957.

They lived in Iron City and pastored a church for two years. During this period of time, Richard completed the pastoral experience needed and Tena completed the required two years of college.

At last, Richard and Tena Morris were ready for appointment. Where were they going? They had read, discussed and prayed over Carl Hunker's book, *Formosa: Beautiful Island*. They were deeply impressed with the challenges and opportunities on this little spot of God's world in the Pacific. During the interviews with the Foreign Mission Board Personnel Department, staff suggested Indonesia, one of the countries newly entered by Southern Baptists missionaries, because of Richard's training in architectural drafting.

Richard and Tena understood the need for architects and builders in these newly entered countries, to supervise the building of missionary homes, hospitals, and churches. Richard had an interest and training in this type work, and he wanted to 'help' with building needs in the country where they were appointed. However, Richard's passion was preaching and starting churches. This passion lasted for a lifetime.

Richard and Tena talked and prayed. As they discussed the options with the Foreign Mission Board personnel, they suddenly knew the place. The Holy Spirit led them to recall *Formosa: Beautiful Island.* They looked at each other and then looked at the Foreign Mission Board personnel and said, "We want to go to Taiwan." There were others in the room that day who shared their passion and love for the Chinese people; they applauded and said, "We are so glad you are going there." Richard and Tena Morris were appointed Southern Baptist missionaries to Taiwan on April 4, 1958.

They had many tasks to do – shopping, packing, speaking in churches, and saying good-byes to family and friends. This was harder than they had anticipated. Tena's mother and sister were proud of her and the man she called husband and partner. Richard's father continued to struggle with his first son going overseas. He was disappointed that his son wasn't going to become a partner at the lumber company. He was also hurt that Richard and Tena were taking his grandchildren thousands of miles away to a foreign country. However, Grandfather slowly came to accept Richard's calling and passion. He and Richard's mother made a trip to Taiwan and were very proud of their preacher/missionary son and his family.

Before departure, the Foreign Mission Board required the family to take specific immunizations for preventive measures in traveling overseas. This wasn't easy on little girls who didn't really "like" needles. After a trip to the clinic, in fear of more painful shots, Rozanne expressed the wishes of the four little girls. "They can go. I don't want to go tell Chinese boys and girls about Jesus. I will stay here."

On August 1, 1958, Richard, Tena, and their four daughters aged seven, five, three, and one boarded a ship in San Francisco and headed to the Far East. They docked in northern Taiwan, the city of Keelung, on August 28! The missionaries and national believers were there to welcome the Morris family to the Taiwan Baptist Mission and to "Formosa: the Beautiful Island."

Their introduction to Taiwan was at the camp on Grass Mountain outside Taipei. They experienced a typhoon that first week, with howling winds and torrential rains like they had never heard before. The children had to be reminded through the noisy night that God would take care of them.

Soon the little family was settled in a large old Japanese-style home with sliding walls and polished floors. They left their shoes at the front door. The children found it fun to slide on the wooden or terrazzo floors in their socks. Marilyn and Rozanne both got hepatitis that first term.

In the late 1950s, Taiwan was populated with refugees from Mainland China and local Taiwanese who had lived there for centuries, and the eight minority nationalities. The Baptist missionaries in Taiwan had transferred from China, with the exception of three couples, who had been appointed to Taiwan. These couples had studied Mandarin which was the language spoken by those who came from Mainland China. There were those in the Mission who felt that the missionaries would soon return to Mainland China, while others thought missionaries would never return to the mainland. A decision had to be made about missionaries learning the local language.

The Mission team, after prayer and an assessment of the situation, came to feel it was time to assign missionaries to learn the local language – Taiwanese. There were millions who spoke that language who had never heard the Gospel. Who would be the first Southern Baptist missionaries to study Taiwanese? It became a strong desire of Richard and Tena to learn and speak the native language of Taiwan. Richard had a strong musical ear and therefore, Taiwanese came more easily for him than for Tena. Tena worked hard, but she never felt she was fluent in Taiwanese. She spoke Taiwanese with a Tennessee Southern accent, to the delight of many. Where she lacked in language skills, she quickly and effectively made up for it in loving people with her southern hospitality. It was often said that Richard spoke like a Taiwanese, but Tena looked Oriental. They were to make a good team in the Taiwanese community.

Meanwhile, Marilyn, who was seven, learned Mandarin on the streets where she played with the neighbor children. She became a helpful interpreter and even invited a young lady to church who actually showed up the following Sunday. They took her with them to Grace Church, and in time, she became a Christian. The children opened many doors for ministry for this young family.

During their first year in Taipei, a man rang their gate bell and asked for any dry-cleaning that they might have. Tena was very trusting and she gave him several of Richard's best suits to clean. They never saw the man or the suits again! This was only one of many cultural lessons that had to be learned.

The Morris family received Chinese names that gave them great pleasure! Their surname was "Ma," which sounded similar to Morris, and is the word for "horse." Bok-su is the Taiwanese word for minister/pastor and Bok-su-niu was the word for pastor's wife. The children were to hear these names many times through the years. They learned to write the character for 'ma,' and had Chinese seals made in their teenage years. Tena and Richard collected beautifully carved Oriental wood and pottery horses over the years. They are proudly displayed in her Arizona home today. These horses continue to remind her of those Taiwan years.

Marilyn, Rozanne, and Melanie were bussed to Taipei American School while Tena and Richard went to Taiwanese class. Richard preached on Sundays with an interpreter until he was able at last to preach alone. As the months moved into years, he was able to pick up a lot of Mandarin just from friendships.

Tena's health took a turn for the worse during these days in Taipei. She spent one year in bed recuperating from chronic pancreatitis, but still managed her household. On many evenings, the family taught English on the second floor of a storefront in Sanjenli. Two sisters had recently graduated from the seminary and worked with Richard and Tena in the Sanjenli ministry, which was later organized into a Taiwanese Church.

The English class was a very popular class, and the girls enjoyed the location and the people. There was a little girl who would wander up the aisle once the lesson started and climb up onto Tena's lap. Just before the end of the class, she would slide down and toddle out. After this happened several times, Tena asked whose daughter she was, and none of the students knew her. This little girl was just one of Tena's many little friends. Her own girls were learning to share their mother with others.

As the family prepared to move from Taipei, it seemed the Lord gave them special fruit for those language years. Richard taught an English Bible class in Banchyau. A young teacher who had recently returned from America with a degree in agriculture came to the class. Richard and a Conservative Baptist missionary, Jim Cummins, worked with the young man, who came to faith in Jesus Christ. He went on to have a very successful career in teaching and later became the first Taiwanese, native-born president of Taiwan, Li Dung Hui.

During their years in Taipei, they became very close friends with three young seminary couples. All of them were native Taiwanese. They had dreams of starting Taiwanese churches. One student was Cheng Da Huh, who was later to start and pastor one of Baptists' leading Taiwanese churches, Mu Yi Baptist Church in Taipei. Tsai Lu Jya moved to Ping Tong in the summer of 1960, and the other one, Chen Dong Bi, to Kaohsiung. They influenced the Morris' decision to move to Kaohsiung in the summer of 1961.

Some missionaries in the Mission questioned their decision to move south and do Taiwanese work, so Pastor Chen and Richard traveled down the island, stopping in major cities to talk with Presbyterian pastors about Baptists doing Taiwanese ministry. Both missionaries and local pastors were dedicated and committed servants of the Lord. Their only motives were to bring the Gospel of Christ to the Taiwanese-speaking people. They realized the needs were overwhelming, and they gladly welcomed Baptists to join them in taking the Gospel to places where it had never been heard.

Consequently, the Morris family moved south to Kaohsiung in the summer of 1961. To the surprise of everyone, especially Tena, she was pregnant again. Daughter number five was born in 1961 and named Grace, "Un-hwi," because she was a blessing from God. This name conveyed their joy to the church family and neighbors that Richard wasn't disappointed that he didn't have a son to carry on the family name.

It was also during this time that the family spent time in the mountains with Pastor Yang Shu at Lyou Gwei, and Mrs. Wang at the Faith, Hope and Love Orphanage. The family took in two children from these mountain towns with heart problems on separate occasions, so that they could come into the city for tests and medical help. One little guy, "Dee-dee," who was about eight years old, really bonded with Richard and called him "Papa." The girls were to admit years later that they were a little jealous because Dee-Dee slept at the foot of Tena and Richard's bed, taking much of their parents' time and attention.

Richard made lots of trips into the mountains to show the Moody nature films that witnessed of God's creation and His love for each person. After the showing of the film, he would hand out tracts and talk to people. The entire family often went on these evangelistic trips. Tena asked one little girl if she knew who Jesus was. With a puzzled look, she answered, "He doesn't live on <u>my</u> street!"

On one of those trips to show the movie and to share Christ, the building was open on all sides and had a concrete floor. There were people of all ages, from the elderly to small children and babies. As the sun went down, the mosquitoes came out. Soon, six-foot pillars of mosquitoes rose up over each person's head. Everyone had mosquito bites on their arms and legs, but that night, Tena must have been especially concerned about Gracie, who was still quite small. She put Grace in a pillowcase and tied it loosely around her neck. Even though Grace looked hilarious, she was protected from the chin down from mosquitoes! Young and old were entertained by Tena's ingenuity. The girls learned from their parents that sometimes life is a little difficult, but there is joy in telling people about Jesus.

The Morris family went on their first furlough when Gracie was not yet one. Marilyn remembers this furlough. "I was about 12 years old when we went on our first furlough. Daddy taught the four older girls how to sing in four-part harmony. At the time, Grace was too shy to join us. That was the beginning of our singing as the 'Morris Girls.' We sang acapella, without musical accompaniment. One of our favorites was a little song called *Yellow Bird*. Mama made us matching yellow dresses to wear when we performed in the U.S."

The furlough was extended to a longer time, because Tena wasn't given medical clearance to return to Taiwan. In fact, it was two years before they returned to Kaohsiung. The family moved back into the same home and the girls attended the same school, Tsoying American School. In Kaohsiung, the entire family was involved in starting a Bible study in their home. They met weekly on Sunday evenings, out on their large screened back porch and in the living room. Their co-worker was Chen Dong Bi, the young pastor who had helped Richard survey the need for Taiwanese work. They worked hard and God honored His Word and their faithfulness in sharing the Good News. This work became the Wen Hwa Baptist Church. It was a blessed day for Richard, Tena and their family, as well as the Chen family, as they realized another dream had come true – an established Taiwanese church where the Good News of Jesus Christ would be preached for generations!

The Foreign Mission Board made available funds to purchase land and build a lovely little church building with windows on both sides. There was a full church when the building was dedicated. Praise and thanksgiving were given to God for His blessing and directing this ministry. The year was 1966.

Richard worked with Dr. Bjorgus, a Norwegian missionary from another mission group. They located children who had polio and needed braces and a place to study. At this time in Taiwan, there were no facilities for handicapped children. They lived at home and lay on mats most of the time. Wen Hwa Baptist Church started a kindergarten for children who had suffered from polio.

Richard and Tena had a burden for this ministry. They wanted God's love to be demonstrated to these children. They shared this need and their burden with Tennessee Baptists. Tennessee R.A.s (Royal Ambassadors) gave an offering to purchase a lift for a bus to pick up the children and take them to the church kindergarten. The bus itself was a witness of God's amazing grace, because it had written in English and Chinese, "Ambassadors for Christ – 2 Corinthians 5:20." The church's kindergarten continues to be very effective even today, even though there are fewer and fewer handicapped children who attend.

The kindergarten was a service of faith for the church, school staff, and the missionaries. The church didn't have the funds to pay the first month's salary to the kindergarten teachers. An American Navy ship docked in the harbor. The chaplain called and said the sailors wanted to help a church in some project, and had taken an offering. Richard and Pastor Chen gladly went to get the offering. What surprised, pleased and thankful men they were when they discovered the offering was the amount to the very cent they needed to pay the teachers' salary. God works in strange and amazing ways. This young missionary and Chinese pastor were learning faith lessons.

The church's kindergarten ministry brought such attention to city officials that they interviewed Richard, asking him why he would go to such efforts. His simple answer was printed in papers for thousands to read, "Jesus loves little children. He would do the same if He were here." All praise and glory were given to the Father who had called him to this beautiful land.

Richard and other missionaries worked with the Kaohsiung and Pingdong churches and they were able to purchase land and establish a Polio Home in Kaohsiung, which was directed by the Kaohsiung Mandarin Church. This was the only home of its kind for many years in south Taiwan. The Christian workers loved and taught the children and ministered to the families. God richly blessed this ministry.

Richard had a beautiful tenor voice and sang the tenor solos for *The Messiah* that term. He practiced throughout the house, until all of the girls could join him in every tune. The girls were all encouraged to take piano lessons, but Melanie is the only one who teaches piano and voice today. All the daughters took voice lessons during one of the furloughs. Their musical talents opened many opportunities for sharing their faith as individuals and as a family.

Marilyn said, "He taught us to love music of all kinds. Much of my knowledge of classical music comes from Daddy playing it at 'concert level' (LOUD!) so that we could hear all of the instruments. I remember sitting at the dinner table listening to the *1812 Overture* at full volume. He would explain all of the movements, instruments, historical settings, etc. He was able to make the music come alive for us."

For more than 12 years, he served on the Board of Scoliosis Association, singing in fundraisers and promoting public awareness to finance corrective surgery for patients.

After a year in Kaohsiung, Tena's health was failing again, so they took medical leave and returned to America for two years. When it was time to go back, they were all excited to go home to Taiwan, this time to Taichung. They lived in Taichung for a year and then moved south to Chiayi. Moving to Chiayi meant that the four oldest daughters had to live in the Morrison Boarding School. They left on Sunday afternoon and returned to Chiayi on Friday afternoon, four to six weeks later.

A new missionary was touring the island the first week of her arrival and stopped in Chiayi to meet the Morris family. She went to the train station with the family to see the girls off to Morrison. She suddenly realized the sacrifices made were not the single missionary's loneliness, but those fathers and mothers who stood at the bus and train stations and watched their young children leave for boarding schools.

It was difficult on all of them, and especially Grace, who was left behind. However, she planned "tea" parties for them when they returned home to Chiayi. Grace attended the one-room school with the few other missionary children in Chiayi.

On one occasion, Tena asked Beverly, age 11, to go to the store and get one pound of eggs, "Jit gin." Beverly was proud of the responsibility and asked the shocked store lady for "Chit gin," seven pounds. It confused her when the store lady left and returned, left and returned, borrowing from family and friends until she had a bushel basket full of fresh eggs. She couldn't tell the lady any different after all her work, so the two of them lugged the basket three blocks home. They had a good laugh over this one, and for the first time in years, the family boiled and colored eggs for Easter hunts. This is an excellent example of Tena's making every situation a "teachable" moment.

Richard and Tena, with their girls, attended the Chiayi Baptist Church and started Taiwanese services in this church. Richard served on various mission committees: evangelism/ church planting committee, housing, children's education and theological education.

Later on, Richard, with co-workers' assistance, wrote and published the first Taiwanese Romanized hymnbook. It enabled many to sing who could not otherwise read Chinese characters. Rozanne says, "I still cannot sing *Glory to His Name, This is My Father's World, Jesus Loves Me,* and *God Will Take Care of You*, without wanting to sing in Taiwanese."

The Morris family returned to America from Chiayi for furlough. This time they stayed in America for a longer time, because of Tena's health and Melanie's asthma. They moved to Tucson, AZ, for health reasons, built a house, and made plans to settle there and take care of their family needs. During these years, the two oldest ones, Marilyn and Rozanne, met their life partners and married. Melanie graduated from high school and began her freshman year at the University of Arizona.

Richard and Tena felt it was time to return to Taiwan. So, along with daughters Beverly and Grace, they arrived back in Kaohsiung in 1973. Beverly traveled to Morrison Academy located in the middle of the island, in the city of Taichung, to study. Grace was a 7th grader. She, too, needed to go to Morrison, because there was no international school in Kaohsiung at the time. Grace went for one week and returned to Kaohsiung and refused to return to Morrison. Grace explained to her parents that she wanted them to home school her. It seemed they didn't get the message, and continued to make plans to send her back to Morrison on Sunday afternoon. Grace, always known for her dramatic ways, on her knees and in tears pleaded with her parents, "Please, please don't send me back to Morrison; I'm only a little girl." This got their attention and of course, all her missionary aunts and uncles in Kaohsiung pleaded with them to listen to Grace and not send her back to Morrison.

Tena became Grace's teacher for this first year back in Kaohsiung. It was a difficult year for both mother and daughter. It was through this experience of home schooling a child that Richard felt an MK school was needed in Kaohsiung. He worked with the Morrison Board of Directors to vote and develop plans to establish a school, grades 1-8, in Kaohsiung.

Richard was invited to draw up the building plans and supervise the construction of the building. It was small, but very attractive. It was a day of rejoicing for missionaries serving in south Taiwan when the new facilities were dedicated. Morrison teachers were assigned to the Morrison-Kaohsiung Branch, and the school opened in the fall with grades K-8. The year was 1974. Grace attended the school for 8th grade, and was ready to go to Morrison in Taichung for her high school years. Today there is a beautiful campus with modern, well-equipped facilities in southern Taiwan that provides quality education, grades K-8, for missionary children.

Tena provided cooking classes and English classes in her home and in the churches for anyone who wanted to attend. Richard and Tena had a very effective ministry among Kaohsiung harbor officials. They continued to assist in the starting of Taiwanese work throughout the island.

In 1981, Richard and Tena answered the Mission's request to return once again to Taipei for Richard to oversee the construction of the new Wan Fu Apartments. He enjoyed supervising this project, and he was blessed when he saw how much missionaries were pleased with the new facilities.

Tena and Richard were called as individuals and as a couple to Taiwan to work with Chinese-Taiwanese people. They taught their daughters to love the Lord Jesus. All of them came to faith at an early age. They taught them to love and appreciate their two cultures and to feel at home in each of them. This was evident in the way the daughters related to people regardless of status, class or position.

The family was called to ministry, yet there were struggles: Richard's father opposing their appointment in the early years, Tena's health problems, children's health issues and lack of medical facilities in the early years, sending children to boarding school, leaving their daughters in America, learning a language, understanding the culture, and lack of responsiveness to the Gospel. These are similar struggles that most missionaries confront working cross-culturally. Yet, they kept their relationship to the Lord strong and their call clear. This made for effective ministry.

In 1981, Beverly returned to Kaohsiung after finishing her first year of college, to spend the summer with her parents. They were living on the 11th floor of an apartment over-looking the Love River in Kaohsiung. Beverly said, "As an adult, I was learning to look at my parents and their ministry in a new way. I was also asking the Lord if He wanted me to surrender for full-time mission work. Looking for words of wisdom from my daddy, I asked him what his greatest accomplishment was in all his years in Taiwan. I could think of several things: churches started on my parents' back porch or in a storefront that were now strong, growing churches with committed believers who were impacting their communities for Christ, the polio home established, churches built, the starting of the Kaohsiung Morrison campus, the printing of the Taiwanese hymnal, English and Bible classes taught, ministry among Kaohsiung harbor officials and U.S. Navy soldiers who docked in Kaohsiung. However, his answer surprised me. Without pausing, Daddy said, 'The greatest accomplishment in my work is that my Taiwanese co-workers see me as their brother in Christ, not just as a missionary. I treasure their friendships. They will be here long after we are gone.'"

Perhaps the most difficult day came when Richard was diagnosed in January 1985 with Amyotrophic Lateral Sclerosis, better known as Lou Gehrig's disease. ALS causes nerve cells to degenerate. The voluntary muscles weaken and become immobile, the senses are unimpaired and the intellect is often unaffected. Tena and Richard confronted the issues and made decisions that needed to be made. Here again, they sold their possessions and packed their freight for another trip to America.

Missionaries and Chinese friends helped, encouraged, and prayed with them. Richard's dear friend, Tsai Lu Jya from Kaohsiung, one of those who had influenced their learning Taiwanese and a long-time co-worker, came to visit him the week before he left. He walked into the living room where Richard was sitting and he said, "Ma mu-shr, I don't need to be polite. We have preached many sermons on heaven. We believe in heaven. I'm just surprised that you are going to arrive there before I do." They talked about their early work in Kaohsiung and the future work in Taiwan, what was ahead for Richard medically, and seeing each other in heaven.

Richard and Tena returned to Tucson, AZ, for medical treatment in January 1985. Their departure from Taiwan was a painful one, but their faith sustained them. Richard underlined Acts 20:36-39 in his Bible, the passage where Paul was leaving the Ephesians, "...Paul went down on his knees and all of them with him, and prayed. And then a river of tears... they knew they would never see him again." It was clear that Richard had experienced the same sorrow at saying 'farewell' to his home of 25 years. Rozanne underlined the same passage in her Bible, and wrote beneath it, "Spiritual heroes leave a trail of tears - Daddy."

Richard lived only seven months after they returned from Taiwan. While Tena held him in a loving embrace, he slipped quietly away and into the arms of the Savior whom he loved and served. It was August 19, 1985. Richard was 57 years old.

Richard lived life to the fullest! He was a talented musician and vocalist. One of his last performances was the lead role in the opera **Mikado**, for the Taipei Civic Theatre. At the time of his death, he was writing several books relating his experiences in Taiwan. He also enjoyed reading poetry, and was an avid golfer, tennis player and swimmer. ALS robbed Richard of his energy, mobility and earthly life, but could never rob him of his love for his Lord, for Tena and his family, and for Taiwanese people. He went to Taiwan with a burden for the souls of men and women, and he left this world with a greater burden for the souls of Taiwanese.

Missionaries and Taiwan churches heard of his death and many thanked God for his life and ministry, and grieved for themselves and his family.

Britt Towery wrote in his weekly newspaper article, *In Kaohsiung, Jody and I lived on Ren Ai Road and shared the same backyard with fellow missionaries Tena and Richard. In our shared backyard there was a mango tree.*

Unfortunately we seldom enjoyed the sweet, juicy, yellow-orange ripe mangoes. Neighborhood children out in the alley would use bamboo poles and knock the green mangos off, scurry over our wall, pick up the loot and disappear. One day Richard came over and with a big smile, said he had solved the problem of the little raiders of our mango tree. Richard always smiled. Not a plastic grin, but a warm smile that God gives to certain people.

So I asked him, "How have you solved the little fellows from getting our mangoes?" "Simple," he said, "I caught one of the little fellows in the yard with a sack of mangoes. I got him before he could get over the wall. I sat him down and gave him a good lecture about how it was wrong to steal.

"What happened after your lecture?" I asked. Goodhearted, trusting Richard said, "After being sure he understood me, I gave him four or five of the green mangoes and walked him out our front gate." The boys continued to come for mango, but they were more careful with their visits.

It was nearly 20 years later, after we had moved to Hong Kong, that Tena and Richard visited us over the Christmas holidays. His faith or his trust in humankind had not changed. He still saw the best in everybody." Richard knew Rudyard Kipling was right when he said, "I always prefer to believe the best in everybody – it saves so much trouble."

Tena received the large crates with all of their belongings from Taiwan the week after he died. It was her 53rd birthday.

They never anticipated their missionary career would end in such way, but with broken hearts they knew they had been faithful to the One who sent them to Taiwan. They planted seeds. They would have to leave the watering to others and the harvest to God.

Grace and her husband, Ed, and Beverly with her husband, Rob, returned to Taiwan in 1989 with Tena. They wanted their mother to bring closure to her Taiwan years and they longed for their husbands to see Taiwan and her people through their eyes. For Tena, it was a time of wonderful reunions with many tears, shared memories, times of worship with Taiwanese brothers and sisters, and incredible Chinese meals. Beverly said, "We were so blessed by the respect and love our brothers and sisters in Christ have for our parents." The memory that is treasured today is, "Pastor and Mrs. Tsai Lu Jya came to visit us at the hotel. My husband, Rob and I walked into the room. Pastor Tsai stood and took off his gold ring and put it on Rob's finger and said, 'Richard Morris was my brother in Christ and my best friend. I cannot place this on his finger but I am giving it to you.'" Rob still wears this ring almost 20 years later.

In 1992, Tena married again. She and her husband, Tommy Putnam, live in Pinetop, AZ. She continues to pray for Taiwan and has contacts with Chinese friends. Her daughters are married and have families of their own. When they are together, they like to sing and sometimes they sing Taiwanese songs. They treasure their Taiwan memories and they pray for Taiwan – their adopted homeland. Grace, the little girl who wouldn't leave Kaohsiung for boarding school, serves with her missionary husband in the Middle East, but she continues to remember her Taiwanese roots.

Marilyn, Tena, Beverly,
Richard, Rozanne, and
Melanie Morris

Hunter and Patsy Hammett
Ingredients for Life

A classmate at Baylor asked me, "Have you ever considered serving as a missionary in a foreign country?" I was not ready for that question, but there it was. I knew I needed to give an answer. I responded by saying, "I know God called me to be a preacher and pastor, but I am not sure that being a missionary is God's plan for me." That was my first real encounter with the question.

What are the ingredients that are poured into a life that enable one to follow wherever God leads? What are the sources from which those ingredients come to be poured into the heart and soul of a person? They come from home and family, schools and teachers, church, the Bible and prayer, first jobs, and work experiences. All of these, mixed up and stirred together, make a person willing or unwilling to seek out God's plan for their life.

Ingredients from Home and Family

My life began at about the same time as the Great Depression. That Depression started about 1929 and continued on for about ten years, all through the 1930s. It left its marks on the times, our family and me. Money was short, and jobs were few, so we moved a lot. We moved as a family. We were a family of five: father, mother, grandmother, brother, and me. Each member of the family unit made a unique contribution to my young life.

Ingredients from Father

The first one took place when my father and I were riding in the car with one of his friends. The friend had a small container of iced down beer. He offered a beer to my father, which he took. Then the friend asked him if he could offer me a beer. I was about eight years old at the time. My father said, "You can offer it to him, but I can tell you beforehand, he won't take it." The friend made the offer, and because my father said 'he won't take it,' I refused the beer. From that day forward, every time someone offered me a beer, I have been able to say, "No, thank you."

The second ingredient that he added to my life came when my father and I were seated on the back steps of our house and he took out a plug of chewing tobacco and his pocket knife, both of which he always carried. He cut off a chunk of it and put it in his mouth and began to chew. The expression on his face said, "this is good." My mouth began to water, and I asked if I could have some too. He said, "You won't like it." "Oh, I will, I will, I will, please let me have some," I said. To my surprise, he took his knife and cut off a big piece and gave it to me. With great delight, I chewed and chewed. He failed to tell me that I should spit out the juice. The more I chewed, the more juice was in my mouth. I chewed and swallowed, chewed and swallowed until I became deathly sick. Then out came the tobacco, juice, and lunch. From that time, on I have not wanted anything to do with tobacco in any form.

I was about nine years old when my father left my mother and family to marry someone else. I missed my father. When my friends talked about where they had gone with their fathers and what they had done together, I knew that something was missing in my young life. I longed for a father-son relationship that was not there.

Some of my friends invited me to go to church with them. I started going, and found a family of friends. At church, I learned that we all are members of the big family of God and that God is our Father. I found the "something" that was missing in my life. I found a father who loved me and would never leave me. I lost a father, but found a heavenly Father.

Ingredients from Mother

I still had a mother, whose love had been crushed and broken. She had a broken heart and broken home, but she was strong and able to pick up the broken pieces and rebuild her life and family. In that rebuilding, she had the hard assignment of giving discipline. This was new to her and she had to develop tough love. At first when I needed discipline, I was told to go get a switch and I would return with a very small branch, only to be sent back for a larger one. When my offenses increased, so did the discipline. I knew what to expect when told to go bend over the old quilt box. Those discipline switches were exchanged for a brush, a belt, and a razor strap.

I shall never forget the day I learned the magic words, "charge it." I discovered that those two little words could be exchanged for candy and gum at the local store. I also learned that "charge it" was followed by a payday. When payday came, it involved more bending over the quilt box. I was marched to a wall on the enclosed back porch, where my mother took a red pencil and drew a small circle about nose high and told me to put my nose in it and not to move until she told me I could. It seemed like I had my nose in the red circle forever. That day, I learned "charge it" was not a good thing, and it was better to pay the price up front, rather than later, plus the interest in punishment.

Ingredients from Grandmother

My grandmother on my mother's side of the family was the third adult member of our family. Even though she had three other daughters and one son, she always made her home with us. She was so much a part of our family that when I went to school, I told my teacher I had two mothers at home. One I called mother and the other I called mama. After some questioning, the teacher learned that mama was my mother's mother and my grandmother.

My two mothers were a lot alike in many ways. One of which was that they both were left-handed. Oh, I wanted to be left-handed like they were. I knew that if I were left-handed, when I played baseball I would be one step closer to first base, and that would be an advantage, but left-handed I was not to be.

My grandmother was the spiritual anchor of our family. She was the one who read the Bible, took me to church and taught me about prayer. When I was six and in the first grade, I helped her dig, plant, and weed the garden. One day in the spring as I weeded alone, I went to one corner of the garden and made a small nest out of grass. Since it was close to Easter, I made the nest hoping an Easter bunny would find the nest and leave some Easter eggs in it.

When the nest was finished, I knelt down and prayed to God for eggs in my nest. I told my Mama about the nest and my prayer. The next day after school, I checked the nest and was delighted to find two large hen eggs in the nest. I rushed home to show my grandmother what I had found in the nest. She smiled and said, "God does answer prayer." In her sly way, she taught me that God does hear and answer prayer.

Ingredients from Brother

The final member of my family was my older brother, Charles. He was my hero. He was a good influence in many ways. One of his outstanding characteristics was that he was always a giver. After my father departed, my brother became the man of the house. He followed my mother's example of not letting anyone take advantage or run over him, or his little brother, either. Besides giving me brotherly protection, he gave me many things. He gladly gave me his outgrown hand-me-down clothes and I gladly received them. I always thought it was an honor to fill his boots, shirts, pants and caps. In high school, I wore his old college freshman cap. When in college, I wore his old Marine shirts and jacket. Many of my classmates thought I was a Marine veteran and I just let them think that. He also gave me my first ring, first watch, and bicycle. While I was in college, he gave me summer jobs working in his service station. He was my best man when I got married. From him I learned the Biblical truth that it is more blessed to give than to receive.

Ingredients from School and Teachers

School and teachers always play a big part in everyone's development. I had the good fortune that a number of my teachers also attended the same church that I attended. I would see them at school during the week and at church on Sunday. I was impressed that church was important to them, and church became important to me.

During high school days, I played on the baseball team. We had a good team and won many games. The sixth period class time was when the team had practice, and on those Fridays when we had a game, we were permitted to cut the fifth period class to go to the ballpark, which was about two miles from school. I did not mind missing the fifth period Algebra class, until our teacher told me we needed to talk. She said my grades were not good, and if they did not improve, I might not be allowed to continue to play on the baseball team. She said she believed I could improve, but I must do each day's homework and must attend each class. Then she asked me if I could think of any way I could do those things.

I told her I could do the homework every night. "Can you be in class every day?" she asked. I told her I would miss the bus to the ballpark, but after class I could put on my uniform and run the two miles to the ballpark to be on time and warmed up for the game. She said, "Why don't we try that plan?" We tried it and it worked. I did not miss a day of homework or a moment of playing time. On the day of the Algebra final exam, I was the last one to finish the test. The teacher asked me to stay while she graded my paper. I watched as she marked a few mistakes in red pencil on my paper, and added up my grade. She marked my paper with a B+. I had been failing and now I had an above average grade. As I was leaving, she called me back to show me something else in her grade book. *We looked at the names from A to Z, and there was only one A+ for habits and attitude in the list, and it was by my name.* In that class, I not only learned how to solve Algebra problems, but also how to solve life problems. That was a very good thing to learn.

Ingredients from Church, Bible and Prayer

Not only did my schools and teachers put life-changing ingredients in my young life, but my church added many as well. In that church family, I saw a real love one for another. I began to understand that their love for each other was an evidence of their love for God. The wonder of it all was that they included me in their love. Their love for God and one another were some of the ingredients that led me to want to be a member of this family of love. As a young member of the church family, I observed that the older members all had their own book, the Bible. They brought it to our weekly meetings on Sundays. They read it, they loved it, and they lived out its teachings. I longed to be like them, so I soon had my own New Testament. I began to carry it in my pocket and read it often. I discovered the more I read it, the more I loved it. It spoke to my heart, and it challenged my life. I began to understand that the Bible had the rules for living, and I needed those rules for guidance in my life.

My new family of friends showed me by example the value of prayer. I saw them pray, and I heard them pray; prayer was important to them. Reading about Jesus revealed that prayer was important to Him. Prayer also became important to me. I began to find time to pray. Jesus made the Garden of Gethsemane his place of prayer, and I made the Oakwood Cemetery my place of prayer. In that cemetery was a concrete bench beside the grave of a former Texas governor, Richard B. Hubbard. That bench became my seat of prayer.

One special night after attending a youth rally at church, I sat on that bench and talked with God. As I prayed, I heard the voice of a Black boy singing as he walked down the road on his way home. I listened and recognized the song he was singing. It was: "Lord, Jesus, remember me when you come to the river of Jordan." As I listened to him sing, I wanted to know, "Does he really know Jesus, does he belong to Jesus, is he saved?" His song was fading in the distance, and if I was ever going to know if he was saved, I would have to run to catch up with him. So I ran and overtook him. It was night and he was a Black boy being chased by a White boy, and before he could run I called out, "Wait, I want to ask you something." I asked him, "Do you know this Jesus you are singing about? Are you saved?"

He said, "I think so, but I am not sure."

"Do you want to be sure?" I asked.

"Yes, I do," he said. As best I could, I explained to him that he needed to believe in Jesus and receive Him as his Savior. Under the streetlight, his face lit up as he said: "If that is it, I have been saved a long time".

We parted, both bound for home singing "Lord Jesus remember me."

Ingredients from Work Experience

I worked in a department store in junior high, high school, and junior college. Up to that time, my ingredients for living had come from home and family, school and teachers, church family, the Bible, and prayer. Now work-related experiences also added their ingredients. I began to learn how to meet the public, relate to them, help them find what they needed and sell it to them. I sold children's clothes and loved to see the children's eyes brighten when mom or dad bought the garment the child wanted. I learned to sell socks, shirts, ties, men's hats, and suits. My real love became shoes; I loved to smell them and sell them.

One experience that made a real impression on me happened when I walked down the store aisle near the shoe department. There I saw a dollar bill on the floor. Without a thought, I picked it up and turned it in to the office saying, "I found it on the floor." Returning back down the aisle, I saw the manager looking at me, smiling. The very next day, the manager called me to the office and told me he had a new assignment for me. He gave me a zipper bag full of all the money that store had from sales the day before, and told me to take it to the bank and deposit it. As I walked to the bank, I thought about that sentence from the Bible, "You have been faithful with a few things; I will put you in charge of many things." It is wonderful how things from the flip of a coin to a dollar on the floor can add needed ingredients to a life. At that time, we needed the money that the job could bring, and I needed the experience to grow and mature.

Experience has always been one of my favorite teachers. In the fall of my freshman year in the local junior college, our church was planning a youth rally on Saturday night. I was serving on the planning committee. We had set the date, invited the speaker, and sent out invitations to the youth of all the Baptist churches in the city. The interest and excitement was high until the Wednesday night before the rally.

After prayer meeting at church, our youth director told me there was a problem regarding the youth rally, which was only three nights away. The problem was that the speaker had phoned that afternoon to say that he had a conflict and would not be able to speak at the rally. We did have a problem, and I asked our director what we could do to find another speaker. She told me she had an idea. Her idea was to suggest that I be the speaker. My immediate response was, "I can't do that; tonight is Wednesday and the rally is Saturday. I just can't do that." She made me promise I would pray about it. I told her I would. On the way home, I stopped at my prayer bench and talked to the Lord about the rally. The more we talked, the stronger I felt the Lord impressing on me that I should speak. I told Him I would, and asked for His help.

The next day, I stopped by the church and told the youth director the Lord was leading me to be the speaker. We prayed, and I went home to prepare my heart and a message. I went early to the rally, and in an empty classroom I poured out my heart to God, asking for His power to speak, and asked Him what He wanted me to learn from this experience. I told Him I knew He would not fail me and I did not want to fail Him, and if He wanted me to become a preacher for Him, then please as a sign, let there be decisions in the rally for His glory. The youth of the city came, they sang, they listened to the message, and then heaven came down.

After I spoke, there was an invitation and I closed my eyes and prayed. My prayer was interrupted as one after another came forward, making the decisions God had laid on their hearts. To my amazement, there were more than 30 young people who made decisions that night. I knew that this was not something I had done; it was God's doing. God gave me a message; God gave good attendance; God gave good results. If God could take me in such a short time of preparation and do such a thing of wonder, then I wanted to give myself to Him for His glory. This experience led me to understand that I needed to be better prepared to serve Him, and it was going to take more than two or three days of preparation.

My thought was to stay in junior college a second year and see where that would lead. I could live at home, continue to work at the store, and take classes at the junior college. We did not have the funds for me to go away to college, like most of my classmates were doing. During that spring while I was sick with the flu, one of my old Sunday school teachers came to visit me. I was impressed that he came to see me while I was sick, but he also had another reason for coming. He wanted to talk with me about my plans for school the next fall.

He then told me he would ask his Men's Bible Class to take up a love offering each month to help me with the expenses. So this became our plan for me to go to Baylor University. Fall came, and I went off to college with high hopes.

Ingredients from College

The college environment began at once to pour the additional ingredients into my life that were needed. The Bible verse: "Old things are passed away: behold all things are become new" was coming true for me. Old teachers were exchanged for new teachers; old tests were upgraded with new ones. The old tests that I had been used to were true and false, multiple-choice, and essay type. The new tests came in the form of open book tests, and researching the answers to a hundred questions. Also there were new kinds of tests that came to try my faith.

In school, the day of testing always comes. One such day came with not one test but two. The chemistry course was divided into two parts, the lab work and the exams. Since I had a good lab partner, we had done well on the lab work, but my grades on the exams were not good. The final exam would determine whether I passed the course or not. If I crammed for the English exam, I knew I could make a good grade, but chemistry was hopeless. Therefore I spent all my time preparing for the English exam, and I asked the Lord to take the one in chemistry for me.

Grades were to be posted in the hallways of the English and the chemistry buildings. I checked the English grade first and was pleased with the grade. With fear of failure, I went to check on the chemistry grade. In my heart, I knew I deserved to fail because I hadn't prepared for the exam. I watched the other students check their grades and saw them turn away rejoicing. After they all were gone, I went with little hope to check my grade. To my surprise, there were no grades posted; just one sentence that said: "Everyone passed, my wife just had a baby boy! Merry Christmas!" God had helped me pass the chemistry test.

The biggest test of all came during my senior year. All the tests were over with, I thought, when the school dean asked me to report to her office. Once there, she informed me that I made only a B on my history exam. I told her I thought a B was not bad. She told me it was good, but not good enough, because I needed an A to have enough grade points to graduate. She said I would have to return next term and take another history course and make an A to graduate.

"What could I do?" I asked her if I could talk to the professor and see if he would change my grade to an A. She laughed and said I could try, but there was no way he would change the grade. I went immediately to his office and was told that he had already gone home. I got his home phone number and pled my case and asked him what could be done. He said for me to wait while he checked his grade book. He came back to the phone and said I had made A's on all the tests but one. He also said he could give me that test again and, if I made an A on it, he would be willing to change my grade so I could graduate. He went on to say, "You don't have time to study. You will need to come to my home right now and I will give you an oral test. Can you do that?" he asked.

Yes, yes, I am on my way, I told him. I called a taxi and prayed all the way there. Prayer was my preparation.

We sat in his kitchen and the test began. His first question was about the crusades, and in my heart I said: "Thank you, Lord, between the two of us we are going to pass this test." I had just finished writing a 50-page term paper on the crusades for a church history class. From writing that paper, I knew the crusades were military expeditions by Christians during the eleventh, twelfth, and thirteenth centuries to recover the Holy Land from the Muslims. From that paper I knew there were seven crusades, and many of the details were still fresh in my mind. I answered his question and gave a few more details about that crusade. This perked his interest, so he asked another question about the crusades. I answered with all the details I could recall and prayed that he would stay with questions about those awful and wonderful crusades. We marched to victory through all seven of them when he closed his grade book. With a thankful ear, I listed to him as he called the school dean and told her he was changing my grade to an A and she could let this boy graduate. I could have kissed him, the History book, his grade book, and the good Lord all at once. I loved history, and from that moment on looked upon history as His Story – God's story.

The classroom was not the only place where testing took place. The nest egg of money that I had saved during the summer was soon eaten up by school fees, rent, and food expenses. I had faith that I would be receiving a check in the mail from the Men's Bible Class. At the end of the first month, there was no check in my mailbox. After the second month, the mailbox was still empty. My mother was limited in the amount of help she could give, but she sacrificed by selling her car and sending me the money. When that money was gone, I began to lose hope and faith – faith in the Men's

Bible Class. That old faith was being replaced by a new faith in God and in myself. After talking it over with the Lord, it was decided that I needed to find part-time work so I could eat. I found a job less than a block away. I started waiting on tables in a café three hours a day, and was paid three meals a day. It was one of the best paying jobs I ever had, because I could eat more in a meal than I could make in an hour. That experience taught me to put my faith in God to supply all my needs.

Ingredients from Plays and Dramas

One of the extracurricular activities that added rich and meaningful ingredients to my life was taking part in church and school dramas. My church had an active drama group in which I took part, and I was also in a few plays in college. While in the Seminary, plans were made for a Christmas drama on the life of Lottie Moon. In the drama, I had the part of Andrew Fuller, who was in love with Lottie. For three years in a row as Andrew, I proposed marriage to Lottie Moon. For three years I asked for her hand in marriage and three times she turned me down. She was called of God to go as a missionary to the people in China. In the cast was a Chinese couple from China and Taiwan named Y.K. and Cherry Chang. Our paths would cross again some time later. In the play, Lottie was faced with God's call to missions, and in real life I was faced with the question of whether or not I was willing to go as a missionary.

For three years, I had a lot of practice proposing marriage to Lottie on stage. I was serving as pastor of a small church in East Texas, and began to feel the need for a wife to join me in that ministry. Coming from a broken home, I knew that marriage was not to be taken lightly. It was among the most important decisions one would make in life. I prayed for God to lead me clearly in that decision.

It was time for the annual homecoming in the church where I was pastor. The date was set, the invitations were sent, and the day arrived. Among those who came was a young red-headed school teacher and her parents. She was teaching school in a nearby town, and we began dating. I wondered if she was in God's plan for my life. One night we attended a revival in another church. Their new pastor was doing the preaching. He recognized me and asked my wife and me to stand. The young lady was a good sport and stood with me. Most of the people in the service knew I was not married and laughed when we stood. Then the pastor knew he had made a mistake. On the way home, she said there was something she needed to tell me. She informed me she had just written a letter to a young man accepting his proposal of marriage. My response was: "This is the first time I have been married and divorced in the same evening." We both had a good laugh. That was God's way of answering my prayer.

Ingredients from Romance to Marriage

When I was a senior in college, my roommate and I went home one weekend and he asked me to double date with him. Not knowing who to ask for a date, I talked with our church youth director, and she suggested I call a young lady named Patsy Price, who was a senior in high school. She accepted and we had a good time on the date. That fall, she was going out of state to college and I was going to the seminary for the next three years.

At that time, finishing my education was my number one priority. A few of my friends put marriage first, and then they failed to continue their education. Finishing school before marriage became my goal. I did not know it, but that was also Patsy's goal. One of my best friends in the seminary began dating Patsy. He wanted a wife; Patsy wanted to get an education. Her strong commitment was to complete college.

144

They never really discussed marriage. He wrote her letters and sometimes he would give them to me to mail and I would write a short note on the outside of the letter. During the Christmas holidays, he met someone else who was "the one."

Patsy and I began dating off and on until her last year in college. Just before the Christmas holidays, I asked her mother if it would be all right if I drove to Patsy's college and brought her home for the holidays. She asked me what Patsy thought about that, and I told her I had not asked her yet. When I did ask her, she said yes. We enjoyed each other's company on the long trip back from her college and also while she was home.

It was during one of those days, about noon, we drove to a spot called Love's Lookout, and after we prayed together, I asked her to be my wife and she said "Yes." At first I told her I could not afford an engagement ring, and she said that was all right. Later I knew I could not let her go back to school without a ring. So I went to the bank and borrowed the money and gave her the ring on New Year's Day 1954, and we set the date to be married on Thanksgiving Day. That day finally arrived, and it was a joy when God made us one. Patsy Price became Patsy Hammett, and I have always jokingly said when I married her I made her "priceless."

Ingredients from God's Call

One month before we were married, I was called to another church as pastor, and we both joined that church on the first Sunday I was there as the new pastor. Those were happy days for us as we worked together in that church. Patsy also had a job working in the same department store in which I had worked as a student. Our combined income helped us meet the financial struggles common to most young couples. During our second year of marriage, the Lord gave us a baby. We named him Joel. The Lord was good to us and we were happy in our work. A pastor friend and former missionary to Mexico told us about a church in Panama City, Panama, that was seeking a pastor, and he recommended us to the church. We were faced with the question of what would we do if that church called us. We prayed it through and felt that if the Lord wanted us to serve there, we were willing to go. God sent someone else – it seemed as if He just wanted to know if we were willing to go overseas to serve Him.

In the fifth year of our marriage, I attended an Evangelism and World Missions Conference in Dallas, TX. Patsy remained home with our young son. At that meeting, a missionary from Japan spoke and in his message he made one statement that touched my heart. He said: "Here in America we have 95 percent of our seminary graduates remaining here working with only 5 percent of the world's lost people, while over-seas only 5 percent of our seminary graduates are working with 95 percent of the world's lost people." He went on to say that was not right and we need to do something to change that percentage.

I agreed, and listened as he outlined what we as pastors could do to change that percentage. "Preach more about missions and increase our church gifts to missions," he said.

Amen, I can do that, I said.

The speaker went on to list the requirements of our mission board one must meet to become a foreign missionary. He named them one by one, and one by one I thought, "I meet that requirement." I met all the requirements.

Then he said, "If you meet all of these requirements, and God calls you to go, then you could help change the percentage and proclaim the Gospel to lost people overseas. If God calls you, you could go." I thought, "That lets me out, for God has not called me." Just at that moment, a small telephone in my heart began to ring. When I answered, it was God calling and asking again, "Are you willing to go?"

I left the conference and could not get home fast enough to tell Patsy that God had called me to be a missionary. I slowed down driving a little as I thought about Patsy and how would I convince her that God was calling us to missions overseas. As I prayed about that, I realized that God knew her number and He could call her too. I promised the Lord I would not say anything to her about my call until He had also called her. All I said about the conference was it was a good meeting, and I wished she could have been there. I waited. Earlier, she had come in from a Ladies' Meeting where she had spoken about missionary requirements and said, "We could go today." We both had wondered.

Two weeks after my meeting, there was a ladies meeting in one of the nearby churches. We agreed she should go in our car and take some of the ladies from our church, and I would stay home and take care of our son. Later that day when she returned, I asked her about the meeting. She said one of our local pastors spoke and gave a report on the Evangelism and World Missions conference that I had attended. She went on to say there was one sentence he quoted that touched her and prompted her to say in her heart, "I'm willing to go." She said she could not hear a missionary speak, or read about missions without wanting to go as a missionary. I said, "Then let's go!" I knew God had also given her a call.

A day or so later she asked, "What shall we do?" We agreed to contact the Foreign Mission Board and see if they would appoint us as missionaries. We went through the application process and were appointed nine months later, in the fall of 1959, to be missionaries to Taiwan. We departed Texas by train to California and boarded a ship for Taiwan. After a three-week journey, with stops in Hawaii, Japan, and the Philippines, we arrived in Hong Kong and spent a few days there. We took a prop plane on to Taiwan, arriving February 1960.

Ingredients for Mission Service

When we arrived in Taipei, the only people we knew there were Dr. Y.K. and Cherry Chang, who were on the faculty of the Taiwan Baptist Theological Seminary. He had been a guest in our home. We found a mission family who welcomed us into their fellowship. Under the leadership of the Lord and the encouragement of the mission, we began studying Taiwanese and spent three years in language study. We worked as church planters in Taipei and Keelung during our first term, mostly with the Mu Yi Baptist Church in helping start four chapels in Taipei, a church in Tainan, and a church in Keelung. Church planting was challenging in the 1960s in Taiwan, and most young missionaries will find it challenging anywhere in the world.

When we returned from our first furlough with two additional children, Lydia and Glenn, whom we had adopted from Buckner's Children's Home in Texas, we were asked to live at the Ling Tou Baptist Assembly Grounds on Grass Mountain. Patsy was to serve as the missionary manager and oversee the Chinese staff. I had been assigned to serve as the Mission Treasurer while the regular treasurer was in the States on furlough. Also during a part of that year, I was asked to be interim pastor of the English-speaking Calvary Baptist Church, which was next door to the assembly grounds. I was asked to serve as the missionary manager of the seven Baptist Literature Centers. It proved to be a busy time for us with two new members in our family and new job responsibilities. Patsy spent 10 years as the missionary manager of the Baptist Camp. Patsy also took on the work of the mission outreach library, which was located next to the Literature Center on Hwai Ning Street in Taipei. Later, she was consultant to the National Post Office, board member of the National YWCA, and board member of the Taiwan Baptist Theological Seminary.

When we elected the officers for our new mission organization, I was asked to serve as the Mission Administrator and served for 15 years. An effective mission organization enables the missionary to be more effective in family and ministry. I cannot say the Taiwan Mission structure was always effective, but we had a desire to work effectively with the Chinese Convention and enhance the missionary's ministry.

The day-by-day work of the Mission Administrator had many joys along with hardships. It had assigned tasks both short and long-term. The on-going tasks had to be completed over and over again, and with the tension and pressure of a deadline for completion. One of the big challenges was to keep calm when working to meet a deadline during endless interruptions. One way to deal with interruptions is to close the door until the task is completed. A good administrator should have an open door policy and I sought to be a good administrator. I was faced with the problem of how to get my work done with all these interruptions. One day I came to realize that those interruptions were an important part of my daily work. That realization removed much of the stress and tension.

Some of the joys that came along the way were to see a new missionary be able to preach in Taiwanese or Mandarin, to encourage a missionary family who was dealing with family issues, serve as negotiator between a missionary and co-worker, see a student graduate from seminary, a pastor ordained, a preaching point, or a chapel become a church, churches become a growing convention, a convention become responsible for agencies, and to send out domestic and foreign missionaries.

One of the ingredients for an effective missionary career is a sense of humor. The missionary must learn to laugh with himself and about himself.

One of the most difficult experiences as a missionary came when I was asked to do something that I really did not want to do. A Chinese pastor called me and said, "I want you to fire our custodian."

I said, "You are the pastor of the church, can't you fire him?"

Oh no, I could not fire him. It would be better for you to fire him.

I agreed to go to the church on Saturday morning and find out why I need to fire the custodian. It was raining when the pastor met me at the front door of the church. Again I asked: "Why do you want to fire him?"

Turning to enter the church building, he said, "Come, I will show you." As we stepped into the entrance way I saw a mess. There was grease, oil, and grime all over the terazzo floor. We walked into the worship center and the pastor said, "We cannot have this in God's house." What I saw was a long rope stretched across the worship center with the weekly wash hanging and dripping all over the chairs, the floor, the Bibles and hymnbooks.

The pastor went for the custodian. I prayed. I told him that I knew it had been raining a lot in the last three weeks and he had found a dry place to work on his motorcycle and for his wife to hang the clothes to dry, but this building is God's house and his responsibility was to keep God's house clean. As his head got lower and lower, I told him the church loved him and his family and wanted to help him move to a better place and help him find a better job and the church would provide four months salary so he would be free to look for other job. He agreed to move within a week to another place.

A few months later, I was invited to preach in this church. As I was seated on the platform, I was surprised to see the custodian and his family in the service. I could hardly wait to ask the pastor what happened, and the pastor could hardly wait to tell me about the custodian.

The pastor said, "Mr. Huang had been a goldsmith, and when he fled to Taiwan he lost all he had. He has now opened a small goldsmith shop and they live in the back of the shop. His business has done well. They ride the bus across the city to come to our church. They are the church's largest tithers. I'm so glad you fired him."

Yes, I thought, The Lord hired him.

God called us as missionaries and gave us 35 fruitful years of service, from 1959 to 1994. We have found it true that God will surely give you the ingredients for life when you are willing to follow His leadership.

We spent our last term on the field working in child evangelism with a church in Banchyau. We had a meaningful ministry with these children, who gave us the opportunity to meet their families and introduce them to Jesus and to the Banchyau churches. Many children, ages nine through twelve, accepted the Lord as Savior through flannelgraph presentations, songs, and fellowship in our home. Some adults also, even after our return to the U.S.

The Hammetts were God's servants in Taiwan. They were available to the institutions, to the churches, to the believers, and to non-believers. They were counselors for senior missionaries, young missionaries and missionary children. Hunter's sense of humor and stories lightened many Chinese pastors' loads and encouraged struggling missionaries. Patsy's sweet, quiet spirit encouraged many missionary wives to understand that taking care of one's children and husband was a calling and precious in His sight. Hunter and Patsy were effective missionaries and their lives and ministries enabled others to be effective.

Hunter and Patsy Hammett with Joel

Herb and Emma Barker
Patiently Run The Race

Prologue

When the writer of Hebrews exhorts us to "run the race with patience," we are reminded of the Apostle Paul's experiences, for he did run his life's race with determination and perseverance. He was constantly "looking unto Jesus, the author and finisher of our faith," and he "kept the faith and finished the course" well.

As I sat down to write about my own journey, especially the grand adventure of trying to serve the Lord in missions endeavors, I was hesitant to do so because I realized that it was not at all about me, but about what the Lord had done. I was a participant, but it was not what I had done that counted. It was all about what He had done in my life and the lives of others as I tried to be available to His call and leading. Paul confessed in II Corinthians 11 and 12 that if he was to go on boasting, it would be of the things that showed his weaknesses, so that Christ's power might be clearly shown, and so that this same power might rest on him. "For," he said, "when I am weak, then I am strong." Through over 35 years of mission service I had the vivid knowledge of God's assignment for overseas service as a confirmation that I was where God had placed me and therefore was able to face whatever difficulty might arise through the assurance of

His presence and guidance. I want to praise Him for every experience He has allowed me to have that glorifies Him and blesses others.

Early Influences

I have to go back to early childhood to see how the Lord planted the seed for missions which grew into fruition as I began to mature. As an eight-year-old boy, I was exposed to mission service through a missions study in my church. We studied the little book, "Whirligigs in China." We made paper whirligigs, or windmills, to spin on a stick and fashioned little Chinese umbrellas from toothpicks and tissue paper while we learned about the boys and girls of China and how they needed to hear about Jesus. Years later, a good friend who never forgets anything told me that I had said during that time that when I grew up, I was going to tell the boys and girls of China about Jesus.

I cannot leave out the influences of a Christian home and my church, First Baptist of Mountain Grove, MO. During that time, our pastor was Earl T. Biven, whom I remember as a kindly man and faithful pastor. Mother and Dad were both church members and led all eight of their children to attend regularly. Mother was my Sunday school teacher at one time. Much prayer, both private and public, placed our family before the Lord for His guidance and blessing.

Conversion and Early Growth in Christ

It was primarily because of these influences and prayers that the Lord convicted me of sin and brought me to salvation through faith in Jesus when I was a lad of nine years of age. Following the Sunday night service when I came under conviction of my sin and made a public commitment to accept Christ, I was questioned about my decision by my mother when I got home. The invitation hymn that night had been, *Trust and Obey*, so when Mother asked me how I knew

I had been saved, I replied, "Mother, all you have to do is to trust and obey Jesus." She was satisfied with my answer.

I began reading my Bible and was faithful to attend Sunday school and worship services as well as the youth organizations of my church. I sometimes fell asleep at night with my Bible in my arms after reading a passage. During high school days, I sang in the church choir and was in a men's quartet that sometimes sang for special services and funerals. I privately thought that some day, God might use my musical talents in His service, and once shared that conviction with a youth leader.

Struggles with God's Call

The next step in following the Lord's leadership came during my sophomore year in college, when I was challenged by Bob Holt, Educational Director of First Baptist Church, Springfield, MO, to find God's will for my life by completely surrendering myself into the Lord's hands. As I discussed with Bob the difficulty of finding God's will, he told me I could only be sure if I gave God the opportunity to lead me by saying to Him, "I am willing to do whatever you want me to do, digging ditches, driving a taxi, preaching the gospel..." When he got that far, it was like a stab to my heart, for I knew I had been refusing to open that part of my life to Christ.

After a few weeks of praying together with Bob Holt each week, the Lord spoke very clearly to call me to the preaching ministry. About midnight one night in March of 1949, as I prayed alone in my room, I made that commitment. I had never before felt the nearness of the Lord as I did at that moment. I made my decision known on the next Sunday morning at the end of the worship service in First Baptist Church. Dr. Fred Eastham, Pastor, invited me to preach my first Sermon a month later at prayer meeting. He encouraged me and the church licensed me to the gospel ministry.

Marriage and Beginning a Family

Following my decision to preach, I looked for a Baptist University to complete my education and begin serious Bible study. I was pointed by Dr. Eastham and Helen Jean Bond, student worker at First Baptist, to Hardin-Simmons University, a Baptist school, in Abilene, TX. That was over 500 miles from Emma Jean Archer, the young lady I had been courting since high school days. She was a student nurse in St. Louis, MO, and a member of the Methodist Church. She had been raised to attend church, but her decision to follow Christ and join the church had been more of an outward display than repentance and trust in Jesus. For those reasons, our courtship began to cool and I became friends with other girls I thought were more suited to my vocation. She also dated other medical students in St. Louis. However, when Emma Jean's church dismissed Sunday evening services for the summer, she began attending Third Baptist Church, St. Louis, and came under conviction that she had never been born again, but only joined a church. She trusted in Christ to save her, was baptized and joined Third Baptist. Slowly we began to reclaim our affection for each other while courting by long distance, mainly through letters we often exchanged. We were married in June 1951, following my graduation from the university.

Seminary Studies

We then began a course of study together at Southwestern Baptist Theological Seminary, Fort Worth, TX, that led us, after graduation, to a pastorate in the West Texas town of Rochester. During seminary days, we had served as the assistant pastor of Vickery Baptist Church in Dallas and later in a weekend pastorate at New Hope Baptist, a country church near Denton, TX. Most of that time, we each had part-time jobs to help support ourselves. It was a struggle to make ends meet, but we were made aware again and again that God was able to supply all our needs. On one occasion when we were running short of funds and could not pay our seminary tuition, a letter arrived from an unexpected source with a check just large enough to meet our obligations. We could see the hand of the Lord in that check and accepted it as a gift from Him.

Following seminary graduation with the Bachelor of Divinity degree, I began a course of study leading to a Master's in Theology. During the second year of that work, I was called by the Baptist Church in Rochester, TX, to be their pastor, and after prayer, accepted that position. It was not until we had been in Rochester for over a year that our son, Jim, was born. Although he was born a few weeks early after a difficult delivery, he was healthy, and Emma Jean recovered after a week in the hospital and two weeks in bed at home. We were happy and the church was prospering, so we felt quite settled among those good people. God was blessing us in many ways, but He had more in store for us.

God's Intervention

While we were in the seminary, we had regularly attended the special mission day services each semester and listened with interest to the missionary speakers and considered whether God wanted us on a mission field. I was under no conviction that He was doing so at that time. While in the pastorate, I often preached on missions and urged others to pray, give and go to tell others about the Lord, but still failed to open my own heart to that possibility for myself. Then in January of 1959, with some nearby fellow pastors, I attended the Evangelism Conference sponsored annually by the Baptist General Convention of Texas. That year, however, they had changed the nature of the meeting to emphasize foreign missions.

On the final evening of the conference, I became aware of the Lord dealing with my heart about missions. The main message of the evening was brought by Dr. Baker James Cauthen, Executive Secretary of the Foreign Mission Board. His text was from John 12:24, "Except a corn of wheat fall into the ground and die, it abideth alone: but if it die, it bringeth forth much fruit." (KJV) As he preached on the importance of yielding to the call of God and sharing Christ with others, the Holy Spirit was simply breaking my heart with His convicting power. When the invitation was given to offer oneself to serve wherever God led, even overseas, I went forward, and with tears made my commitment to follow that call.

When I arrived home around two a.m. the next morning, Emma Jean was still awake, waiting for me. When I walked into the room where she was, she took one look at me and said, "God has called you to missions, hasn't He?" She said that the look on my face was of a broken man or one "who had lost his last friend." She related how, in my absence, she had begun to pray and think about what she would do if God should call me to overseas service as a missionary. After prayer, she committed herself that if the Lord called me, she was willing to go, a decision she had never made before. So it was evident that the Holy Spirit was working in two hearts that night and won the victory in both.

Appointment for Mission Service

We soon contacted the Foreign Mission Board and began the process of application for appointment. They urged us to pray about the needs in Taiwan, since no one had been appointed to serve there for 18 months, so as we wrote our life histories, had physicals and psychological tests, we also met with some who were serving in Taiwan, including Miss Pearl Johnson, and Oz and Mary Quick. Through all that process, the Lord was opening doors for quick appointment, just six months following our decision. We qualified in every category, including the needed three years experience as pastor of a church. Our appointment service in Richmond, VA, in October of 1959, in which Billy Graham brought the main message, was followed by a week of orientation there in December. We spent Christmas with our families and left for Taiwan in February of 1960, sailing aboard the *President Cleveland* on a 21-day trip to Hong Kong. After a week there spent in quarantine, during which our son recovered from the measles he had caught on the ship, a short 500-mile flight took us to Taipei.

Looking back, I can only shake my head in wonderment. Why would God tap me on the shoulder, a young man from an inconspicuous background in a small Ozark Mountain town, send me halfway around the world, and allow me the privilege of being His messenger for over 35 years? And although I was a flawed witness at best, during that time I was able to see many people in 10 different countries or political entities where I had some semblance of witnessing opportunities, come to know Him as Lord and Savior. I can only stand in awe and give praise and glory to His wonderful name.

Wrestling with Language and Culture

Our first week of introduction to Taiwan was provided by Dr. and Mrs. Carl Hunker, in whose home we stayed. Just driving the narrow lane through the rice patties and military unit on the way to their house at the new Taiwan Baptist Seminary was a cultural eye opener. They became our beloved friends and mentors for missionary service. Our first home in Taipei was in one of the apartments at the old Grace Baptist Church compound. Hunter and Patsy Hammett, also newly arrived language students, lived on one side, and Miss Ola Lee and Miss Josephine Ward shared the other apartment. We all shared an automobile driven by Mr. Wang or rode pedicabs nearly anywhere in Taipei for the equivalent of 25 cents U.S.

Culture shock was to continue over the years, but immediately the different repugnant smells, crowds of people, difficult traffic conditions, noises – especially the booms of fireworks and clanging of cymbals and drums when they paraded different idols through the streets – and the radically different forces of nature, both earthquakes and typhoons, made life seem very different to us. The first two years in Taipei were spent in full-time language study, five hours per day, five days each week in class at the Taipei Language Institute, with plenty of the preparation and practice both listening and speaking required.

Church Planting in the Chiayi Area

Following two years of language study, the mission asked us to move to Chiayi, in southern Taiwan, where we were to continue studying part-time with a teacher at home while working with the three churches in the area; Chiayi, Huwei, and Hsinying. During the three years we lived there, I took turns preaching, visiting, encouraging and challenging the pastors and congregations in those churches to start new preaching points, which we hoped would grow into churches. As we continued language study with two teachers who came to our home for a couple of hours each day, we did what we could to help support and encourage the pastors and members of the churches in our area. Emma Jean attended the women's meetings and worked with Marie Conner, the experienced co-worker there, in ministering to the women in the churches. She played the pump organs for services and joined in teaching classes during Vacation Bible Schools. She served as station treasurer for the year when Miss Conner was away. Together with our Chinese pastors, we went visiting in member's homes and with them to their non-Christian neighbors and friends. We were learning through experience more than we were actually ministering during those days.

Getting Our Eyes Opened

The Chiayi area is a Buddhist and local god stronghold, where evil spirits are feared and continual sacrifices made to placate them. Especially notorious is the ornate temple dedicated to Ma Dzu, "goddess of the sea," in the fishing village of Bei Gang. There an annual celebration of this idol's "birthday" attracts huge crowds to a parade and feast in her honor. Many pigs are slaughtered and placed on stands in the temple courtyard and along the streets, accompanied by rice and steamed breads, dyed red, offered to the idol (and eaten by the participants later), and the usual incense sticks and paper "spirit money" burned to supplicate their ancestors in the spirit world.

As we traveled to Taipei one day on the railroad – the easiest transportation in those days, even though they were coal burning steam engines – we met a young college student from Bei Gang. When he discovered we spoke some Chinese, we visited together and I began to try to witness to him. He was attending Taiwan University in Taipei, just across the street from the Grace Baptist Church compound where we had lived during language study. I will never forget his response that day. He said, "I have been to church, but I can never become a Christian as long as my parents are alive." I already knew by that time what difficulty Chinese young people have in breaking from the family traditions and control, and was aware of the influence of the temple in Bei Gang on anyone in that area. But, I was amazed at what else he said, and it has forever been a challenge to me. He continued, "But we need missionaries to come to Taiwan, not just to the big cities, but also to places like Bei Gang, *where my parents sit in darkness, and tell them of the love of God.*" The insight of that young man, I believe, is the hope of the Chinese people.

A New Challenge: Radio and Television

In late 1964, the mission executive committee asked us to move to Taipei and develop the radio ministry that had been started earlier using English programs sent from the United States and a weekly Mandarin preaching program on the government-owned, China Broadcasting Company Education Network. My main qualifications for that work were one radio course in college, musical training in choirs and voice class, plus some language ability and willingness to try new things in using it.

The radio studio at that time consisted of one room with a desk and microphone facing a smaller control room with a tape recorder and small mixer. Gu Dzu Ying, the part-time engineer who did the recording, soon left to fulfill his military service. We were able to hire Frank Wu, a young man who had some experience recording with another mission group, to fill that position, and since our language teacher from Chiayi, Mrs. Christine Mao, had recently moved to Taipei, we were able to engage her as announcer. Those two became the nucleus for a staff that grew slowly over 15 years to number at its highest 23 Chinese and missionary workers.

Almost immediately, we were able to add several Mandarin, Taiwanese, and Hakka dialect programs consisting of music and message each week. The messages were recorded in the studio by various Baptist pastors and music added later in the control room. A weekly children's program also proved very popular. The tapes for these programs had to be duplicated for the various stations and mailed to them each week for transmission. These were to grow over the next decade to a total of 27 radio programs with various formats in three dialects broadcast on both government and private stations in Taiwan. Some were also aired on the shortwave facilities of Far East Broadcasting, Trans World Broadcasting, and the

China Central Broadcasting companies, transmitted to the mainland of China.

Television Beginnings

By using the film series, "The Answer," produced by the Southern Baptist Radio and Television Commission, we were able to begin the dubbing of movies into Mandarin for broadcast on the Taiwan television station. At that time, all programming was in black and white, as were our films. A rather primitive system of dubbing using a 16 MM film projector and tape recorder proved slow and difficult because of the need for lip synchronization, but we were able to complete a couple of films. It was a major breakthrough for religious programming in Taiwan, because most imported films of any kind were then shown with burned-on Chinese captions, which were unsteady, causing the Chinese characters to be difficult to read. We realized that new equipment and perhaps professional help would be necessary to accomplish an acceptable job.

First Furlough

There was much to do during that first furlough, getting more training, attending mission conferences, doing deputation work by speaking in the churches and associational meetings, and visiting with relatives and friends. My father was injured in an automobile accident and was in the hospital only a few months before passing away. I was blessed by being able to spend some time by his bedside and comforting Mother after the funeral.

The Taiwan Baptist Mission was committed to building a new recording studio, so funds were requested from the Foreign Mission Board for that purpose. Since I was asked to get more training during our first furlough, I enrolled in the courses offered by Southwestern Seminary in Fort Worth, and was accepted as an apprentice at the Radio and Television

Commission for eight months. During that time, I worked with the Chief Engineer J.O. Terry, to arrive at proposed plans, and later with an architect in Taiwan to design a state-of-the art recording facility for Taiwan Baptists.

It was also during our furlough at home that we were notified to come by the Missouri Baptist Children's Home for an interview. We had applied to adopt a child and had done the necessary paperwork before leaving Taiwan. After about 45 minutes of questions by the caseworker, he excused himself to confer with the director. In a few minutes, he returned and said, "Congratulations, you are the parents of a baby girl." Thus, our lives were blessed by a beautiful, three-week-old blonde and blue-eyed baby whom we named Jeanette Marie. She had her first birthday as we sailed back to Taiwan.

A Second Term of Media Growth

When we returned to Taipei, we proceeded to work with the mission to secure the land and build a radio and television studio with three floors and a basement containing offices, dining facilities and three recording studios, one of which could be used for either media. Although there were many difficulties in securing the property rights, removing a squatter, and building the studio, we finally were able to dedicate the Taiwan Baptist Mass Communications Building in 1968.

Our first television programs consisted of the films from "The Answer" series, as previously mentioned, dubbed with Mandarin sound. Later, a weekly television program, *Wan Fu Lin Men,* was produced locally by us and broadcast by China Television Company for several years in the 1970s. These were locally written drama series that ran for 10 or 11 weeks each. Between series, we used special music programs featuring either local Christian musicians, our own studio choir, or well-known Christian music artists sent to Asia for special concerts by the Foreign Mission Board. To accomplish this, it was necessary to hire and train a Chinese staff. I will ever be grateful to the above-named Christine Mao, who became the head of the program department, and Frank Wu, control room Chief Operator and sometimes announcer. To these were added Mrs. Chen Lin Rwei Tsau, program engineer, Mrs. Nora Li, book keeper and secretary, Mrs. Gau Lyou Li Hwa, Taiwanese Announcer, Wu Wen-Hwa, Administrator, James Liu, engineer, and a host of others through the years, too numerous to name here.

Besides radio and television program production, a multiple media approach was designed both to promote and to follow up the broadcasts. A Bible correspondence course, written by two of our Baptist Pastors, Li Jung Shan, and Teddy Jang Ji Jung, were printed and offered free to listeners. A monthly magazine, *Gan Lu,* was produced and mailed to churches and listeners who requested it. Christian booklets, outlining the plan of salvation, or encouraging Christians in their walk were also offered and mailed to the seekers among our listeners. A Christian film and slide library had been begun by the mission, so it was housed at the studio and enlarged to include video tapes and other visual materials for loan to churches and Christian groups.

Response to the Broadcasts

A family of six, named Wang, wrote to us after hearing one of our programs in the Taiwanese dialect, saying that they each wanted to trust in Jesus as their Savior. They asked how they could join a church. The six of them each signed their names to the letter. We immediately notified a pastor of a Taiwanese Baptist Church near them and he went to visit the family. They all attended church together the following Sunday, even though the father had to ask off from work to do so. They were given a Bible and began study in the church's enquirer's class leading to baptism and church membership.

In 1972, our television program was given the "Golden Bell" award by the Cultural Bureau of the Ministry of Education, the Republic of China. It was in the category of "Service to Society," which is as close to a religious classification as the government had. The citation read "for excellence in programming," and it was significant in that it showed that our programs were culturally acceptable by the industry as well as the people of Taiwan. When the Baptist Radio and Television Commission produced a religious cartoon called "JOT," we were given permission to dub it into Chinese and broadcast it following our regular program on China Television. It received an unusual amount of response from young readers. Over 10,000 wrote to us during one month, asking for the children's stories and finger puppets we were offering.

Music Hath Charms

A staff choir was organized in early years to record music for the programs and present special music in churches. Later, with the addition of a music missionary, Milton Lites, to our staff, a more professional group was constituted as the "Hwei Sheng Gu" (Reverberations) choir and fellowship that continued to present concerts in churches and other venues, as well as record more indigenous music for use in the programs. This choral group appeared on some of our television programs and presented concerts in local churches that we billed as "Radio Listener Rallies." In these rallies, they helped us attract a larger audience to hear testimonies of other listeners who found Christ through the messages in the programs or through the Bible correspondence courses.

Some Changed Lives

One such dramatic testimony was that of a Taiwanese lady, Mrs. Lin, who came to the rally in her wheelchair to share her story. She had been so stressed and despondent in her messed-up life that she had decided to end it. She took an overdose of sleeping pills, but was discovered in time and rushed to the hospital, where she was resuscitated. After some time, her situation had not improved and she again became depressed, so she went to the ocean and waded out into the waves, intending to drown herself, but she was saved by a young man who rescued her. Finding no relief, for a third time she tried to end her life. This time she selected what she thought was a foolproof method, jumping from an eight-story building, where she presumed she would surely die. However, she landed on a structure that deflected her fall and only succeeded in fracturing her spine. As a result, she was totally paralyzed.

In the hospital and at home she could do little else except listen to the radio. And so it was in God's providence that she heard the sweet Gospel music and beautiful message of Jesus, the one who came to rescue her from sin and its woes, being broadcast in her heart language on one of our Taiwanese programs. She had her family contact the studio to send her some of the materials and music tapes being offered. Later, a Taiwanese-speaking missionary, Richard Morris, followed up with a visit and continued to witness and show her Christ's love. As a result she was truly converted and wanted to be baptized. An ambulance was hired by Richard to transport her to church, and she was taken into the baptistery on a stretcher. After the baptism, the church members gathered around her and prayed for her healing. She miraculously was able to sit up on that stretcher. She soon became able to use a wheelchair, and would go to the vegetable market to sell small objects and add to the family income. In so doing, she would often have opportunities to tell others about her experience and Jesus' love for her. Her life had been completely changed and her family blessed. In giving her testimony, she often ended by saying, "Oh, if only someone had come to tell me about Jesus before I tried to take my own life!"

Showers of God's Blessings

For several years, the combined efforts of the media ministry produced an average of about 500 who registered decisions for Christ annually after completing a Bible correspondence course. Many of these were followed up by local Baptist Churches, as we shared with them the names and addresses of those who indicated their desire to trust Jesus. The highest number of professions of faith, over 700, came in 1983, following the partnership evangelistic campaign between Taiwan Baptists and the Missouri Baptist Convention. That campaign, financed by Missouri Baptists, was the climax to a media blitz utilizing all the resources of the Mass Communications staff, plus many church coworkers and missionaries.

A Harvest of Gold

One morning, Mrs. Gao, the Taiwanese program producer and announcer, rushed into my office and said, "There is a man downstairs who is trying to give me some gold jewelry. I don't know how to deal with him and besides I need to be producing my program. Can you go down and talk to him?" I went to the small reception room and met a middle-aged Taiwanese man who was holding a large gold medallion and some small gold bars. He told me this story. He said he had been a farmer who lived with his mother at the edge of Syin Jwang, a suburb of rapidly growing Taipei. The land on his little farm, as in all surrounding areas, had become very valuable and a developer had offered him a lot of money for it, so he sold it. Suddenly, he found himself to be a popular person with many new fair-weather friends who showed him a good time and plied him with drink. He drank so much that he ended up in the hospital. While recuperating, he heard our programs and found new peace and meaning to life. He said, "That program saved my life and I have brought some gold bars and this necklace to show my gratitude." He said, "If this is not enough, I have much more." I rejoiced with him on his newfound faith and explained to him that we did not want his gold, only to help him know Jesus. He insisted he wanted to contribute the gold to us to help us make the programs, so on those terms, as an offering to God, we accepted it. When our staff took the gold to be valued and sold, we found it to be worth well over U.S. $500, a very worthy offering for a new believer in those days.

Other Preaching Opportunities

Preaching was my first love, and although I did not actually pastor a church, I was asked to be pastor-advisor by Mei Ren Baptist Church. Helen Liu Sung Syu Syan was the evangelist in charge and the pastor in actuality, even though she refused ordination. She and I worked well together for over 20 years. I preached at Mei Ren once a month and administered the ordinances. One other Sunday each month, I was at one of the four mission points the church began over a period of 10 years. She took me visiting house-to-house and was a bold witness as well as a great prayer warrior. At least one Sunday each month or two was given to speaking in one of the other Baptist churches up and down the island, promoting the radio and television work, as I sought to inform and inspire churches to reach out for Christ. Many times, the staff choral group would accompany me to present special music during the service. It helped them to make contact with some of our listeners, too.

The Nurse in the Family

During the first few terms of our mission service, Emma Jean continued her language study part-time, served on mission committees as requested, and played the piano at Mei Ren Baptist Church or the pump organ in the mission churches where I preached as needed. Although she was a Registered Nurse, little opportunity to use her training was afforded in Taiwan, because our mission had no medical work as such. That was primarily because of a strong government medical program and other earlier missionary work in this area. She did get to participate in a few special projects, such as the blood pressure checking station at the downtown Hwai Ning Baptist Church, which was used as an outreach and service project. She was always active in one of the churches, serving as pianist much of the time and working with the women's organizations. She often invited the women into our home for special meetings. Another area of service was in the hospitality area, arranging meals and lodging for visiting mission personnel. In this work, she became known as "the hostess with the mostest."

Breaking New Ground

In 1975, a new media missionary, Mike Wolf, who had more experience in the Mass Communications field than I, finished his language study and was ready to take his place as leader in our radio and television work, so the executive committee asked me to become the Research and Design Consultant for our mission. The first assignment, however, was to place me on loan to the Billy Graham Association for four months to help prepare for Billy's Taipei Evangelistic Campaign.

My job was to serve as coordinator for the School of Evangelism, which met each morning during the crusade to train local pastors and leaders in evangelism methods. Besides arranging for an auditorium for the main sessions and rooms for break-away sessions, we helped find suitable accommodations for those who wanted to attend. Although finding a suitable venue for the over 1,800 registrants was a formidable task, everyone prayed fervently, and finally we were offered the newly completed gymnasium of the Taipei Athletic College, which adjoined the soccer stadium where the crusade was to be held. The Lord quietly intervened to supply in a gracious way that facility. The college's rental condition was that we cover the gym floor with rubber matting to protect it from the rented folding chairs. This we were able to do at the last minute.

The Graham Crusade

That winter I wrote to my family at home the following brief summary of the crusade results. "The wonderful part of it was the way the Lord overcame all the obstacles for us. We saw so many victories it is hard to single one out. It rained four out of the five services, but still the crowds came. Our goal for the final service was 50,000, the seating capacity of our largest soccer stadium, where all services were held. There were more than that present in the rain on the first night and we probably had 70,000 crowded in on the closing Sunday afternoon. Some papers estimated 80,000, but you could not tell as most of them were seated on the mud of the soccer playing field. We originally prepared 10,000 Styrofoam cushions sealed in plastic for them to sit on, but the majority stood jammed together. We later doubled the number of plastic seats, but there was no way for all to sit. The 2,000 sets of new believer's printed materials and Bibles prepared for each service were always used up and most of the 2,000 counselors had to talk with several persons each service. Over 11,500 decisions were registered. The follow-up work will go on for some time yet, but I have baptized five in one small church from the crusade and 20 persons came forward at Grace Baptist Church the Sunday following the crusade confirming their decisions."

The Beginnings of TEE

The Taiwan Baptist Mission in its annual mission meeting of 1976 asked me, in my role as Research and Development Consultant, to research and design a plan for Theological Education by Extension in Taiwan. During our furlough in the States that fall, I attended Southwestern Seminary again and studied under Dr. Leroy Ford. At that time, I prepared a proposed curriculum design for TEE in Taiwan. Returning to Taiwan in 1977, I organized a committee of six men selected by the Taiwan Baptist Convention and six from the mission to finalize a TEE plan for Taiwan, hoping to make it as indigenous as possible. We met once each month for one year, following the plan I had originally prepared in principle, but changing the details to fit the culture and actual conditions facing the churches of Taiwan at that time.

A TEE office was set up at the seminary and work was begun preparing materials and enlisting teachers from among the Baptist pastors. The office secretary, Mrs. Fu Weng Shu, was herself a seminary graduate and proficient in using the Chinese typewriter. We worked together to prepare programmed instruction materials for the classes. Cheng Feng Yi, seminary graduate and pastor of a local church, helped with translation and teaching material preparation on a part-time basis. A short training class was held for interested pastors who wanted to lead classes in their churches. The first TEE classes soon were underway.

Overcoming Cultural Resistance

Classes were begun in a few churches in 1978, in spite of the lack of support from some seminary leaders who resisted anything other than "complete dedication" and centralized seminary education. But one class was led in Sya Men Street Baptist Church by Dr. Carl Hunker, former President of the seminary, so I have always been grateful for his leadership and example. Some of the students in different classes later felt called to full-time service and went on to enroll in the seminary.

Most of my weekends were spent traveling to different cities, speaking in the churches and promoting TEE to the membership. I wrote home in May of 1979 that TEE enrollment was up slightly for the second semester, from 55 students in 10 classes to 68 in 11 classes, with several more ready to begin. These were in different Baptist churches and various cities of Taiwan. The flexibility of beginning a class at any time was one of the advantages of this type education. In the space of three years, there were 15 TEE classes meeting in several cities over the island, with over 150 students enrolled. Those who completed several classes were recognized during seminary graduation services.

During those years, I continued to teach both in TEE classes and in the seminary as an adjunct professor as needed, teaching classes in Paul's Epistles, Church Growth, Principles of Teaching and Homiletics. I enjoyed teaching, but was seldom given the opportunity to teach the same subject twice, resulting in the necessity of continued study and preparation to keep one step ahead of my students.

Family Life

Emma Jean was also active in seminary life, teaching English and piano. She continued working with the women at Mei Ren Baptist Church, visiting hospitals and prisons to comfort and to witness to those in need. Later she was asked to help in the mission office as assistant to Herb Barrett, the mission Business Manager who sometimes had to double as Treasurer, too. Our daughter, Jeanette, became a teenager during those years at the seminary, with the usual struggles of growing up in a different culture. She began to show signs of having entrepreneur talents when she enlisted elementary students in the neighborhood and began teaching English in our basement guest room. Later, she taught at an English *Bushiban* or Make-up School in downtown Taipei.

Our furlough in the U.S. was particularly enjoyable in 1980, because I got to officiate at the wedding of our son, Jim, to Nancy Martin. They married in Nancy's home church, the Park Cities Baptist Church, in Dallas, TX.

Several missionary kids and friends were able to participate and enjoy the festivities with us.

Bold Mission Thrust

In 1980, as a part of Southern Baptist's Bold Mission Thrust program, Taiwan Baptists entered into a three-year partnership with the Missouri Baptist Convention. A number of specialists in different areas of church life were sent to lead conferences or to provide support in their particular expertise. It was dubbed, "The Modern Plan of Evangelism" by the Chinese Baptist Convention, who joined in the effort.

Our mission asked me to head up the Church Growth Committee for that effort. In that role, I had opportunity to speak to co-workers groups in nine different areas of Taiwan. At first there was little response. I was openly accused of being impractical in asking for churches to grow by dividing and reaching out to begin new work. One pastor openly said it was only *"Jr shang tan bing,"* (talk of battle on paper) something like "armchair strategy." In 1982, we scheduled a Church Growth Conference at Sun-Moon Lake, and the participation was good. Many of the pastors caught a vision for beginning new churches in their area, and a goal of 30 new places of work was set for the next two years. By counting a couple of places that had begun the year before, we were able to start 27 new chapels and preaching points during that time, short of the goal, but many more than had been begun in previous years.

The Mass Media Campaign

In 1982, there were personnel changes at the Mass Communications Center, with Mike Wolf, the Director, resigning and returning to the United States. Because the climax of the three-year Modern Plan of Evangelism was to be a simultaneous revival effort in all the churches, a mass media campaign was projected to coincide with it. The mission asked me to return to Mass Communications to plan and coordinate this effort. We packed up and moved our home for the sixth time in 12 years, this time to the newly constructed mission apartment building, Wan Fu Da Lou, next to Grace Baptist Church.

A mass media blitz committee was elected and met several times, struggling with ideas to best implement this plan. A $200,000 budget was provided by Missouri Baptists and the use of all media was projected, including radio, television, newspapers, other printed media and billboards. A logo and theme was needed, so there was much discussion as to the best plan to use. On a day when I was ill at home and praying about this need, the Lord suddenly revealed a plan to me. After presentation to the committee and much discussion, it was adopted. It became known as the *"Renshr Ta"* (Know Him) plan. For one week, ads would appear in all media, simply asking, "DO YOU KNOW HIM?" without revealing who "him" was. The second week, testimonies of 11 Christians from different walks of life in Taiwan would appear under the banner, "THESE PEOPLE KNOW HIM." The third week, just before the evangelistic meetings, the message was "YOU CAN KNOW HIM, TOO," followed by the addresses of the churches that were participating in the revival, and an invitation to attend.

The Testimonies of Faithful Christians

The media campaign was centered on the televised and printed testimonies of 11 outstanding Chinese Christians, most of whom were well-known in Taiwan, including our own Dr. Leon Chow, Pastor of Grace Baptist Church and seminary professor, and Mr. Lee Deng Hwei, who was Governor of Taiwan at the time, and was later elected President.

A total of 123 spot announcements were placed on three television stations, 644 radio spot announcements were broadcast over the 11-station network of the China

Broadcasting Corp., and the three-station hook-up of the Jeng Sheng Radio Station, and 19 different ads were placed in nine different newspapers. Contents of the ads featured the testimonies and pictures of the same persons seen in the TV spots and the announcements of the evangelistic crusade. Besides these mass media outlets, ads were placed in seven different magazines, including two in the Chinese edition of *Reader's Digest.* Other media included car stickers, bus ads, cloth banners, posters, tracts, booklets containing the testimonies of the 11 persons seen on TV along with the plan of salvation, and lapel pins with the campaign logo. Other than the bus ads, most of the latter were distributed by the churches. Three areas used small broadcast trucks and five different telephone hotlines were advertised in the major cities to counsel inquirers and give out information.

Campaign Results

The 106 pastors and laymen from Missouri were divided into teams to serve in the 109 churches and mission points which participated, 53 in northern Taiwan the first week and 56 in the south during the second. As a result of the media blitz, when the Missouri teams and their hosts visited door-to-door in their neighborhoods, they found a ready response and open doors because people recognized the lapel pins and the literature containing the testimonies, because of the "Know Him" logo seen on TV and in newspapers, etc. During the revivals, many churches reported the largest number of first-time visitors to ever attend their services. During the crusade, there were 2,300 professions of faith in the churches, the united rallies and in homes. Many who made professions said they came because of the ads they saw. Testimony booklets offered on TV, radio, and in other ads, drew a large response for several months. Churches also distributed them. Over 5,000 letters were received requesting them. They contained a decision card and a Bible correspondence course registration blank. In excess of 700 of the decision cards and more than 1,000 new correspondence course registrations were mailed back to us in September and October of that year. Christians reported that witnessing was easier during the crusade because everyone recognized the logo and were more ready to accept tracts and other literature. We all gave thanks and glory to God for His harvest of souls.

The Decline of Mass Communications

Before he resigned, Mike Wolf had discontinued the television programs in favor of producing Christian videos that could be used in churches and perhaps later on TV. He would have stopped the radio programs also, but the Chinese trustees and the churches stepped in and raised the needed budget to keep most of them on the air. Budget problems were intensified by the government's revaluing of Taiwan's Currency, which in effect cut our available funds from the Foreign Mission Board in half. At the same time, television broadcasting fees had escalated. Some staff members had been dismissed and other personnel problems arose among the remaining staff, both Chinese and missionary. 1985 was a very stressful year for me, and Emma Jean wrote home that she thought I was in "burn out."

In January of 1986, we were finally able to complete the production of a 13-episode Christian drama series, the true story of a young Chinese drug addict and his life-changing experience through faith in Christ and began broadcasting it on the China Television station. But it appeared that other parts of our operations would have to be cut, such as *"Gan Lu Magazine,"* which contained the monthly follow-up and discipleship articles we used with the programs. I could not see much future for Baptist Mass Communications as we had known it, so began praying about what the Lord would have me to do.

Missionary-Led Evangelistic Teams

Our mission voted to form missionary-led evange-listic teams and asked me, as chairman of the evangelism committee, to organize and lead them. I participated in several, either as preacher or song leader. These were mostly two or three-day meetings held in small or weak chapels or churches that could not finance their own. I felt that evangelism and church planting were the areas in which the Lord wanted to use me. After much prayer and consideration, I decided to leave Radio and Television work in March of 1986 and to re-enter full-time church-related evangelism.

The East Coast of Taiwan

After considering several cities of Taiwan where new work was needed, and praying for the Lord's leadership, we decided on the East Coast region. We moved to Hualien in the summer of 1986, while Jeanette was home on her one board-funded trip back to the field during college. We shipped our household goods in a container on the cross island railroad, and Emma Jean and Jeanette rode the train while I drove the car loaded with our plants. I had to travel around the southern tip of Taiwan because the cross island roads were blocked by landslides.

The day before we arrived in Hualien, they had an earth-quake registering 6 on the Richter scale, killing one person and injuring several. The first week in our new home in that volatile seismic area, there were many tremors. Otherwise our reception in Hualien was a warm one. Both the Chinese co-workers and the missionaries from other denominations welcomed us. We spent the first year or so doing what we could to support them and to investigate the possibilities for beginning new churches in the area. Both Emma Jean and I taught English classes in the Mei Lwun and Bwo Ai Baptist churches, and I preached in each about once a month as invited, as well as in the Bi Yun Jwang Chapel near our home. The other churches on the east coast in Ilan and Ping Tung also made use of our near presence by inviting us for regular or special services. Much of the time Ilan, a home mission chapel over an hour away, was without a regular pastor, so we tried to help them as often as possible.

During the first two years of laying groundwork and establishing relationships with co-workers in Hualien, I continued teaching English classes in the churches, preaching in the churches there or in Pingtung and Ilan when invited. After more than a year of these activities, seeking to gain the confidence of our pastors and asking often the possibility for beginning new work, Pastor Hsiao Ping, Pastor of Mei Lwun Baptist Church, approached me, asking if I would partner with his church to start a new mission on the west side of Hualien. Of course this was what I had worked and prayed toward. A comprehensive plan was drawn up, and he secured the support of the Mei Lwun Church deacons. A mission committee was formed to guide the work and the church voted to invest $10,000 N.T. (about U.S. $400 at that time) and contribute $2,000 N.T. a month toward rental of a storefront building on the main east-west street, near the new train station and not far from where the new north-south East Coast Highway One Bypass was being constructed. The mission granted N.T. $20,000 for the purchase of equipment, consisting mostly of folding chairs. The new church start was finally underway with a low-key approach to cultivate the area by offering activities that would interest and help people.

The Baptist Gospel Activities Center

A dedication service of the Activities Center was held in May with a capacity crowd attending from Mei Lwun Church, sister churches and the missionary communities. We canvassed the area, asking people what services they would prefer for us to offer for themselves or for their children.

English rated high, but cooking and sewing were indicated by many women. We quickly enrolled good-sized classes in these activities. A children's ABC English class on Sunday afternoon, the only time when they had no public school classes, soon attracted a dozen or so youngsters. The class also included oral Bible stories and slide sets consisting of Mandarin Bible stories in cartoon form. Thus was born the Hualien Activities Center, where we offered free classes in English for children and adults in which the Bible was used as a part of the curriculum. Western cooking and quilting was also taught by Emma Jean, and flower arranging by ladies from our mother church. In August of 1989, we wrote home that the first phase of cultivation, which began in May, had enrolled over 100 persons and about 20 had indicated a desire to seek Christ as Savior. Thirty children had attended the Sunday Afternoon Bible classes where ABCs were taught as an extra attraction.

In September we began a Sunday afternoon worship service, which was moderated by one of several deacons from our mother church. Young people from the church came to present special music and help teach the children in Sunday school. It was a small beginning, but a profession of faith, a local doctor, was registered at the first service. We averaged 25 in attendance the first few months. Dr. and Mrs. Liu of the mother church helped with the classes, and she served as Sunday school superintendent for the first few months. However, they soon had to drop out.

At the beginning of 1991, the worship services were changed to Sunday morning, which, although it prevented any of the congregation from the mother church from attending, gradually attracted more people from the Center's community. In February, a Winter Vacation Bible School was held, which enrolled 68 children and young people. It was led by Pastor and Mrs. Paul Fu and a team of workers from Mu Yi Baptist Church in Taipei. These activities continually attracted new people and helped us reach a host of people with a witness for the Lord.

The Jau Family's Conversion

A breakthrough came about when two of the children in the Sunday school class the previous year, Susan and Edith Jau, went home and told their mother, Mrs. Jau Wang De-nyu, about the slide set Bible story they had seen of Jesus dying on the cross for our sins. The girls had been deeply moved by that event and wanted to believe in Jesus. At home, they told their mother about what they had learned. Mrs. Jau, head of the International Commerce Bank's accounting department, who used the English name Alice, began attending our English classes and worship services and seemed moved by God's word. I approached her with a witness and met a teary reply that I just did not understand about Chinese families. I did understand a little about those strong ties, so continued to pray for her. Her husband, Jeffrey, said that if Alice became a Christian, that would be a miracle, because she had a volatile temper. But, she did trust in Christ! Then she said if Jeffrey became a Christian, that would be a great miracle, but before long her husband received Christ, too! At Easter, the entire family of four was baptized at Mei Lwun Church. Their testimonies and influence helped lead others to trust Christ and other inactive believers to unite with our church.

The Day the Idol Moved

Early in 1991 a new business – an idol shop – moved into the storefront building adjoining ours. Inside, one could see displayed images of every description, from wooden carvings to polished marble and gilt-gold, life-sized ones. Outside under the covered walkway and only a few feet from our entrance was placed an eight-foot tall replica of Guang Yin, the "goddess of mercy." We were very sad to have to face that idol daily, although the proprietor, Mr. Wang, assured us he was not in opposition to our work, "Only a businessman, trying to make money," he said, and that he would be happy to make us an image of Mary at little or no charge!

When Pastor and Mrs. Hsiao came to the center on Wednesday for our monthly prayer session a few weeks later, they were very upset, saying no one would want to come to worship in a place next door to those idols. As we prayed, the two of them, and especially Mrs. Hsiao, were very bold in telling the Lord that He had to move those idols. I confess that my faith was small, because businessmen do not pay six months rent plus the key money that was required for those store buildings, then move out in one month. Besides, that location was perfect for his business. Bus loads of Buddhist "pilgrims" came to visit the big Buddhist Hospital a few blocks away, and many of them stopped at the tea store on the other side of us so the passengers could buy Hualien tea, so I knew his business had every opportunity of succeeding.

That weekend we were involved in our mission's winter prayer retreat in Taipei, where we requested that they join us in prayer for that situation. When we returned to Hualien on Monday morning, Emma Jean went to the center for her women's class. When she returned home, she told me that she did not see the Guang Yin idol, and the door to the idol shop was closed. When I went to the center that afternoon to meet my class, sure enough, the big idol was gone and the shop door shuttered! I went to the tea shop on the other side and asked about it. They told me that the idols had all been moved out on Sunday and the shop shut down. No reason was ever given, but we knew – God had answered some prayers! The next weekend, we had scheduled evangelistic services led by Mrs. Helen Liu Sung Syu-Syan from Mei Ren Baptist Church of Taipei. Those services resulted in a good attendance, and 10 persons made public decisions to trust in Christ. Among them was a young man, 27 years of age, the son of Mr. Wang, proprietor of the idol shop. We had come upon him while visiting up and down that street where he was watching the empty shop for his father until it could be disposed of. We witnessed to him and invited him to the services. That night he was present, but did not make a decision. The next night he came back, and at the end of the service confessed Jesus as his savior. So, the Lord not only moved the idols, He saved the son of the shop owner!

Emmanuel Baptist Church

In May of 1991, on the second anniversary of the opening of the center, a Thanksgiving and Dedication Service was held with 37 in attendance, led by Pastor Hsiao of the mother church. At that time, the name of the center was changed to Emmanuel Baptist Church. A new sign with a large cross was purchased and hung on the front of our building. The membership was growing, and in June we averaged 23 in attendance at the worship services. The church began to plan for the purchase of our own facility in that area, and Mei Lwun Church voted to make a challenge gift of US $20,000 (NT $500,000) if the members of Emmanuel would match it. During a morning service in June, the small congregation of 13 baptized members and several "seekers" pledged a total of NT $354,000 to add to the NT $125,000 already on hand to make a first payment of one million yuan toward purchase of a three-story town-house (row of adjoining houses) type building, in which the new church could meet. An application for a loan was made to the Chinese Baptist Convention's Loan Fund, in hopes that a building could be bought by the end of the year.

Fellowship in the Body

A capacity crowd of 75 persons attended our Christmas dinner and program at the end of 1991. We had expected and prepared for only 55, but since most of them also brought food, there was plenty to eat. It did tax our facilities, as we only had 60 chairs. Chinese people do love crowds and noise. We had plenty of both. Goals of 25 church members and 10 baptisms for 1991 were reached, and the average attendance in the worship services grew to 30 by the end of the year. We were blessed by the addition of a couple of Baptist families that moved to Hualien. By the middle of 1992, our worship attendance averaged around 30 and there were 33 baptized members, including Emma Jean and myself.

As the Lord built his church in that area of Hualien, we just watched and applauded. A real fellowship developed as we began discipleship classes that met following the morning service on Sunday. We took turns preparing a simple lunch and enjoying it together. After completing a Masterlife class, all seven adults in the group accepted positions as teachers in our newly graded Sunday school, and otherwise served as leaders in various capacities. We quickly grew to love this small congregation and stand in awe at what the Lord was doing in their lives. I wrote home about this growth and my sister, Juanita, replied, "It appears you are re-living the Book of Acts."

The New Worship Center

As we neared the time of leaving Hualien for retirement, we were anxious about two things; the purchase of a building to house this growing congregation, and the calling of a national pastor to lead them. Each of these items was made a matter of much prayer, both by my wife and me, and by the members of the congregation. The building was needed to provide adequate space and keep the church from the burden of paying rent. The Chinese pastor was absolutely necessary for future leadership and more indigenous growth.

As we priced the available buildings, we realized that we were still in need of U.S. $40,000. The Baptist Church Loan Fund had approved $100,000, but even with the $40,000 raised earlier by our members and the mother church, we were still short of our goal. Dr. Yang, who had given earlier, reserved the last $2,000 in a promissory note as his own gift. Jeffery Jau, Chairman of our Building Committee, mortgaged a building he owned and took a bank loan for U.S. $40,000, which he loaned to the church at no interest. That put us over the top. We purchased a three-story house in a row of adjoining houses only one block from East Coast Highway One Bypass and a few blocks from the planned Buddhist Medical School. Another church member donated a used 15-ton air conditioner for the use of the church. The Lord is faithful and he provided for our needs!

The New Pastor
After much prayer and conferring with the seminary and the convention office, a young man soon to graduate from the seminary, Gau Chang-Sheng, was recommended by one of his teachers. His talents included playing the guitar, and he seemed at first to be well accepted by our people, especially the young people, even though he was not Chinese, but an Ami Tribal person, one of the nine indigenous groups in Taiwan. After we left, he moved on the field, but cultural differences soon alienated many of the members. After a few years, he left the ministry and took a commercial job. A woman graduate of the seminary, Miss Lee Chwun-Mei, was invited to lead the church, but by that time many of the charter members had moved to other churches in the city. This has been a big disappointment for us and for those original members, but we are still looking for the Lord to bless that church in an unusual way.

Leaving Taiwan
After a round of farewell dinners, we left Hualien on November 11, 1992, to spend a few days in Taipei checking out at our mission office and saying goodbye to friends and

coworkers there. We left a big chunk of our heart in Taiwan. I had what I would describe as "withdrawal symptoms" for many months, and even now, many years later, I still have deep feelings for our Christian friends there.

An Unusual Welcome Home

Just two short weeks after arriving back in America, our grandson, Kelsey, was born to Jim and Nancy, our son and daughter-in-law. It was a grand welcome home. We quickly visited family and began to accept speaking invitations in churches and summer camps. It was good to be home, but we had "withdrawal pains," thinking of our friends and coworkers in Taiwan and remembering the struggles of new Christians in the church at Hualien. Following our final furlough, we journeyed to Richmond, Virginia, for our retirement ceremony at the International Mission Board. On the last day, Dr. Sam James, Vice President for Asia, asked us if we would be willing to go to Paris, France, to fill in for the Tome Halsell family for five months while they came home on furlough.

Beginning a New Church in Paris

We arrived in Paris in the spring of 1994, and quickly began working with Pastor and Mrs. John Hung in their Cantonese-speaking East Paris Chinese Baptist Church, while exploring the possibility of beginning work with the Mandarin speakers among the 300,000 Chinese there. Many of the Cantonese were former residents of Viet Nam and were among the boat people who escaped to Hong Kong or the Philippines following the Communist takeover, and were later accepted by France. Now other Chinese were arriving from Taiwan and the China Mainland, mainly students or business people. We began visiting the many prospects in the area and started Bible study in the home of the Wang family, who were recently from Taiwan. Several others in the neighborhood began attending the class.

Table-top Evangelism

One of the most effective ways of witnessing among the Chinese community in Paris was what we began calling "table-top evangelism." It was named that because we were invited to eat in the homes of the Cantonese-speaking church members, who also spoke some Mandarin, a total of 27 times in the five months we were there. They would also invite their friends, many of whom were non-Christians, and we would spend several hours around the dinner table, eating and conversing while waiting for the men to come home from their restaurant work around 9:00 p.m. Each family that arrived would bring another dish or two, so we remained around the table, eating a bit of each delicious offering. The host would introduce each guest and tell us they were "seekers" or "interested in Christianity" or "not yet believers," etc., thus giving us an opening to witness in a casual way. The believers in the group also would add their testimonies of the Lord's goodness in one way or another, making an effective and natural progression of presenting the Word of God to non-believers.

As we began reaching more Mandarin-speaking families, we looked for a place to open a new mission. It was difficult to find any place to rent, and almost impossible to buy at the high prices in France. Also, the government restrictions for church meeting places were very strict, requiring a certain height of the ceiling, and a number of parking places that are available, etc. Finally, we were able to rent a hotel conference room for $U.S. 2,000 per month for a morning worship service on Sundays. With the help of two Chinese short-term mission teams, one from Hong Kong's Kowloon City Baptist Church, John Hung's sponsoring church, and one from some Chinese churches in Toronto, Canada, we held special services there featuring the visiting choir and evangelist. The new Mandarin Baptist Mission of East Paris was under way. Rapid growth followed as several new families were reached and baptized.

Singapore Calling

After returning home, we were contacted by Dr. Clyde Meador, Area Director for Southeast Asia, inviting us to teach for one year in the Baptist Seminary in Singapore. That was a big challenge to me, because it had been several years since I had taught seminary classes, especially to teach in Chinese again. But after prayer, we determined that this was the Lord's will for us at that time.

We arrived in Singapore in September of 1995 and received a warm welcome from missionaries and seminary faculty. Danny Hsia, President of the seminary, asked me to teach the Book of Galatians, Principles of Teaching, and the Paul's Prison Epistles during the first term and Paul's Pastoral Epistles, Church Growth and Homiletics (Preaching) in the second term. Although I had taught these before, either in Taiwan Baptist Seminary or a TEE class, they were more than enough to keep me hitting the books to prepare and keep ahead of my students. There were only 17 enrolled in the small seminary during the first term, nine of them in the Chinese stream where I was teaching. We also added a night course in Principles of Teaching during the second term, to accommodate some of the lay teachers from Singapore's Baptist churches.

American Samoa's Chinese Baptist Church

An opportunity for evangelism in American Samoa arose in 1995, when a Chinese businessman built a clothing factory there to make T-shirts for Wal-Mart Discount Stores. He imported 300 young workers from China to staff it and to train Samoan workers. The little church, which had nine members at the time, began to minister and witness to them. A Chinese pastor from Hong Kong, who was studying at Southwestern Seminary in the U.S., was sent by the Home Mission Board and the South Pacific Baptist Convention to hold an evangelistic meeting there. During those services, there were a large number of professions of faith and the convention was looking for someone to go and disciple them. After much prayer, Emma Jean and I agreed to go for three months.

My job included preaching in the Chinese worship services, visiting with Chinese families, and witnessing to them as much as possible. They were the businessmen of the island and difficult to find at an off time. We set up discipleship classes for those young workers that had already trusted the Lord, and offered special activities to try to reach the others. They lived in the factory dormitory and were not available to be visited in the plant area, so we needed to invite them to special occasions, loading them on the back of the rusted-out pickup that was our only available transportation. The final Sunday I was in Samoa, we held a baptismal service for seven new believers in the ocean at a beautiful beach. Several of the young workers were included, as well as one business woman, Mrs. Huang, who had been attending some of our services and was transformed by the power of Christ in her life as she accepted Him.

Back to Myanmar

The Sunday before we were scheduled to leave Singapore, I had preached at a local Baptist church where our friend, Buddy Morris, was pastor. Following the service, a Chinese woman, Wen Hwei Ai, came up to me and asked me if I would be interested in going to Myanmar to teach in a Chinese Bible school. After returning home, I continued to have correspondence with Miss Wen, who was a teacher at the Chinese Christian Institute in Pin Oo Lwin, Myanmar, and with Jim McAtee, the missionary in charge of the work there. Miss Wen was able to send me an official letter of invitation to teach for six weeks at the school. Using the letter, I applied to the Myanmar government for a business visa, which would allow me to stay in the country two months. It had one drawback – it would require that I have the visa extended after one month, and it had to be done in the capital city of Yangon.

Over the months that followed, I was successful in securing that visa and arrived in Pin Oo Lwin, Myanmar, in February of 1997. However, by the time I arrived there had been some problems at the school and most of the students had left. I was then asked to teach the faculty a concentrated course in Church Growth for a few weeks, until arrangements could be made for the students to return. The teaching faculty was joined by two local pastors for part of the course.

An Unexpected Witnessing Experience

One day as I walked from my classes back to the motel, I met Ji Syau Hwei, a young Chinese businessman from Beijing, who asked me to teach him some English. I told him that although I was busy with classes, I would have some time on Sunday afternoon. Since I was to preach during the morning worship service at the school chapel, I invited him to attend and we could study English in a classroom after church. He accepted the invitation and came to the first Christian meeting he had ever attended. Following the service, he was simply beaming with joy. In the classroom, he immediately began asking questions about the message he had just heard. He was no longer interested in studying English, but wanted to hear more of the story of Jesus. Within two hours, with lunch totally forgotten, he prayed to receive Christ as his Savior.

On the Burma Road

After consultation with Pastor Yan Da An, president of the school, I was asked to travel up the Burma Road to the city of Lashio, near the China border, and conduct a training course each morning for two weeks for the 45 or so young "missionary" teachers the church had sent out into the countryside and villages of upper Burma, to begin small primary schools for Chinese children, who otherwise had no opportunity for an education. Their objective was to lead the children to faith in Christ and seek to win their parents, and then undertake to start a church. They also wanted me to preach a two-week *pei-ling hwei,* or church revival at night in their church.

Early one morning, we left Pin Oo Lwin in a rented station wagon with a local Burmese driver and started up the Burma Road, which the National Geographic called the road you never ask when you will get there. Although it had been paved at one time, the roadway was in such disrepair that it was easier to drive in the oxcart path alongside the broken pavement much of the way. We were stopped at military checkpoints along the way, and I had to show the copy of my passport that had been made for me to use while mine was sent to Yangon to get my visa extended after the first month. I was told by my companions not to say I was a missionary, but a teacher or a tourist. At the first checkpoint, I was passed through with no problem. However, late in the afternoon a few miles outside Lashio, I was ordered out of the car along with my companions and ushered into the military station behind the armed guard. As we followed him into the shack that served as the army post there at the military checkpoint on the old Burma Road, outside the city of Lashio, I felt a strange feeling of calmness come over me. I actually wanted to goose step as I marched behind him! I felt no real sense of anxiety or apprehension as Pastor Wang, Pastor Yan's son, and I were taken into custody and detained by these Myanmar Army guards. The peace that only Christ can give settled into my heart.

The Interrogation and Detainment

Inside the building, I was interrogated for about an hour while the Chinese were searched and also had to give proof of where they had been and their business with me. The army interpreter helping to question me finally said that because of the condition of my passport, I was to be detained and sent back to Mandalay. No traffic was allowed on the road at night, so it would be at least the next day before I could be returned. The Chinese men were released and went into the city to report on my plight. While they were gone, the interrogator asked me if I taught Bible. I could not lie to him, so I said, "Sometimes." After a while, when we were alone, he told me, "I am also a Christian, and a member of the Kachin Baptist Church in Lashio." He said, "I do not belong to this detachment, but just happened to come by to say goodbye to some friends here because I am being transferred to another post, and I was asked to interpret because I speak some English." It was then that I began to realize why I had not been tense or worried about the situation. Things like that do not "just happen." They are the Lord's provision.

House Arrest in Lashio

Within an hour, Pastor Yan Da An and two of the deacons from the Chinese Baptist Church had arrived and had lively conversations with the captain and the interpreter, explaining why I was there and why I only had a copy of my passport. The captain agreed that if the army commander in Lashio gave his permission, I could be released into house arrest in the home of Pastor Yan, who would guarantee me. One of the deacons remained to keep me company, while the pastor and other deacon went back to Lashio to find the Area Commander. Within another couple of hours, permission was granted and I was released into their custody until my passport could be returned. When we arrived at the church around nine p.m., most of the congregation was still there where they had gathered earlier to greet me. What a prayer meeting they must have been having!

The irony of it was that the pastor, in whose home I was sentenced to live under house arrest, resided in the very church where I was supposed to teach and preach for two weeks. How perfect are the provisions the Lord makes! The accommodations in the church were only a *tatami* bed, a table and a chair, with toilet and a separate bath on the hall, but I had ample space in the "upper room," a prayer and study area in the church attic, to prepare for the classes and revival services. It was a real challenge because I had arrived only prepared to teach on church growth, and the last minute change plus the need to prepare messages to the church for 16 services and several home worship services stretched me considerably. I spent much time on my knees, and as I became more acquainted with the situation under which the members and people of Lashio lived, found myself weeping more than I had in years. They were serving the Lord there under appalling conditions!

After I received my passport back from Yangon and was released from house arrest, we visited one of the small schools, the Manna Baptist School, several miles out from Lashio, meeting in three bamboo shacks. I wished I had been able to visit them sooner, so I would have had more understanding of their situation and would have been better prepared for the classes. Teaching under those conditions must have taken real dedication and I grew to greatly appreciate those young workers. Starting a church in those facilities would not be easy, to say the least.

Hong Kong and Beyond

As I prayed about further short term-mission opportunities, the Lord impressed me in 2001 with one of the personnel requests listed in the International Mission Board's quarterly personnel request bulletin. It was listed as an English teaching opportunity, but also mentioned evangelism as one part of it. When I wrote to the Board, they put me in contact with the person on the field who had made the request. As a result, I flew to Hong Kong, where he met me and took me by train to the city where he was working with one of the large minority people groups. Because it was one of the Autonomous Regions in China, the work he was doing in teaching English and operating a small café could be done pretty openly. He supplied a large number of English teachers to different schools in the city during the summer months, so was permitted access to many students and their teachers in several settings in that city.

Since there was only one open Protestant church in the area, and it had limited seating capacity, several house churches related to that church were permitted to openly hold services. As a result, I was given opportunity during the four weeks I was there to preach seven times in four different house churches, and to work with student groups three times each week. For three weeks, I met several times a week with house church leaders to train and encourage them. There were as few as three leaders in attendance on one night, and as many as 15 on others. In the final meeting with the students, an opportunity to trust Christ as savior was given, and nine of the 25 in attendance made that decision. When we met with them the following Wednesday evening to give some discipleship training, they had already won one of their fellow students to the Lord. I look back on that brief time as a very unusual period and unique opportunity for sharing the gospel in a very special place.

Hong Kong Revisited

In 2002, Emma Jean and I were again invited to live in Hong Kong and take part in leading some training sessions in methods of starting Church Planting Movements across the border in East Asia. For five months, we lived in a high-rise apartment in Kowloon, Hong Kong, and I traveled to a city where arrangements had been made to hold several training sessions for different groups, some of whom were house church members who had dedicated their lives to sharing Christ with the minority peoples of their nation. Some of these were mature Christians who were white hot in their devotion to the Lord, but had not had much training. Other classes were themselves members of one of the minority people groups who, as new Christians, wanted to receive training in discipleship and witnessing methods. Then they would be able to start small groups and lead them to grow into viable churches, which although small, could continue to train others who would do the same, repeating the cycle. In this way, a Church Planting Movement – a multiplication or explosion of churches like those happening in other parts of the world, could be initiated among their own peoples.

These groups represented a variety of people groups, age levels, and different maturity of Christian experience. One group, for instance, contained schoolteachers, a former Buddhist monk, an ex-convict, and business people. Another group contained several older people who had little formal schooling and were functional illiterates. One attendee was a brand new Christian; several had not yet been baptized, but were happy to be immersed in the bathtub at the meeting place during the week. An older man showed us his Evangicube, a folding set of blocks with pictures of the life of Christ, which can be used in witnessing to those who have never heard the Gospel. Although he is illiterate, he has a small restaurant and often uses the cubes to share with his customers. I asked him what percentage of those to whom he witnessed indicated a willingness to believe in Jesus. He replied, 80 percent. Unlearned and ignorant men (as found in Acts) have often through history made very effective evangelists, and still do. When I returned one year after the first series of training sessions, I was able to visit one of the men who had participated in a class the year before. He was a new Christian and had received baptism during that week. He and his wife had a small shop selling children's clothes and shoes. As I visited with them, I asked if they had been able to use any of the things they had learned. He replied that they had been able to win some friends and were meeting twice weekly with about 15 in the group. He added, A friend and I have baptized 12 new believers this year. That, of course, was thrilling to hear.

Back in the Ozarks

My wife and I are retired and now reside in an independent living apartment at The Baptist Home in Ozark, MO. We are still active in our church, where teaching and serving opportunities are afforded us. Until recently, we were able to teach some Bible studies to Chinese students from several places in the Orient. Our children live in Texas, where Jim is the Minister of Worship and Young Adults at First Baptist Church, Copperas Cove. His wife, Nancy, and son, Kelsey, are both very active in school and church activities. Kelsey, our only grandchild, is a freshman in high school and provides us with plenty of excitement with his excellence in music, athletics, and scholastic achievements. Jeanette is a flight attendant for American Airlines, still single and active in her age group's Bible studies at her church, as much as her flight schedule allows.

One day we may have opportunity to once again travel to Asia for short periods of sharing the gospel, and we can tell "the rest of the story." Until that day, my only regret is that advancing age and need to care for my wife, who has various health problems, has curtailed our ability to travel very far from home. Still, our constant consolation of it now.

Jim and his wife Nancy,
Herb, Jeanette and Emma Jean Barker

Ruth and Art Robinson
Dreams Come True

Chosen

It all began for Annie Ruth in the early hours of April 13, 1925. A devout Christian couple, Jasper Thomas and Annie Lou Smithson McIntosh, added another child to their already ample number of eight. Ruth, as the family called the new baby, was born in San Gabriel, CA, which later was incorporated into a new town called Garvey. Their home was only one block from the Frances E. Willard Elementary School, the school which several of her siblings and she attended.

As a preschooler, Ruth believed Jesus loved her, would forgive her for the naughty things she did, and would come into her heart and make her a child of God. With her mother kneeling by her bedside and leading Ruth in a prayer, she sincerely prayed after her mother, asking Jesus to come into her heart.

One day at school, when she was seven years old, she prayed an important prayer. Standing on the playground at recess time, Ruth prayed that Jesus would show her what was right and what was wrong. She told Jesus she was not always sure. If Jesus would show her what was right and what was wrong, she promised to try to always do what was right. One of the things that helped Ruth to realize the differ-

199

ence between right and wrong was Bible study. She made a decision as a ten-year-old to read her Bible every day, and daily Bible reading became a lifetime practice.

At the age of nine, Ruth attended meetings planned and directed by J. Irwin Overholtzer, the founder of Child Evangelism. She found his Bible stories very interesting. One day he asked the children. "What do you want to be when you grow up?" Ruth had not given any serious thought to this. Good teaching in her home once again helped her to know what to do.

Quickly she prayed, "God, what do you want me to be?"

Mr. Overholtzer asked her, "What do you want to be, little girl?"

Her quick response was, "A missionary."

Ruth could have forgotten this response, but as missionaries from time to time spoke in her church, the Holy Spirit continued to speak to her about missionary service. It became a frequent tug upon her heart as she entered her teen years. Ruth felt heavily convicted about the fact she did not have the courage to tell others about Jesus. She wondered: What kind of missionary would she make?

God continued to deal with Ruth until she prayed, "Here I am, God. I am turning my whole life over to you. If your will includes success, a success I will be. If your will includes a failure, a failure I will be. I submit myself to whatever Your path for me entails." She had found glorious freedom and a new confidence.

During Ruth's high school years, God gave her leadership positions in church and in her school. She was a good student and was valedictorian of her high school graduating class of June 1942. She attended Pasadena Junior College (Pasadena City College) and University of California at Los Angles (UCLA).

It was a struggle to work her way through college. God provided jobs – babysitting, a seamstress job and work in the university library. She received a scholarship her last year in college. Ruth said, "I was broke, or nearly so, most of those college years, but I never went hungry."

Also Chosen

Back in 1925, when Ruth was born, a couple by the name of Burton Kenson and Mabel Helen Michaelson Robinson were expecting a child. They lived in another city far from Ruth's southern California home. Their city was Klamath Falls, OR. It was here that their baby boy, their first child, made his appearance on August 26, 1925. They named him Arthur C. Robinson. He, like Ruth, came from a dedicated Christian family. He was raised in the church.

At the age of ten, during a revival, Art, as he came to be known, went down the sawdust aisle of the tent with penitent tears streaming down his face, and accepted Jesus Christ as his Savior and Lord. Shortly thereafter, he was baptized and became a member of First Baptist Church of Klamath Falls, the church to which not only his immediate family belonged, but also his aunts, uncles, and cousins. Art attended one of the local elementary schools and went on to Klamath Union High School, from which he graduated.

Fresh out of high school at a crucial time in American history as World War II was being waged, Art volunteered for military duty. He joined the U.S. Navy. He saw God's hand in this decision and made a promise to God, "I need you to help me face an uncertain future. I need You to help me in my weaknesses. If You will help me, I will give my life to You to serve You." God heard that prayer, and Art began to honor that promise.

The Navy sent Art for officer's training, first to the University of Washington for one year, and then to the University of California at Los Angeles (UCLA) for the rest of his college education. He sought out Christians, studied his Bible with intensity, and became involved in Inter-Varsity Christian Fellowship, which met right off on campus.

The Chosen Ones Meet

Ruth was serving as an officer in Inter-Varsity Christian Fellowship. As secretary, it was her responsibility to register newcomers. At one of the meetings, she noticed a newcomer, an NROTC student; young, clean-cut, and good looking. She thought, "There is a young man from a good home." Thus, she and Art met.

When Ruth's mother was killed in a train accident in 1945, Art got some of the other Christians together. They went to the sorority house where Ruth was living and prayed for her. Ruth knew this was an unusual young man.

While both of them were still students at UCLA, World War II ended. One evening, they walked the campus with great gratitude to God that this nightmare was over. They were falling in love. However, Ruth had some reservations, as she knew she could not marry someone who was not called to be a missionary. She had settled the issue with God. She was called to serve God as a missionary. She was afraid to mention this to Art, for fear he might decide he too would be a missionary so that their relationship would not be short-ended.

One evening, as Art was sharing from his heart, he told Ruth that he felt God had called him to be a missionary. He told her about a word picture a missionary to India had given, of ten men carrying a heavy log with nine of them on one end and only one man holding up the other end. From this, the missionary had drawn the comparison of American young men and women going into the ministry who stay in America, and those who go abroad to share the Good News. More than 90 percent stay in America and less than 10 percent go with the Gospel to the ends of the earth. Art confided that he felt he must go where fewer had the opportunity to hear the Gospel.

They knew God had directed their lives to serve together. On August 10, 1947, they said their vows and were bonded together. They chose as their life verse, "Whatsoever you do in word or deed, do all in the name of the Lord Jesus, giving thanks to God and the Father by Him." (Colossians 3:17 KJV)

Early in the 1950s, Art and Ruth began attending Golden Gate Baptist Theological Seminary in Mill Valley, CA. When they learned they were expecting a baby, they felt they needed a job to support their growing family. Art accepted a teaching position in the high school of Weed, CA. After a year there, they moved to Malin, OR, where Art taught high school for two years. Then they moved back to California, where Art taught high school for 10 years. During these years, they attended Humboldt State University and both earned Master's degrees in Educational Administration and Supervision.

As they neared completion of their advanced degrees, they began to seek appointment with the Foreign Mission Board of the Southern Baptist Convention. Their first application for missionary service was turned down by the Board. There was some doubt in the Board's mind that they were called. However, Ruth and Art knew they were called. They had to be faithful and let God work out the details and the timing for their appointment.

They were active members of the church. At one time or another, Art and Ruth held every office there was in the Sunny Brae Baptist Church of Arcata, CA. They were making a contribution to their community by teaching in the public schools. They started a Christian teachers' group that met once a month, and Art started a "Christians Living on Campus" club for the students at his school. God was using them, and they were content.

God had also gifted their home with three children during the 1950s: Trudy Elise, born August 12, 1952; Mark Winslow, September 24, 1955; and Daniel Craig, February 3, 1957.

Finally, Commissioned for Mission Service

They were blessed and they knew it. However, they also knew they were called to serve God overseas. In the summer of 1964, they drove across the United States to Ridgecrest Baptist Assembly for Foreign Missions Week. This gave them the opportunity to visit with Mission Board personnel, who now understood their commitment to the Lord Jesus and to missions. Art and Ruth were commissioned as missionaries to Taiwan in the October Board Meeting, 1964, for one term of service with the possibility of one additional term of service if the Taiwan Baptist Mission requested it. The mission voted and then requested the Board to appoint them for career service, which the Board did. The year was 1966.

Children and the Mission Field

Ruth and Art, like missionaries before them, wondered how living in a foreign country would affect their children. Would they be deprived of things that were essential to their growth and future? Would they become resentful of their parents uprooting them from friends, family and their homeland to take them overseas? They prayed and asked God to prepare their children for their move overseas. Trudy was the oldest and would be in junior high when they went to Taiwan, and she would have the biggest adjustment. They prayed especially for Trudy. Then, at a summer camp, Trudy surrendered her life to God for missionary service. When her parents told her that they were seeking appointment to Taiwan, she was not only ready to go, but looked forward to going overseas.

Mark and Dan were in their early elementary grades, and they took the news of their parents considering missionary service without noticeable reaction. They were happy to join their parents as they made preparation for their new home thousands of miles away from California. They arrived in Taiwan July 29, 1965. The temperature was more than 90 degrees and the humidity matched that. There were adjustments to be made, but they had no doubt about God's place of service.

Ministry in Taiwan

Their assignment was to teach at Morrison Christian Academy in Taichung, Taiwan. This was a match for both Ruth and Art. Together, their years of teaching experience added up to nearly 25 years. They were gifted teachers. They loved working with students. Trudy, Mark and Dan were happy to be in Taiwan and living next to the school they would be attending.

From 1965 to 1980, they were involved in Morrison Christian Academy, a school which has educated scores of missionary children who are now successfully working around the world.

Art served at Morrison, first as a teacher and coach, then as an administrator at the junior high level, and later as high school principal. Ruth taught English, Bible, and music. These were rewarding years as they had opportunity to share Christ with missionary children and youth from Norway, Sweden, Japan, Korea, India, U.S., Germany, and Australia. The school also offered an education to American military children.

Ruth also became increasingly involved with Chung Hsing University. She taught English to majors in mechanical and civil engineering, as well as to students in the Department of Western Languages. She was challenged by these students, and there were many opportunities to answer their questions about faith and life. The Robinsons lived and worked in an international community where there were many needs among students and faculty. They were available as God directed their steps.

Their fourth child, Heidi, was born in Taiwan, January 19, 1967. Heidi was God's gift of healing to Art in the loss of his mother, who passed away in November 1966.

As they prepared to return to America in mid-1980 for their third furlough, Art began to feel God speaking to him about working full-time in the Chinese community. During their years at Morrison, they had taught English Bible classes in their home and in the Chinese Baptist Churches.

They had been involved in evangelistic ministries. For example, they had a Christmas party for the blue collar workers who helped build their home next to the Morrison School campus. They wanted to express their appreciation to the laborers for the good job they had done, and they wanted to share God's love as portrayed in a film about the first Christmas. What a wonderful experience to watch the men and women enjoy the Western refreshments and the story of that first Christmas. Many of them heard it for the first time.

The ministry with Chinese people, with the English Bible Fellowship, which Ruth started in the late 1970s, resulted in a significant number of decisions for Christ. EBF met during the Sunday school hour of Immanuel Baptist Church. Immanuel served primarily the American community, including U.S. military men and Morrison Christian Academy students. Though the Chinese were not part of Immanuel's target audience, they were welcomed to its services. The EBF students would attend the English services of Immanuel Baptist Church, which was held right after EBF. A few missionaries and some Christian Chinese interpreters helped Ruth with this ministry. Converts were baptized in the swimming pools of Morrison Academy.

By 1981, three of the Robinsons' children had graduated from Morrison and were either in college in the U.S., or had graduated from college. Their children had made them proud during the years they lived in Taiwan.

They participated in the various school activities: sports, drama, music, and school government. They were good students and never embarrassed their parents. The children were always happy to participate in the activities for the Chinese to whom their parents were ministering, such as parties, classes, movies, and tours. Their exposure to both the Chinese and American cultures, plus their opportunity to study with students from a number of different countries, made them far more world conscious than most students in America.

Only Heidi was still at home. When asked how she would feel about the family moving from Morrison Academy to a Chinese community which had few missionaries, without hesitation she responded, "I think you should do what God tells you to do. Besides, I think it would be fun to live in the dormitory at Morrison."

After furlough in 1981, Art, Ruth and Heidi moved to south Taiwan to the city of Tainan. They opened their homes for English activities and ministered as pastor and wife to the English-language congregation of Trinity Baptist Church. Ruth taught English Conversation classes at Cheng Kung National University in Tainan. Ruth and Art had their most rewarding ministry and perhaps their most fruitful missionary service during the next eight years. They were able to walk with many students and young adults to faith in Jesus Christ. Many of these men and women are faithful church members in Taiwan and other countries.

Heidi did have fun in the school dormitory, did well in her studies, was an asset to the school's volleyball, track and basketball teams, and was a blessing to her parents' ministry when she was home from boarding school on weekends and during the summers.

Art and Ruth were cooperative members of the Taiwan Baptist Mission. They felt so privileged to have missionaries as their friends and co-workers. They served on various committees. Prayer times with fellow missionaries were especially heartening. Ruth was coordinator for the "Home and Church" division of the Mission. This entailed writing a strategy for 'homemakers' in the Taiwan Baptist Mission. These wives and mothers were able to encourage each other to be better wives, mothers, and missionaries.

Retirement and Beyond

In 1989, they returned to the U.S. for their final furlough. This one, like all the other furloughs, was busy as they spoke in churches in both the United States and Canada. They were blessed to share what God was doing in Taiwan among His people.

Ruth and Art have continued to be involved in the teaching ministry. Ruth has participated in mission trips to every continent (except the South Pole). These trips have taken her to Russia, Kazakhstan, India, Brazil, the British Isles (England, Scotland, Wales and Ireland) Australia, and Mexico. Ruth has had the dream of teaching God's Word on every continent fulfilled.

She has written a book, whose title, **Silk Bird Net,** is the story of God's faithfulness to them. In her book, she tells the story of God's faithfulness to them and how delighting in the Lord and serving Him have resulted in their being given the desires of their hearts.

Art and Ruth are active members of the church in Klamath Falls, where they have retired. They continue to study God's Word and encourage others to read and study it. They hold a number of positions in their church. They promote missions, encouraging all age groups to carry out the Great Commission. They participate in and promote prayer. They assist in helping to meet community needs.

In retirement during the 1990s and early 2000s, Ruth substitute taught in the public schools of Klamath County and of the city of Klamath Falls for 13 years. In recent years, she served as the prayer coordinator of Basic Women's Connection, a dinner program in which Christian women invite their non-Christian friends to a meal and a program that always includes a testimony about the change that Christ makes in one's life. She belongs to the Toastmasters, a club which allows her to not only work on her speaking skills, but to also relate to people, some of whom are not Christians.

They are pray-ers. They pray for their church and their country on all levels of society. They pray for international events and needs. They lift their children and their ministries and their grandchildren and their activities to the throne. They remember their extended family in prayer. They are burdened for the American churches, for the Taiwan Baptist Mission, and for missionaries who serve around the world. They always remember to pray for their Taiwan "family" – Christian brothers and sisters – whom they came to love during their years in Taiwan. They learned together. They worked together. They played together. They prayed together. They worshiped together. They continue to keep in touch.

Art and Ruth spent a quarter of a century in Taiwan. It was a busy time, challenging and a blessed time. As they saw lost people come to Jesus Christ, as they discipled believers, worked cooperatively with Chinese pastors and church leaders, and ministered to people with special needs, God kept His promises to them that He would never leave nor forsake them.

Serendipity

Dan, their third son, before leaving for Taiwan as a seven-year-old asked, "Will I become Chinese in Taiwan?"

They assured him that he would remain a little American boy, but he would enjoy playing with Chinese children. They wonder today if they answered him correctly, because he is far more Chinese than was anticipated, for he, his wife and three sons live on the campus of Morrison Academy, where they teach and serve as missionaries. Dan has interaction with Chinese people every day, speaks their language, works with them, worships and serves with them in a church plant called House of Blessing.

Rewards of Obedience

Art and Ruth believe that there are rewards of obedience. God knows His creation far better than they know themselves, and He wants the very best for each of His children. Jeremiah 29:11 says, "I know the plans I have for you, says the Lord, plans to give you a future and a hope." (Living Bible Version)

As Ruth has delighted in the Lord and in His plan for her, He has given her the desires of her heart. Ruth desired to travel. She has been able to travel to and minister on every continent. She desired a family. Today she has four children who have Godly spouses, nine grandchildren, and four great-grandchildren. How blessed they are.

She desired to be a missionary. She, alongside Art, served in Taiwan for 25 years.

She desired to have a singing family. The family not only loves music, but can perform together. Their children sang at their parent's 60th wedding anniversary in 2007, and this time the grandchildren accompanied them with musical instruments.

Ruth desired to teach. She loved teaching and thought she was giving a teaching career up when she surrendered to being a missionary. What a wonderful surprise when she discovered that on the mission field, she could be a missionary and a teacher. She has had more than 60 years of teaching in schools and churches, and is still teaching.

She desired to tell others about the love of Jesus. Ruth and Art wanted to win souls for Jesus Christ. Many of their prayers were focused on this need. There was no way this desire could be fulfilled, except by the power of the Holy Spirit and God's intervention in people's lives. The more they allowed God to guide them, fill them, and use them, the more they saw people coming to faith in Christ.

Two forces in the lives of Art and Ruth that motivated them to stay faithful to their task were the Great Commission, "Go into all the world and preach the Gospel to every person," and a true adage, "Only one life; 'twill soon be past. Only what's done for Christ will last." And, to God be the glory!

Art and Ruth Robinson

Jack and Ruby Gentry
A Perfect Fit for Taiwan

The Beginning

What a blessing to be born to two dedicated Christian parents! Ruby Hickman would say after she was a retired missionary. Ruby's father was an ordained Baptist minister, as well as a school administrator. After one year of college her mother, when only nineteen, married Ruby's father-to-be. He was ten years older than her mother, but the age difference was no problem for them. Her mother was a loving homemaker as well as an effective pastor's wife and principal's wife. Her mother not only nurtured her own family, but several young teachers who lived with the Hickman family. This family was a perfect fit for Ruby.

Going to church was an important part of Ruby's life from the time she was born. Her church family was loving and kind. Her parents not only taught her how to live, they showed her how to live. Ruby was blessed by being introduced to God's love very early. Not only did she learn about God's love for herself, but she learned God's love included everyone, "red and yellow, black and white." She became a Christian and was baptized at age nine. Even before that time, Ruby knew that God wanted her to share His love with children. She dreamed of becoming a missionary in another country, where people had not had the opportunity to hear about Jesus and His love. Participation in the mission organizations at her church was an important part of her life.

At age 13, Ruby made a public decision to commit her life to God in His service. It was not a struggle for Ruby. It was the natural thing to do. From that time on, most of her education and decisions were consciously done in preparation for following God's call. As a high school senior, she wrote a term paper on Baptist work in Nigeria. She took college courses that would be helpful to her in mission service. She was very active in mission organizations during her college years. At the end of her sophomore year in college, she worked as a summer missionary in the bayous south of New Orleans, LA. She was involved in visiting families with a strong French background, leading Vacation Bible Schools, and playing the piano for worship. That summer deepened Ruby's commitment to missions as she worked in this subculture. A perfect fit — to prepare for missionary service.

Ruby's plans were to complete college and enter seminary in preparation for missionary service. She did this, but not the way she had planned. God had other plans.

Here's Jack

Jack Gentry was born September 14, 1931, the first child of Harvey and Loraine Gentry. He was dangerously premature, and his survival was a surprise to most of the extended family. Jack grew up in a lower middle-class North Carolina home. They lived near the intersecting crossroads of a small town in northwest North Carolina. Three years later, a baby sister joined the family. Jack and his sister's home life was similar to many children of that generation. They were a part of a three-generation household.

Jack's father supervised an electric power company crew who lived and worked out of a large, three-story house that Jack called home. Jack's mother was a homemaker who had a wonderful capacity to enjoy almost anything she did

– almost non-stop. A non-spoken family motto was "Make do with what you have." He learned that it was a perfect fit for missionary service.

Jack felt deeply loved and cared for by grandparents, parents and other family members. Friendship with his paternal grandparents as a preschooler through age nine seems to have been foundational to his early development. He learned much from them about family history and learned to appreciate the importance of family. For example, "Grandpa 'got religion' late. Granny got religion early in life." These stories and experiences helped to shape Jack's philosophy of life.

Jack was often sick in his early childhood. On the days that he could attend school, he was usually welcomed home by his granny's words, "You work hard and someday, you'll be at the head of your class." A blood transfusion from his father, following a tonsillectomy, was the turning point for better health for him.

Jack spent some of his summers working on his grand-parents' tobacco farm. He had the responsibility for planting, caring for, and harvesting the tobacco. Even then, Jack felt a dichotomy of 'it is okay to produce tobacco, but not use it.' With his mother's help, he was able to earn approximately $3,500U.S. He spent his summers working, as well as part-time work during the school year, until he left for his first semester of college.

Jack's parents were very active, dedicated church people. Church-related matters remained impersonal for Jack until a couple of months before his 12th birthday. By the third night of the annual revival that year, he recognized that Christ's death on the cross was for him. The next night when the invitation was given, Jack says, "I was drawn, as if by a magnet, to profess my need and my faith in Jesus Christ as Savior." Within a couple of weeks, personal relationships, especially with his mother, took a very different, harmonious character.

The daily life of one person above all others, a great-grandmother, demonstrated the potential joy and meaning of Jesus Christ as Lord. Jack struggled with a clear sense that Christ was not the Lord of his life, but should be. That matter was settled, the first time, soon after his 13th birthday. Some time within the next two months, Bun Olive, a missionary who had to leave China due to war-time conditions, was scheduled to speak at his mother's home church, and Jack asked his parents to take him. As Jack listened to the missionary, he was greatly surprised by a deep, quiet awareness that God was calling him. The call was to prepare himself to take the Gospel to Chinese people, specifically that the Gospel be shared with Chinese youth and children similar to himself. Jack did not tell anyone about his decision, fearing that they would laugh at him, so he kept the matter to himself.

He slowly began to see himself, school, church, and personal relationships differently, following his experiencing a sense of call. When he tried to share with classmates, they laughed because what he shared with them seemed so far-fetched. So, a call to missions came months and years before a call to any other sort of ministry.

As Granny had predicted, her grandson was valedictorian of his graduating class in 1950 and was also class president. Just days after Jack's high school graduation, the Korean conflict started, June 1950.

Jack entered college that fall and, as the end of the first semester in college neared, what he was doing there did not seem as important as doing his part for his country. He enlisted in the U.S. Navy for four years as a hospital corpsman. After almost a year-and-a-half of intensive training, Jack was stationed aboard a 555-foot-long, sea-going tanker that hauled up to 1 million gallons of oil, gasoline, or jet fuel. He was one of three corpsman responsible for the medical needs of a crew of 180 men. There was no doctor aboard the ship. There was also no chaplain. With the encouragement of a para-church group called The Navigators, he started a Bible study group. When they were in dangerous situations, the attendance would be good. For many of the crew, Jack became an informal chaplain. A perfect fit – preparing one for missionary service.

On two different occasions, for about one month, Jack's ship was docked in the Kaohsiung harbor. These experiences really stirred his sense of call to relate to, appreciate, and work with Chinese people. God would not allow His call on Jack's life to disappear. A perfect fit – reminding him of God's call on his life.

Jack was discharged from the U.S. Navy in 1955. He entered Wake Forest University, a North Carolina Baptist-supported institution. He participated in church and mission activities and related to persons who were preparing for various kinds of pastoral ministry. He also served as a summer missionary among Hispanic people in Barstow, CA. This was a challenging experience that provided learning in a sub-culture. A perfect fit for missionary training.

When Jack returned from his summer mission experience, a church in his home county extended a call to him to serve as their "quarter-time" pastor. This was a growing experience. One of the interesting facts of this experience was that the usual attendance at Sunday school and worship was about 180. This was the same number as the crew members aboard the Navy ship where he had served.

A Great Team

Jack's participation in mission activities at Wake Forest changed his life forever! Near the beginning of his senior year, as he prepared to attend a mission conference, he met a young woman who was also attending the mission confer-ence. Her name was Ruby Hickman. She was a junior at

Wake Forest University, majoring in English. She was beautiful, cultured, smart, gifted, dedicated to the Lord Jesus, and was focused on God's direction. This was the beginning of a relationship of equals. Jack and Ruby begin dating and were married after her graduation from college. The day was July 11, 1959. Jack was a year ahead of Ruby in college, so he had already completed one year of seminary when Ruby entered Southeastern Baptist Theological Seminary at Wake Forest, NC, in the fall of 1959. They were the first husband and wife to graduate together with a Bachelor of Divinity, in 1962, (now Master of Divinity) from Southeastern Baptist Seminary.

During his first two seminary years, Jack continued to serve the "quarter-time" church. Their first year of marriage, they traveled back and forth between the church and the seminary. This was a meaningful experience for the young couple. When they resigned in 1960, the church was, marginally, into the full-time category and was preparing to build a parsonage for a full-time pastor and family. During those years, often there was no money and even less time, but God was always faithful and took care of them.

Since both of them felt a strong sense of call to overseas mission service, they went to a second church, with the understanding that after three years of ministry, they would seek appointment as overseas missionaries. Rather than being located in the open countryside, their second church was in a small, very active manufacturing town. The issues centered primarily around restoring the church, made up of both labor and management-related families, into a united community of believers. Indeed, again by the Lord's grace, this was what happened.

The Ramseur Baptist Church was a good experience for the young couple, but another "joy" was given to them at this place. Their first child and only daughter, Jan, was born

January 27, 1963. She was a petite little angel that blessed them then, and continues to do so!

On Their Way to Taiwan

The time had come for them to seek appointment for missionary service. Their lifetime dream. Jack felt a call to China from his childhood, and Taiwan was the closest they could get. They completed application forms, received physicals, had interviews and were appointed to Taiwan, the Republic of China, December 10, 1964.

The shopping was done. The packing was done. The good-byes were said. Jan had just turned two years old when Jack and Ruby took her to Taiwan. It was very difficult for their parents to let them go, and especially to take their granddaughter. However, the four grandparents believed in the Great Commission and were thankful God had called their children to be missionaries. They were very supportive of them during their years in Taiwan.

Home In a Foreign Land

Jack and Ruby found following God's plan for their lives involved taking steps into the unknown and taking risks. They were willing to do this but it wasn't always easy. They arrived at the Taipei airport on April 2, 1965. They could see people gathered who had come to meet family and friends. They only knew two missionaries in Taiwan, and they did not see them among the gathered people. As they went through Customs, the officials wanted to know where they were going to live. The only information they had was the postal address for the Taiwan Baptist Mission. The officials said over and over to the young couple with the beautiful little girl, "But you cannot live in a post office box." Finally, they saw an older American lady in the crowd and asked her for assistance. Fortunately, she was one of the Southern Baptist missionaries and had indeed come to meet them. Jack and Ruby were finding cross-cultural missions had its challenges, and this was only the first day. But they were a "fit" for this new land.

Like all cross-cultural missionaries who are appointed as career missionaries, they faced the tremendous and nerve-wrecking task of learning the language. Jack felt strongly that he and Ruby should learn Mandarin. However, the Taiwan Baptist Mission had other opinions and the official response was, "Who are you, in your total ignorance of the realities of the setting, to make such a decision?" They expressed their sense of call, but the final decision was the Mission leadership. So, they started where the established mission organization instructed. A mission organization is not always correct, and many difficult experiences can happen for both the missionary and the organization. The Gentrys studied Taiwanese. A perfect fit but a difficult decision!

Jack and Ruby lived in Taipei. Both of them were involved in language learning, attending five hours of class each day, Monday through Friday. At that time, it took them an hour of travel each way, so they were away from home and their daughter Jan seven hours each day. The lady who took care of Jan had six little girls of her own, and spoke Mandarin with a Shandong accent. It was humiliating when their three-year-old daughter became their translator. Becoming a preschooler again after having received advanced degrees was not an easy thing, and especially having their daughter say to her parents, "Chinese is so easy, what's wrong with you?" A perfect time to be taught more humility and flexibility. Two qualities required for missionary service.

During their two-year language experience in Taipei, their second child, Jay, was born in 1966. What another "joy" in their lives. He blessed their lives then and continues to do so. This meant that Ruby needed to spend more time at home, so a private tutor was found. The tutor came to the home, and Ruby continued her studies.

After Jack completed two years of Taiwanese language learning, the Mission asked the couple to move to Chiayi. Ruby and Jack made plans to move south, and then it was decided that the Gentrys should move to Kaohsiung, of all the places in Taiwan, where Jack had been ashore many times as a U.S. sailor. God was even then "fitting" the sailor for the years ahead, when he and his wife would serve as missionaries in Kaohsiung. The years in Kaohsiung were good ones. Jack worked in church planting with a young pastor.

Hwang Syun Liang and his wife had recently returned home to Kaohsiung, following their seminary graduation. They conducted Bible studies, showed movies in the Taiwanese communities, visited the sick, preached on Sunday, and built relationships. The Ai Chuan Baptist Church was started during the three years they lived in Kaohsiung.

Ruby, as a mother of two small children, considered her main responsibility to be caring for the children and taking care of the home. However, she found time to minister to pastors' wives and their families. Jan attended kindergarten at the Kaohsiung Mandarin Church, and Ruby had fellowship with the families who had children in kindergarten. She used their home for fellowship and Bible study for women, as well as entertaining missionaries and other foreigners.

A new missionary visited Kaohsiung on her orientation trip around the island. Jack took her around the city to introduce pastors, co-workers, visit the churches and the temples. As they walked into a temple, she was keenly aware of the people everywhere, the darkness, and the sense of lostness. She turned and said to Jack, "How do you deal with the lostness every day?" His response was, "When there is no longer a burden for the lostness of this land, I will go home."

Jack and Ruby kept their burden for the lostness of Taiwan until retirement, and beyond retirement.

One of the most difficult experiences of their first term of service was the sudden death of Ruby's father a year before they were scheduled to go on furlough. Travel, financial resources and communication at that time made it difficult for missionaries to return home for such occasions. This was a time of suffering, because she was not able to be with her family. But even in this situation, she felt the loving presence of her heavenly Father, and was comforted by friends, both missionaries and Chinese.

Their first furlough came after five years, two months and fifteen days – June 1970. It was a time to visit family and friends. It was very beneficial to Jan and Jay to spend one year in America. This gave them time to learn about life in the U.S., and also have one year in the western education system. Ruby and Jack spent much time speaking in churches, conferences, meetings, classes, etc., about their lives in Taiwan. Jack was pursuing another seminary degree and Ruby was a grader for one of the professors and was Jack's typist.

Their furlough was over too quickly, and they soon found themselves shopping, packing, and saying good-byes again. Back to Taiwan and to Taichung, where they would study Mandarin. The year was 1971.

They worked with both Mandarin and Taiwanese churches. The two languages made it possible to have many meaningful relationships. Jan attended Chinese kindergarten. She went to the American Military School in Kaohsiung for the first grade, then second grade in North Carolina. She attended Morrison Academy from third grade through high school graduation, with the exception of furloughs. Jay had kindergarten in North Carolina and entered Morrison Academy after they returned to Taichung. They were involved in various activities – basketball, soccer, swimming, tennis, piano, drama, hiking, mountain-climbing and cheerleading. They attended Chinese services with their parents and also worshiped at the International Christian Church services held on the Morrison Academy campus.

Jack's call as a little boy was to help Chinese children know about Jesus. The burden of his heart to reach children, young people, and especially their leaders, was still in his heart when he arrived in Taichung. In God's timing, he found a pastor, Hwang Wen Siung, who shared a similar burden – to train lay-leaders to be effective Bible teachers for children and youth and assist churches with discipleship training.

Jack and Ruby, along with Pastor and Mrs. Hwang, slowly found their way in training lay-leaders to become all God wanted them to become. A short while later, a seminary graduate, then another one, and then another one, and another one came asking to join the team. They, too, wanted to be a part of training lay-leaders to be effective in Bible teaching and discipleship training. The ministry needed an identity – so the Church Education Center was established. It was not always easy. There were times of disagreement about the work of the center among the Chinese church leaders and the missionaries, and this made the ministry difficult at times.

Jack was qualified for this ministry as he started preparing for God's timing to work in church training and development in 1970-71, when he selected his Th.M. thesis title, "Teaching the Christian Faith in the Chinese Educational Context." In 1975, "The Development of a Communication Model for a Cross Cultural Setting," was the theme for his D.Min. thesis, and he wrote "Pre-requisites for Faith Development in Church Related Chinese Children in Taiwan," for the MA thesis.

Ruby served as English secretary and English teacher for the Education Center. She hosted in their lovely home many special gatherings and parties for the staff, taught English in local churches, formed a fellowship for Chinese pastors' wives, served as chairperson for the Taichung International Christian Women's Club, and as an officer in the Taiwan Missionary Fellowship.

Jan and Jay had a happy childhood and teenage years in Taichung. Twelve years before Jack and Ruby were to retire, Jan returned to the U.S. for college. This was a painful experience, yet they knew the God who called them to Taiwan would provide for their daughter. She had her grandmothers nearby, so this was a comfort to daughter and parents. The summer after her sophomore year, both grandmothers came to Taiwan with her for three weeks. Three years later, Jay returned to the U.S. for college. After his sophomore year, he returned to Taichung and studied Mandarin at Tung Hai University. He spent a semester in China, where he studied Mandarin and taught English drama and literature. Jan and Jay were blessed to have grown up in Taiwan. They learned to love and understand another culture, which has been very beneficial in preparing them to live in a global world. They received a quality education at Morrison Academy and made life-long friends with other missionary children and classmates.

Ruby and Jack were actively involved in the activities of the Taiwan Baptist Mission. Ruby was the treasurer for the Taichung station. Jack served as the Research and Design Consultant for the Program Base Design for the Mission, and Ruby wrote the historical section for the Home Program and served as the Home Program leader for a period of time. Jack was a long-time trustee of Baptist Press, located in Hong Kong (now Chinese Baptist Press International, Inc.).

Jack had chronic back problems throughout his missionary service, and in 1992, Ruby had cancer. They took a slightly early retirement because of health concerns. They left Taiwan on November 10, 1993. They officially retired on January 1, 1995.

Retirement was bittersweet. They loved the Chinese people. Taiwan was home to them and their children. They appreciated and enjoyed the Mission family. They had strong, workable relationships with co-workers in church education and pastors in the churches. They had planted their lives in the soil of church training and development.

After 1995

They returned to the hills of North Carolina, and pur- chased a home near their children and grandchildren. It is a joy to be with their grandchildren, and attend their sport activities and church events. They are privileged to have their mothers nearby. God has blessed them with good health. They have been involved in the Cooperative Baptist Fellowship. Jack has opportunities to preach, and they continue to tell the mission story.

A few months after the Gentrys arrived in Taiwan, a respected, senior missionary came to their home for an unexpected visit. He was soon weeping bitterly. He recited the story of the Taiwan Baptist Mission and the Chinese Baptist Convention agreement to call a qualified missionary church education specialist. Such a person came, learned the language well, and as he waited for an opportunity to serve, no doors of opportunity opened for him. A few months later, the young, frustrated, disappointed missionary had a nervous breakdown. Why should there be a wall of resistance to church education?

Jack and Ruby, under the leadership of the Holy Spirit, helped to break down the wall of resistance toward church training and development. They were there to listen, encourage and love. These are the qualities that will break down any wall. There are few times when church educators meet in Taiwan that Jack and Ruby Gentry's names are not mentioned. They made a difference in church education. Jack and Ruby continue to pray that Chinese people will find the Lord Jesus as Lord and Savior early in life – childhood and youth.

They treasure countless memories: trips to O Lan Bi with their children, Christmas parties with the Church Education

Center staff, developing Sunday school curriculum, promoting **Master Life,** hosting a group of missionaries in their home, praying with a co-worker, preaching in a small church, baptizing a new convert, and sharing the Gospel with the man who delivered their groceries – and memories of the faithfulness of the ONE who called them.

He called and equipped Jack and Ruby Gentry for 30 years of ministry in Taiwan – their call was a fit for Church Education in Taiwan – yes, a perfect fit. All praise to the God who kept all His promises to them.

Ruby, Jack and Jan Gentry

Ben and Bettie Tomlinson
Steps of Faith

Growing Up Days

Ben was born in south Georgia and Bettie was born in East Texas. Both of them were the children of farmers, and later both of their parents changed careers. Ben's dad became a self-employed cross tie and pulpwood broker for southeastern railroads and paper mills. Bettie's father became an employee of Humble Oil Company.

Ben and Bettie attended small country schools and transferred to middle schools and high schools in nearby towns. Naturally, the city schools had larger enrollments and more extracurricular activities, which provided a strong educational background for them.

Coming to Jesus

At the age of 11, in a rural church, Ben heard a bi-vocational pastor say, "You are a sinner!" The pastor then said, "You need Jesus Christ!" Those two statements are not the whole Gospel, but they were all Ben knew about God's Word at the time. The Holy Spirit opened his mind and he understood that he desperately wanted Jesus Christ in his heart and his life as Savior and Lord. That was 66 years ago, and the Jesus who entered his heart then is still in his heart now. As a 13-year-old, Bettie asked Jesus to come into her heart and

227

save her from her sins. She was baptized the same day as her father and brother. She began attending a mission organization in her church and heard the story of a missionary, which inspired her to begin thinking about missions and praying for missionaries.

High School Years

Ben and Bettie were good students and very successful in academics and extra-curricular events. Ben received five awards during his senior year at Lanier County High School: Mr. L. C. H. S., Most Dependable, Best All-Round, Most Studious, Most Likely to Succeed. He was very involved in sports: football, basketball, tennis, etc. During Bettie's senior year in high school, she started playing the French horn and was a majorette in the marching band. She was elected as the "Friendliest Girl" at Tyler High School. She was also chosen as one of the most ideal girls (21 were chosen) in her senior class, out of a class of 350 students.

College Ahead

Ben had finished two years of college when his father died. His older brother, Cecil, invited him to move to Texas, live with his brother's family, and attend the small community college, East Texas Baptist College, in Marshall, TX. Ben was enticed to move to Texas when his brother said, "I think you can play football." Thus began Ben's journey of going west: from Georgia to Texas, from Texas to California, and from California to Taiwan.

Bettie's Call

Bettie was called to be a missionary at the age of 16. She was willing to commit her life for His service. It was a year later when Bettie committed her life to be a foreign missionary. She knew she needed a college education to apply for missionary service. She felt East Texas Baptist College in Marshall was the right school for her, so she found herself on the same campus as Ben.

Bettie's father was supporting 12 children. He felt Bettie needed to go to a business college in nearby Tyler, so she could pay her tuition. She said, "Daddy, God didn't call me to be a secretary. He called me to be a missionary." Her father did what he could. He gave her $50.00 and his blessings. So began her journey of faith. She worked, prayed, and with the support from her home church, First Baptist Church, Tyler, TX, and her friends, she always had the money to pay her tuition, books and lodging.

Life Partners

The first Sunday Ben was in Marshall, TX, he went to Central Baptist Church for worship. As he entered the auditorium, two college students were sitting in the choir. One of the young ladies said to the other one, "One day I'm going to marry him." The young lady's name was Bettie Ruth Adair. According to her prediction, three years later, she became Mrs. Ben Tomlinson.

Ben's Call

Ben's call to missions came in two steps: First, he was called to preach and secondly, he was called to be a missionary. He struggled to discover whether God had called him to be a minister, teacher or a missionary. God used Matthew 6:33 to help him understand that God was the "boss" in his life, and if Ben put Him first in all things, God would also take care of the details and that included finances, his home, his children, his marriage and his ministry. God used this simple idea to break his stubborn will. Ben decided to tell his pastor that he was dedicating his life to be a committed layman, but out of his mouth came the words, "I give my life to preach the Gospel." At that moment, great joy filled Ben's soul. That happened in 1951, and one month later, the second step was taken.

While Ben was walking on campus one day, God further enlightened him through His Word – II Timothy 1:11, "To which I was appointed as a preacher, an apostle, and a call to ministry." God used this verse to help Ben understand that Paul was a gifted and intelligent man who did not limit his types of ministries. Paul was involved in both the Jewish and Gentile ministries of the early church. He did church planting in some places, and other times he was involved in discipleship. Paul's experience stretched Ben's faith and challenged him to realize that in God's power, anything was possible. Ben surrendered to whatever God had ahead for him – a pastor, a teacher, a church planter, a missionary, an administrator – and God prepared and equipped him for the tasks ahead.

Wedding Bells

After Ben and Bettie graduated from East Texas Baptist College, Bettie spent the summer in Alaska serving as a summer missionary, and Ben stayed in Texas and led youth revivals in Baptist churches. Both of them had productive and meaningful summers, returned to Tyler, and were married at First Baptist Church. It was August 27, 1953.

Seminary Life

Like Abraham, they had great faith, but unlike Abraham, they had no money. Ben borrowed $300 on their wedding day. Their honeymoon was driving across the country to Berkeley, CA, where they were enrolled at Golden Gate Theological Seminary. Ben worked in a factory and pastored a small church while studying at Golden Gate Seminary. Bettie only studied one year because she was pregnant with their first child.

Ben and Bettie found God to be faithful and kept His promise that if they would put Him first, He then would take care of their needs. They discovered that through testing, the Lord creates growth and obedience. There were hard times, but God was preparing them for missionary service.

Early Days in Taiwan

One health problem threatened to prevent Ben and Bettie from missionary appointment. At that time, the Foreign Mission Board would not appoint anyone who suffered from asthma. Ben insisted, and finally he was given medical clearance. All other requirements were met and Ben and Bettie were appointed to Taiwan. The year was 1965.

Ben was/is allergic to grass. God used grass to test Ben's faith and his persistence. Taiwan has grass year round, and is called, "The Emerald Isle." The Tomlinson's first home was located on Yang Ming Shan which is translated "Grass Mountain." Ben had less allergy problems in Taiwan than he did in California. Yet, they were serious and remain serious to this day.

Ben and Bettie both struggled with learning Taiwanese. Ben is a visual learner. As is well known, language learning is auditory. It is important that one learn with one's ears, not one's eyes. Ben thought that Taiwanese tones were absolute and not relative. He tried to imitate the sounds of a high soprano or low bass, and this strained his vocal chords. Ben's teachers thought he was tone deaf and Ben thought the teachers couldn't find the tones either. A book written by a teacher at one of the Catholic Language Centers saved Ben's mind, his throat, his sanity and his missionary career, and he learned to simply put the proper tones in his own range. He learned to enjoy Taiwanese and preaching in Taiwanese. He later studied Mandarin and was able to use it in conversation.

Bettie's problem with language learning involved the stress of trying to balance lessons with her duties as a mother of five children and a wife. She tried to be perfect in pronouncing every tone. She worked with limited language skills, and for her to find satisfaction in ministry, the Tomlinsons formed a team. Bettie is an excellent communicator, both verbal and non-verbal, in her mother tongue. God used her million-dollar smile and her body language to communicate "I love you," and Ben interpreted the spoken words. God blessed and used the team.

Ministry

Bettie was appointed as a "home and church missionary." She was an excellent cook, a talented artist, and a gifted floral arranger. She used the gifts and talents to entertain scores of friends around her lovely table, to decorate both Chinese and missionary homes, and add beauty to many conference rooms, churches, chapels, and meeting places. These gifts were used as an avenue of sharing her faith in the Chinese and international communities. Bettie also served as 'dining hall hostess' for the Morrison Christian Academy while Ben was on the faculty of the institution.

Ben's original job description was "field evangelist." It was later changed to "church planter." He also worked in church development. He spent many hours in administrative tasks for the Taiwan Baptist Mission. He served at Morrison Academy on a part-time basis – a teacher, a coach and one year as Superintendent of the Morrison Academy system.

His original goal was to plant a church each year he served in Taiwan. Perhaps the goal was too high. Perhaps other reasons were: rural Taiwanese people were resistant to the Gospel. Lack of unity between the missionaries of the Mission and pastors and co-workers of the Chinese Baptist Convention. Reviewing what he did, Ben feels today that much of the blame for poor relationships should be assumed by the missionaries. Unilateral actions without consultations caused dissatisfaction among the pastors and co-workers.

It took a long time for Ben to realize the extreme need for unity and cooperation among the local pastors and missionaries who were working in church planting. His most successful and satisfying church planting was with and under his Chinese brothers. One example: The Taiwanese speaking missionaries attempted to compile and print a Taiwanese Baptist Hymnal. They were unsuccessful. Ben and a Chinese pastor were elected to lead this committee. Not long after they were elected as co-chairmen, Ben went to the pastor and said, "You need to be the chairperson and I will support you." He agreed. Within one year, the pastor had organized the committee. The hymnal became "their" project and not the missionary's. They completed the compilation, transla-tion, and published the hymnal. "Love, unity, cooperation are not just desirable qualities, but they are absolutely essen-tial for being effective missionaries and pastors." This is the philosophy of the now-retired missionary.

Another example of Ben and Bettie's cooperation is found in working with a local church in starting an ESL program for a village populated by a resistant ethnic group. The church wanted Ben and Bettie to develop a program for all levels of English speakers. Bettie taught the intermediate and advanced classes. Ben taught the beginners. He also directed an English choir for local pastors. The classes were held once a week, and follow-up with those who showed an interest in Christianity was done during the week. Over a two-year period, more than a thousand people visited and/or enrolled in the program.

When Bettie and Ben announced their retirement, class members sought to persuade them to move to the village to teach English, and the community would purchase them a retirement home. They worked cooperatively with the pastor and the church. They had planted the seeds of the Gospel.

They spent time watering the seeds dropped in good soil, and they saw good results. They know the Holy Spirit will continue to open doors for the pastors and the believers to share their faith, and gather new converts into the church through the seeds they planted.

Ben and Bettie served their last term with a young pastor who was a recent seminary graduate. Most of the deacons had Ph.D.s, and were teaching at a nearby university. The young pastor felt inadequate, but he was wise beyond his years. He said to the deacons, "I am not qualified to be your pastor. Let me serve as a deacon among deacons. Teach me how to be a good deacon and then I can become a good pastor." At present, he has served more than ten years as their pastor, and he is loved and respected by the academic community, society, and the church.

Yet, the young pastor had to cross another obstacle. What about the older missionary who had come to work with him? One day, the young pastor came to Ben and Bettie's door and called, "Grandfather, grandfather." Ben knew in his heart the young pastor was saying, "I will give you respect. I give you the right to make suggestions. I will ask for your opinions. However, the day-to-day operation of the church is my responsibility." Ben gladly and humbly accepted the new position and the new title. One of the suggestions that Ben made to the young pastor and to the deacons was that they accept the revolutionary role of being deacons like Philip and Stephen, who were full of faith and the Holy Spirit, witnessing, preaching, baptizing and starting new chapels and churches. They humbly accepted the challenged. They divided the church into districts. The deacons became responsible for the well being of the church members who lived in the districts for which they were responsible. They led in evangelistic meetings. They worked with the pastor and the missionary in starting new chapels.

Retirement

Ben and Bettie retired, but the pastor and deacons continue to strengthen the mother church, which is located near a university campus. The church has a strong college ministry and a community ministry. They are actively involved in overseas ministries. Ben and Bettie returned to Taiwan a few years ago to attend the anniversary celebration of this university campus church. They were met at the airport by the pastor and the chairman of deacons. The first words they heard were, "Welcome home, grandfather and grandmother." Ben would say to new missionaries, "The missionary has many names throughout one's years of service. The missionary must earn the right to be heard and must earn the names of respect given. Perhaps, the sweetest one is 'grandfather and grandmother.'"

In retirement, they serve as ministers to senior adults of First Baptist Church, Dallas, TX, visiting the sick in many retirement homes, performing a few weddings and more than a few funerals. As they recall their Taiwan years, they are truly thankful for the "grandchildren and great grandchildren" who caught the vision to share the Good News with the villages across Taiwan. To God be the glory!

Ben and Bettie Tomlinson

Leroy and Janell Hogue
A Rich Pilgrimage

The Guy

He was born in Oklahoma City, in the very southeastern corner of the city, in a neighborhood that might be described as "lower middle-class." The neighborhood, then and now, could be classed as "poor." And it was true enough, because Leroy Hogue was born in 1930, the year after the big stock market crash and the beginning of the Great Depression. He was the youngest of four children. And if he ever thought about it, about being poor did not disturb him.

Leroy's elementary school was five blocks north of his home, and their church was about two blocks to the south. Those two institutions defined his world. In school, Leroy followed in the footsteps of his older brother and two sisters, so he was known to the teachers at the school before he even came into their classrooms. Their church was very important to his family. This was the Wilmont Place Baptist Church, and the Hogue family was there just about every time the doors were open. It made a great impact on the little fellow's life. The pastor set an example of what a pastor ought to be. His ministry was that of a shepherd, and years later, Leroy tried to model his ministry after the older man.

Leroy's daddy was a deacon in the church, and his mother was a teacher in the children's department of the

237

Sunday school. Not much took place in the church that they didn't know about, including the internal squabbles among the members. This is just to say that the church was a major factor in their lives, and it was a formative influence in the life of each of the children.

At the age of seven, Leroy made a profession of faith and was received into the membership of the church. To tell the truth, Leroy didn't know if he was saved. At the age of 15, he had a far more significant experience with Christ. He knew without a doubt that he was saved, and his life underwent a great change. He began to read the Bible very earnestly. He had such a thirst for the Word. And the next year, when he was 16, Leroy received a very vivid call to the ministry, a "call to preach" that was so very clear and certain. He later said that he might possibly have doubted the existence of God, but he could never doubt his call to preach. Whatever his ministry, wherever the place, the call was always to preach!

One other major influence on Leroy's life at this time was his work in a nearby grocery store, a supermarket called "Jones Boys #6." He started working there when he was 13 years old. Leroy worked there for more than five years, until he went away to college. The importance of it for him was that it helped him to be able to meet people, because he was painfully shy. He was a good student at school, and he knew it, but he was scared to death of being in front of a crowd, or of being singled out in any way. The work also helped him to develop his work values and save the money he needed for college.

OBU and Janell

Leroy began his college education at Oklahoma Baptist University, Shawnee, OK, in 1949. It was close at hand, just 40 miles away from his home. That first year in college, he hitchhiked home every weekend to teach a Sunday school class at his home church, and also to get his laundry done.

College was an eye-opener for Leroy. He had led a rather sheltered life, and suddenly, at OBU, he was introduced to young people who were much more worldly-wise than he was. However, it was still OBU, a rather conservative Baptist school, in rural Oklahoma. The most significant thing that happened to Leroy in those four years at OBU took place on the first day of his third year. He saw Janell Ohagan sitting at a table in the registration area. It was her first day at OBU, and she was working for the Dean's office, helping in registration of students. Leroy was no longer shy, for he immediately went up to her and introduced himself. He wanted to make a positive impression on the new student. They became friends that first year, but did not begin dating until his senior year in college and Janell's sophomore year.

Janell Ohagan was born in Kiowa County in southwestern Oklahoma. Her family was probably even poorer than the Hogue family. Her father was a carpenter and worked incredibly hard to make a living for his family. He was also a devout Christian, who loved the Lord and His church and was very active in his church. He was a deacon and a Sunday school teacher. Leroy had a deep respect for Mr. Ohagan back then, and he still looks back with great appreciation on David Ohagan as an example of basic, genuine Christian character. Janell's mother was a "country lady" all of her life. She, too, was a sincere, deeply committed Christian and tried to protect her three children from the world and its temptations. Janell came to OBU from such a home and family, protected and sheltered in many ways from the evils of the world.

Leroy did not know it at the time, but Janell had come to OBU with the belief that God had called her to be a preacher's wife. As she has said so many times, "That was where the preachers were." And so it seemed to be some kind of omen that on that first day, Leroy introduced himself to her. How God arranged the events in their lives! It seems that about the same time that God was calling Leroy to be a preacher, He was also calling Janell to be a preacher's wife. However, they were not aware at that time of God's plan.

On June 28, 1953, just after Leroy graduated from OBU, Leroy and Janell were married in her home church, South Memorial Baptist Church in the southwestern part of Oklahoma City. She knew that she was marrying a pastor because Leroy had become pastor of the Paruna Baptist Church in far northwestern Oklahoma. Talk about a small church! Paruna was 14 miles out in the country from the nearest town. Their salary at the church was $30 a week, and it was necessary for both of them to work as well as pastor the church. They learned a biblical phrase by heart, and they have repeated it often over the years, both in Oklahoma and in Asia: "Jehovah-jireh," the Lord will provide. And He always has.

They continued their pastoral work in various parts of Oklahoma, moving to eastern Oklahoma, then to southeastern Oklahoma, and back to southwestern Oklahoma, where Leroy was the pastor of Lone Wolf First Baptist Church. God was blessing their ministry in these churches, and He was also blessing their family with children. First, Sue Ann was born in 1954, when they were at Paruna. Then, Charles David was born four years later in Hugo, where Leroy was pastor at Grant Baptist Church. Tom was born in 1961, when they were living at Lone Wolf. Andrew, their youngest, was born in 1964, when Leroy was pastor of the Second Baptist Church, in Vernon, TX. Four children in ten years! And that kept Janell busy at home and also in their churches.

In the meantime, Leroy had begun his studies at Southwestern Seminary in Fort Worth, TX. The year was 1955, when he was pastor at Onapa Baptist Church. It was not easy, because their salary was still only $30 a week, but again, "Jehovah-jireh." Wherever they moved, Leroy was able to continue his seminary education, commuting long distances to do so. Janell also traveled with him from the church field to Fort Worth, keeping residences in both places. Sue Ann loved this experience and felt the family had lost something when they only had one house in one state. These were good years for the family.

That first year at Fort Worth, Leroy first became aware that God had some plan for them, other than pastoral ministry in Oklahoma and Texas. He attended a Missions Day chapel at the seminary, where Keith Parks and his wife were the main speakers. He felt deeply impressed that God was speaking to him that day about missionary service, but he said, as he sat in that chapel service, "Lord, you know that I can't go because of my physical condition." He has a rather severe case of scoliosis, spinal curvature, that had prevented him from serving in the military. Leroy says he heard what seemed to him almost an audible voice, saying, "Who says that you cannot go?"

He went back to Fort Worth Hall, the men's dorm, and in earnest prayer, he promised God that he would go anywhere He wanted him to go. Leroy was so thrilled to be called to missions, not knowing as yet where God would want them to go. He had made a genuine commitment to missions. Now he needed to tell Janell the good news.

When he went home that Friday, he said to Janell, "Guess what, Janell? God has called us to be missionaries!" Leroy still remembers Janell's stunned look and her instant response, "Well, He may have called you, but He hasn't called me!" And that was that for the time being. Wisely, Leroy did not pursue the matter any further at the time. But God did.

Leroy continued his studies at the Seminary. When he received his B.D. degree (now Masters of Divinity), he was presented with the possibility of working toward a graduate degree, which would equip him to teach at a seminary level.

In 1959, he began working on his Th.D. with a major in Church History. It meant seven more years of studies at the seminary, but it became much clearer with each passing year that this was what God wanted. Sometimes, people have asked Leroy why he spent 11 years at the seminary. His response has been, "I went on the 20-year plan and finished early." Leroy knew God was preparing them for missions service.

What about Janell's call to missions? Well, God took care of that, too. It turned out, as Janell remembers, God had already called her as a 13-year old girl to be a missionary to China. How could she have forgotten that? The pastor, in his kind way, had suggested to Janell that she should not say that God called her to missionary service but she should say, "Wherever He would lead." He meant this to be a kindness to her, so she would not be embarrassed when people asked her about missionary service. He knew that young people often make life commitments that change shape and direction over the years, and he wanted to spare her any disappointment or embarrassment. Gradually, Janell felt that God really was leading the two of them to overseas service. She came forward one Sunday evening at the close of a service in their church in Vernon, TX, to state her surrender to God's call to missions.

They had been in touch with the Foreign Mission Board for about eight years. At one time, they were told that they would not be able to go because of Leroy's scoliosis. He had responded to that disappointing news by saying that surely his years in pastoral service in the hinterlands of Oklahoma would equip him for just about anything that he might face on the field. The next letter from the Board was permission to proceed towards appointment. God had not wasted any of their work and ministry experiences. He was leading and directing their lives, and on March 10, 1966, they were appointed as missionaries of the Foreign Mission Board, to

Taiwan, with the expectation that they would join the faculty at the Taiwan Baptist Theological Seminary.

Sometimes people ask the Hogues why they decided to go to Taiwan. Leroy usually replies with the words, "It was not us but the Lord who decided." They had always known, somehow, that it would be in Asia, and at first, they were looking at southeast Asia, either Indonesia or Malaysia. This may have been the influence of Keith and Helen Jean Parks who served in southeast Asia. In 1965, the situation in southeast Asia was very unsettled. There had been an attempted Communist coup in Indonesia, and also some unrest in Malaysia, along the Thailand-Malaysian border. The FMB suggested that they consider three other fields in Asia: the Philippines, South Korea, and Taiwan. As they prayed about it, they looked beyond Taiwan to Mainland China. China was completely closed at that time, but they felt that it would not always be closed. Taiwan was the place God had arranged for them. When they are with Chinese people, they feel a deep sense of "belonging," of being where they ought to be.

Language Learning Is Painful

In August 1966, Leroy, Janell and their four children boarded the *President Cleveland* to sail to Taiwan. It was such a wise thing that their Board did at that time, permitting the newly appointed missionaries to sail to their intended fields of service. Each day spent on board the ship gave the missionaries an awareness that they were really leaving their homeland and going far away to a new country and a new culture. New missionaries really needed that. It was also a fun time for the children – watching movies, swimming, table games, and eating all kinds of food. The last portion of the long trip was by air, from Japan to Taiwan. When they finally landed at the Sung Shan Airport, in the east part of Taipei, they were met by a large body of Southern Baptist missionaries, who had come to welcome these new missionaries to Taiwan.

The Hogues felt so honored by the reception they received. Some of the missionaries at the airport that day were veteran missionaries who had served in China and had fled to Taiwan at the time of the Communist takeover. Leroy stood in awe of these colleagues.

The next few weeks were spent in getting settled into their new home. A house had been found for them, in what is now an upscale part of Taipei. It was a nice house, sufficiently large for their family. Living behind a wall, with barbed wire and broken glass on top of the wall, took some getting used to, but they finally accepted it as a necessary part of life in Taiwan. Their children were enrolled in school. They were remarkably good in their acceptance of a totally new environment and in their adjustment to it. They might have done better in some ways than their parents.

One thing that Janell struggled with was the necessity of having live-in household help. Leroy and Janell had never had this experience before, and they didn't know how to relate to the two very nice Chinese ladies who moved into their home and began cleaning their house, doing their laundry, and doing their cooking. They didn't speak any English, and obviously, Leroy and Janell didn't speak any Chinese. So it was a trial for the ladies and for the Hogue family. Janell and Leroy feel they must have made a lot of mistakes in those early days, due to their ignorance of the language and the Chinese culture, but that was a part of the learning process, too. They are so thankful Chinese people are very forgiving.

Their primary task those first two years in Taiwan was to learn the language. Both of them spent a certain number of hours each day in class at the Taipei Language Institute (TLI). Language study was their full-time job. Leroy began attending class from 7:30 to 12:30 every day, Monday through Friday. Janell had a less rigorous class schedule, because she had to manage the home and get the children off to school every day.

Leroy found language learning to be difficult. He says, "I was already 35 years old, and I had been serving as a pastor for the previous 15 years. Suddenly, I was thrust into the situation where I was a student again, and many of the simplest things that needed to be done in regard to our family business, I was unable to do because of my language limitations. Also, I was under the pressure of knowing that I had to acquire a sufficient fluency in Mandarin to teach at the seminary and also to preach in the churches. I was often discouraged, and I wondered if I would ever acquire the ability to preach the Gospel in Chinese. But God is faithful, and He helped me during those first two years to continue at the task. Also, I should say that Janell believed in me, and she often encouraged me to believe that the same God who had called us to the mission field, would also enable us to speak the language." Today, both Leroy and Janell feel comfortable in the language and in the culture.

Sunny Kaohsiung

When Leroy finished his two years of language requirements, the seminary administration felt that it would be helpful if they would move to the south for the rest of their first term, to get a bit of "seasoning," both in the language and in acquaintance with the Taiwan churches. They were very open to that suggestion, and they came to see the wisdom of this approach when they moved to Kaohsiung. It was a wonderful time to meet the pastors and believers in the churches, and they had many opportunities to use Chinese. They continue to be grateful for the wise counsel of senior missionaries who were thoughtful of the Hogues' needs. Those next three years, from 1968-1971, were very enjoyable years for the whole family.

Once again, Sue, Charles, Tom, and Andrew showed their adaptability to a new living situation and a new environment. The three boys attended school in Tsoying, at a Department of Defense elementary school, and Sue went daily to a high school in Tainan, also a military-related school. These schools were basically intended, of course, for the children of military personnel, but missionary families were kindly given the opportunity to send their children there. This was a tremendous help to Janell and Leroy, who would otherwise have been forced to make other arrangements for their children's education.

Leroy's responsibility in the Kaohsiung-Pingdong area for the next three years was to work rather closely with the churches scattered throughout the cities and towns, and to help them build their congregations. For the most part, the churches were small and struggling, and so the work was to some degree a "caregiver" kind of work. This was not an ideal situation, of course, but it was what was needed at the time. The co-workers, the pastors and preachers in these churches, were good men, dedicated men, but the rural areas of Taiwan were very traditional in regard to religion. For the most part, the people in these places were not very responsive to the Gospel. Buddhist and Taoist temples were abundant and prominent in every village. Out in the open country, there were many shrines, especially those of the "god of the soil," the Tu Ti Kung. Evidences of animistic worship were everywhere. Many of the large banyan trees in the countryside would have some kind of shrine under them, dedicated to the spirit that lived in the tree.

Leroy and Janell owe much of their successful ministry to their years in Kaohsiung and to the people – co-workers, pastors, and believers – who loved them, taught them, believed in them, and gave them opportunities to serve. Three examples are given to point out relationships with co-workers.

The church in Meinung, which was a Hakka community, was very small, and was largely supported through the income from a kindergarten operated by Pastor and Mrs. Su Yin Chuan Leroy later said, "The struggles and sacrifices of that pastor and wife should be recorded for the benefit and inspiration of the present generation of Christians in Taiwan. They were such a blessing to us then, and we still consider them as among our dearest friends in Taiwan. What a privilege it was to teach Pastor Su's oldest son at the Taiwan Seminary and later work with him in the Hsiao Kang Baptist Church in south Taiwan."

Another person who influenced the Hogue family was Mrs. Wang Shou Syin a Bible woman, and the founder of the Faith, Hope, and Love Children's Home at Hsin Guo Hsin Tswun, "Rock Village." This was a terribly poor area at the time. Many of the people were refugees from the Chinese-Burma border area, who had fled to Taiwan and been given land in this rocky riverbed by the government. In that very unpromising area, Mrs. Wang had established the children's home, and it was a tremendous witness for Christ throughout that whole area. The Buddhist community knew about the Syin, Wang, Ai Orphanage, and they knew the name of Wang Shou Syin. Mrs. Wang received a lot of the needed financial and material support from the non-Christian community and also from the Taiwan military personnel. There was a little Baptist church in Rock Village, and Leroy often went to that church to preach and to administer the Lord's Supper. Quite often, on his visits there, he would stay overnight at the orphanage and eat a meal with the children. What a blessing that was! Many years later, when Mrs. Wang died, her son, James Wang, asked Leroy to speak at Mrs. Wang's memorial service. This experience is one of the great honors of his missionary career.

Two other individuals with whom Leroy and Janell came to have an enduring relationship are Pastor Yang Hsu, and his wife, Yang Shr Mu. Pastor Yang served as pastor of the church at Lyou Kwei, and he and his wife had also founded an orphanage up in the mountain areas of Lyou Kwei, "The Christian Mountain Children's Home." The home's focus was on the aboriginal children. Leroy loved the orphanage and Pastor and Mrs. Yang from his first visit to the children's home. He saw firsthand the sacrifices that the Yangs made for the sake of their "children." In those early days, food was scarce for the children. Sometimes, the rice would be supplemented by shredded cassava root, which would help the children's stomachs, but did not have any nutritional value.

The Hogues recall, on one of Pastor Yang's visits to their home in Kaohsiung he was looking for a refrigerator for the orphanage. Refrigerators in those days were scarce and expensive, and Leroy did not have any funds available for that purpose. He told Pastor Yang he didn't have any funds. Pastor Yang asked him to pray with him about the orphanage's need for a refrigerator. They stood in the living and prayed. Leroy recalls he had little faith.

The next week, an American Army sergeant, who was a good friend of the Hogues, told Leroy that a new refrigerator had arrived at the American military base and they did not have any current need for the refrigerator. Oh, Leroy knew where the need was. Jehovah-jireh! Leroy called Pastor Yang and they made arrangements for the refrigerator to be delivered to the orphanage in Lyou Kwei.

Leroy still recalls this experience with laughing eyes. "U.S. Army personnel, a U.S. air force truck, and two missionaries were involved in the delivery of that refrigerator. The refrigerator had to be carried across the swinging suspension bridge across the Lao Nung River. Was that a problem? Not to Pastor Yang! A long, sturdy bamboo pole, a long piece of rope, and two strong men carried that refrigerator across the swaying bridge, while the military men and missionaries stood there, expecting to see the refrigerator fall into the river 100 feet below. Of course, it also had to be hauled up by rope, in through the window on the second floor of the building where it would be placed, but that was easy!" Suffice it to say that the Hogues' relationship with the Yangs has grown and deepened over the years, and they think of them among their dearest friends in Taiwan. These are the kinds of experiences where the missionary learns culture and develops strong, lasting and meaningful relationships.

When the Hogues left southern Taiwan in 1971 at the end of their five-year term, to return to America for their furlough, they were deeply touched by the expressions of love and appreciation from the churches and co-workers. Mrs. Wang said to them, "Pastor Hogue, don't forget us." Leroy and Janell stored away in their hearts the love and appreciation of the co-workers as they visited family and friends. They were also strengthened and blessed as they shared from the pulpit, in the classrooms, in conference rooms, around coffee tables, sitting in living rooms and on university campuses, the need for the Good News to be shared in Taiwan.

Seminary Hill

The Hogues had a restful furlough. Sue Ann graduated from high school during the year and enrolled in Oklahoma Baptist University in the fall of 1972. Leroy, Janell, and the three boys were ready to return to Taiwan at the same time, fall of 1972. Leroy and Janell were thrilled to be going to the seminary. Leroy's vision of going to Taiwan was being realized. They lived in the house on the far corner of the campus next door to John and Jean Chang.

Leroy remembers the student body was very small – about 14 students – at the time, and it was a bit doubtful the school could continue with so few students. There were so many terms in Church History that had to be translated. How did one say, "Constantinople" in Chinese? Or Alexandria? Or the Roman Empire? That first term was a discovery and learning process for Leroy, and also for his students. Thank God for the patience and courtesy of Chinese students! It had to be a trial for them, too. Leroy discovered that he loved teaching, he loved students, and he loved the seminary. Again, it was the story of relationships, with students, and fellow faculty members.

Janell and Leroy loved living on seminary campus. All three of their sons, Charles, Andrew and Tom spent some time on Seminary Hill. Andy and Tom graduated from Morrison Academy in Taichung, but Charlie graduated from Shawnee High School on their next furlough. The boys loved Wu Hsing street. They loved all of the little shops and interesting little lanes. They also loved the mountains nearby. They would often climb Thumb Mountain and Elephant (Long Life) Mountain. As a matter of fact, Leroy enjoyed the mountain climbing opportunities and spent time up on the mountains whenever he could spare the time. Leroy's mother came to Taiwan on several occasions, and it was a blessing for faculty, both Chinese and missionaries, and for the students to have Grandmother Hogue on campus. She was an inspiration and blessing to everyone.

One of the rather pleasant aspects of living on the seminary campus was the opportunity to have a family dog. Actually, the Hogues had several dogs during their years on the campus. The boys always thought up the strangest names: Christo Belito and Brownie and Clyde. Brownie even eloped with the neighbor's, John and Jean Chang's dog. Some of their dogs just "disappeared," perhaps stolen for somebody's table. But the most famous of their dogs was Crow, a beautiful black German Shepherd, that more or less owned the campus for nearly 15 years. He was such a good dog, and Andy trained him when he was just a puppy.

Crow was such a smart dog, he would obey just about any of Andy's commands.

Eventually, Crow had some sons, and one of them came to live with his father at the seminary. What to name the pup? The boys settled on "Crude," as in crude oil, which is also very black. Because the dogs were big and black, they attracted quite a bit of attention on campus. Some of the students told about coming back to the campus late at night, when the gates were closed, and it was very dark, and they were afraid. Suddenly they were aware that two big, black dogs were walking along with them on either side, as guard dogs. But some of the students were afraid of the dogs, so they had to be kept at home during the day. There were other times when Leroy would bring the dogs to the freshman orientation to introduce the new students and "nice evening guards" to the freshmen. The Hogue boys loved their dogs, and would often take them along up on the mountains, when they went mountain climbing.

Leroy, Janell, and Andrew returned to Taiwan in March of 1982, just after Sue got married. They had been in the States for several months, during which time Leroy's father was in the hospital. Leroy had tried to spend as much time as he possibly could with his dad. When they left Oklahoma for Taiwan, his dad was back home and seemed to be doing rather well. They had not been back in Taiwan very long when Janell came down to Leroy's office and told him that his brother had just called, and said that his father had passed away. Leroy went to their house for a little while and then called Charles Culpepper, Jr., and asked if he could go down to the old farm house where the Culpeppers were living. He told Charles what had happened, Charles made a pot of tea, and they sat and talked for a long time. Leroy was always so appreciative of the kindness that Charles showed him that day.

In June of 1982, a rather momentous thing happened in regard to their ministry. Leroy received a call, asking if he would become the English pastor at Grace Baptist Church. It did not mean that he would do any less teaching at the seminary, but that he would be involved every Sunday at Grace Church. Also, it offered an opportunity to work under the senior pastor, Chow Lien Hwa, who had previously been a professor at the Taiwan Baptist Seminary. One thing that Leroy enjoyed about his new work at Grace Church was the preaching opportunity. The church was located directly across the street from National Taiwan University, the largest and most prestigious university on the island. That meant that every Sunday morning there would be a number of university students present in the congregation who came, as much as anything, for the opportunity to hear English. He rejoiced in the opportunity to share the Gospel with so many young Chinese students. For the next ten years, he served at Grace Church in the capacity of English pastor, while continuing his full-time teaching assignment at the seminary.

Janell was also very busy during these years. She taught English at the seminary and at various times she served as business-manager-treasurer for the seminary. Janell was very involved in the various ministries at Grace Church. She also taught at Bethany Elementary School, a Morrison Academy Branch in Taipei.

By this time, all of the children were gone, but each one, from time to time, would return for a few weeks or for summer vacations. They still enjoyed the walks down Wu Hsing Street and the mountains around the seminary, not to mention their trips to O Lan Bi and Sun-Moon Lake.

Beyond Taiwan

In 1991, Leroy and Janell left Taiwan for furlough and for a new field of service in Singapore. Leroy had been invited to teach at Baptist Theological Seminary Singapore

(BTS). They began that ministry in 1992, and they thoroughly enjoyed their ministry there. Living in Singapore opened up a whole new window on Asia for them. They became acquainted with the neighboring countries and had preaching and teaching opportunities in several of them. The culture, even among the Singaporean Chinese, was a good bit different from the Chinese culture in Taiwan. So their brief two-year stay in Singapore broadened their understanding of Asia.

Back Where They Started

Leroy and Janell returned to Taiwan for another two years of ministry, again in Kaohsiung, the place where they first began their Taiwan ministry. They worked with several churches in Kaohsiung, including the one in Hsiao Kang, where Pastor Su's son, Su Cheng En, was the pastor. But very quickly, Leroy was invited to teach at the seminary – Church History and New Testament – the courses he had taught for so many years. This invitation was totally unexpected, but was such a wonderful blessing to Leroy.

What is Retirement?

They left Taiwan in 1997 and officially retired in 1998. They continue to have many opportunities to work with the Chinese people: trips back to Taiwan for ministry opportunities and serving in Shandong, China, where they were able to walk the same alleys that Lottie Moon walked.

Their children have a global view – Sue and her husband live in Louisville, KY, where she teaches high school math, and he teaches philosophy and other courses at Sullivan University. Charles and his family live in Perth, Australia, where he is employed with an Australian oil company. His wife is Australian and they have two daughters. Tom and his wife, Putu, who is from Bali, live currently in Bangkok, Thailand, where Tom is an editor for Associated Press. They have a three-year-old son. Andy and his Beijing wife live in Phoenix, AZ. Their first child, Katherine, was born in Beijing, and did not speak any English until she was about three years old. Little brother Charles joined the family four years later.

When Leroy and Janell return to Taiwan, they have an instant sense of "returning" home to the place where they belong! They would be closer to three of their grandchildren, but for the moment, they are in Shawnee, OK, a mile from Oklahoma Baptist University, where the "shy" young man welcomed a freshman girl to a university campus. They have many opportunities to work with the Chinese churches in central Oklahoma. Leroy is currently serving as pastor-advisor for one of those churches.

Their verse continues to be: "Jehovah-jireh – The Lord will provide." He has all these years, and to HIM they give praise!!

Leroy and Janell Hogue with Pastor and Mrs. Su

Bob and Nell Beard
Reaching Two Worlds

A little boy born into a loving, caring, family on September 2, 1927, was named Charles Robert Beard. His family called him "Bob." He grew up in Memphis, TN, the heartland of the South. His parents were active church members. His father was a deacon. Bob was an official member of the nursery department of Temple Baptist Church in Memphis, so church life started early for the little fellow.

Bob received his education in the Memphis Public School system. He was active in sports: football, basketball, baseball, golf, tennis and swimming. His interest in sports lasted all of his life. He also enjoyed a paper route during his junior high years. He was a good child, but like many members of the Beard family, he had a quick temper and a quick sense of humor. His temper came quickly, but he was quick to forgive. Bob came to realize that he needed a Savior, and he accepted Jesus Christ as his personal Savior at the age of ten and was baptized into the membership of Temple Baptist Church on April 25, 1937.

After high school graduation, he joined the U.S. Navy and served one year in China and Japan. It was during this year that Bob matured and realized that the world was filled with suffering and sorrow. He said, "I had my first unsheltered view of the world." God placed a seed in his heart that was to grow and mature in the years ahead.

Bob entered Memphis State University after his stay in the Navy to major in engineering. He soon learned that engineering wasn't the major for him, and he transferred to the University of Tennessee and changed his major to sociology. He was active in the Baptist Student Union on campus and served as president of the state organization his senior year in college.

It was during his college days that he came face-to-face with God's purpose for his life. He loved God. He loved God's Word. He loved the church. He loved telling others about Jesus Christ. He couldn't escape the impressions made during his Navy experience. He wanted to make a difference in a suffering world and made public his decision to follow the Lord's plan for his life. He knew in his heart that God had called him to preach, and he was willing to be obedient to the King of Kings. He made plans to attend Southwestern Baptist Theological Seminary after university graduation.

Bob had dated several girls, but he had not found the right girl. He prayed that God would bless him with a godly wife, who was willing to walk beside him in Christian ministry. He came home for the weekend, and as always he attended his home church, Temple Baptist. He met the new youth director, Saranell Head Beard. God does have surprises! Who is Saranell Head Beard? What do we find about this young woman?

Saranell Head Beard was born October 17, 1925, in Fairfield, a suburb of Birmingham, AL. Fairfield was built by and existed only because of the Tennessee Coal, Iron and Railroad Company. Its population was approximately 10,000. There were only Protestant churches: Baptist, Methodist, Presbyterian, and Episcopal in the order of their membership size. Everyone was about on the same economic level. There were many nationalities living in the small town of

Fairfield: Italian, Greek, Swedish, German and Dutch. This background was a good foundation for Nell's future.

Nell's father was an employee of the T.C.I. Her grandfather was reared on a fairly large farm in rural Alabama. He was a prosperous farmer until he lost his life savings in the bank failure of 1929. The worry resulting from this experience finally caused him to have a mental breakdown, and he was committed to a mental institution and died there. Of course, this background affected her father's life.

He wasn't a Christian and seldom attended church with the family. He was a clean moral man, a good provider for his family, and an honest citizen. Nell's mother was a nominal Christian, but she had a strong Baptist background. Mrs. Head played the piano in the children's Sunday school and attended worship services. She demanded that Nell and her two sisters, Marjorie, four years older, and Frances, four years younger, attend youth meetings and worship services.

Nell says her home life was comfortable, but not affectionate. However, they were close and enjoyed doing things together – picnics, nut hunting, flower picking, and visiting both sets of grandparents and other relatives in the summer months.

She was a very active little girl and was an extrovert, but years later she saw herself as an introvert. It was during the seventh grade that the doctor discovered that Nell had almost no use of her left eye. This was an inherited condition and she was born with this problem. She wore glasses, which was a difficult experience for a seventh grader. Nell was a good student and she loved books, books of all kinds.

After high school graduation, Nell entered Birmingham-Southern, a Methodist College. She had no idea what she wanted to do, but the college had offered her a work scholarship. After one semester, Nell decided to work for a while and save money, and perhaps, she could decide what she wanted to do with her life.

Nell's mother forced her to attend church and she joined the church; however, she didn't have any interest in church nor was she saved. It was during her work experience that she met a young man who was active in church. They started dating, and church was the place where they went. It was during one of those services that Nell was seized with the conviction that she wasn't a Christian. She made a public decision for Jesus Christ and asked for believer's baptism. She said, "No doubt the person having the most to do with my conviction and subsequent life dedication was my first boyfriend. It wasn't anything he said, but what he was and still is. For this, I thank the Lord for providing such for me."

During a revival in the spring of 1944, Nell felt God calling her to dedicate her life to full-time Christian service. She had an interest in church education and enrolled in a very conservative school, Bob Jones College, to pursue her education for ministry. She spent one year at Bob Jones College, which was a very negative experience; yet she said, "I had an excellent OT Bible teacher and it was a very cultural school – concerts, operas, and I found all of this of great value." She left Bob Jones College after one year and enrolled in Southwestern Baptist Seminary. Nell worked at the Mexican Chapel and taught children at the orphanage during her seminary years. Nell was single when she received her Bachelor of Religious Education in July 1947. She worked in her home church as educational secretary for a short time before becoming educational director for Parker Memorial Baptist Church in Anniston, AL, in 1949. Nell learned from this pastor and this church how to listen to people and lead them, instead of forcing them to do it "my way."

In May 1950, Nell was invited to become youth director at Temple Baptist Church in Memphis, TN. One good and lasting thing came in Nell's youth director's days. Nell says, "I heard often about Robert (Bob) Beard. He was a student at the University of Tennessee and had been State Baptist Student Union President. His home church, Temple Baptist, was very proud of their young man. I knew I had to finally meet him. He came home for the weekend and this weekend changed my life, my future, my attitude."

Nell liked Bob from the beginning, but she had serious doubts about the friendship. She did not think it had any future because of two reasons: they were the same height and she liked to wear heels and the other one was Bob was two years younger than she. However, as she got to know Bob, she wasn't too worried about the height, nor the age. Bob graduated from University of Tennessee in March 1951, with a bachelor of arts degree. They were married on July 6, 1951.

Bob was already prepared to attend Southwestern Seminary in the fall of 1951, so Nell found herself returning to Southwestern. Nell worked in the registrar's office, as Bob was a full-time student. They, like most of the students attending Southwestern, were poor. Bob had a paper route in the beginning and later worked as a sales clerk in a department store. Seminary was a meaningful and growing experience for the young couple. Bob graduated in July 1954 and they accepted the pastorate of a rural church in Nell's home county. They found this experience to be very difficult, and were asked to leave after one year. They were called to another Alabama church, and this experience wasn't any better, and they left after one year.

Nell was pregnant when Bob graduated from seminary and Becky was born in 1954 during their first pastorate. After they left the second pastorate, both Bob and Nell were discouraged and wondered how the Lord could use them.

However, God had other plans, and the first Sunday after Bob left the second church, he was invited to preach at Calvary Baptist Church in Bessemer, AL. It was in a very poor section of the city, but they were willing to accept the invitation to serve as pastor. The church couldn't pay a full-time pastor's salary. Bob worked as draftsman for a while, and later taught in the junior high school. Nell would later say, "Those were some of the happiest years of our lives." Their second daughter, Bobbie, was born in August 1957.

Bob worked with the men in the church, and several of the men became active church members who were faithful in sharing their faith. Bob was able to guide the church in purchasing property and building a suitable church facility. Nell found her place in ministry. She became very active in teaching women's Bible classes and working with women and children in missions programs. And, third daughter, Betsy, was born in 1964.

Bob and Nell resigned from Calvary Baptist Church after eight years. Bob returned to the university to complete his degree in counseling. This was a struggling time for the Beard family. Finances were tight. Bob taught and also worked in a department store in the evenings and on weekends. They had little time as a family.

Bob and Nell were active members of a local church, and one day as they read the Foreign Missions Board's monthly magazine, *The Commission,* they were touched by the needs of the world. They began to talk about the possibilities of serving overseas. Were they qualified? Where would they serve? What job would they fill? They contacted the Mission Board.

The Foreign Mission Board was entering new fields of service in the 60s. One of the countries that spoke to their hearts and their qualifications was Taiwan. Taiwan was the home base for many American military, and the country was encouraging foreign investors. The Taiwan Mission voted to request the Mission Board to appoint a couple to work with the American military in south Taiwan, the city of Tainan.

Bob had never been able to escape the impression made during his Navy days. He had seen China and Japan up close, and he loved the places and their people. He had seen suffering and pain up close, and he wanted to make a difference in an unsheltered world. He also understood the needs among internationals living and working overseas. Bob and Nell were appointed to do English language work among English-speaking people in Tainan, Taiwan.

Bob and Nell could not seek career appointment because they were over the age limit. At the time of their appointment, this age level group was called "missionary associates." The Beards were appointed July 1967, to work in an English language church for five years.

The daughters were an important part of this family. Becky was an extrovert and made friends easily. As the family looked forward to overseas service, Becky was excited. She was 13 when they departed for Taiwan. Bobbie was nine when they left for Taiwan. At first, Bobbie reacted tearfully to the family's interest in missions, and Bob and Nell waited until she was willing to go. Bobbie loved life in Taiwan and made many friends. Betsy was only two-and-a-half when they left the U.S. She had a sunny disposition, made friends easily, loved church and loved to travel. She was made for Taiwan.

The Beards, with their three daughters, arrived in Taiwan in August 1967. Missionary associates were required to spend one year in full-time language learning. This gave the missionary associates a foundation in the language. Missionary associates were allowed to continue to study, but not on a full-time basis. Bob was one of those associates who studied language and the culture until the last months of his missionary career.

They spent their first year in Taipei and moved to Tainan in the fall of 1968 to pastor Trinity Baptist Church. The city, the church, the people, both locals and foreigners, were a fit for the Beard family. God had used all the experiences of those little undeveloped, rural churches to prepare Bob and Nell for Trinity Baptist Church.

Bob had many opportunities to visit American military on the base and off. He was introduced to Chinese military personnel. He was there to listen, encourage, counsel and supervise. His master's in counseling was being used.

Bob rode his bicycle almost all the time, so this provided an opportunity to meet people at the bus stops. One day he met a young military wife at the bus stop who said, "Last night, I prayed for someone to provide spiritual help for me."

Nell was active in Bible study groups, women's ministries, children's ministry and playing the piano for Sunday worship services.

During the years the Beards lived and ministered in Tainan, they were able to do effective evangelism and discipleship training. Their ministry included working with Chinese and American military personnel: locals and foreigners; international and local businessmen and women. The world had come to them. They served an international community at Trinity Baptist Church. They were appointed for five years, but the five years became ten years.

Their daughters loved Tainan and stored up many happy memories of their years in Tainan. They attended the Jonathan M. Wainwright School in Tainan. It was located on the American military base and operated by the U.S. Department of Defense. The missionary children living in Tainan were able to attend this school. Each one found her own interests and talents – sports, music, art, drama.

There were other memories of their Tainan days. Betsy was hit by a motorcycle. She was bruised and had a broken jaw from the experience. She was also bitten by a dog, and Becky was burned trying to light the gas water heater.

The Beards grew up in the southern part of the United States, and typhoons were not a part of their history. However, it seemed typhoons were frequent and very strong in Taiwan. This was especially true for the Beards. They lived in a section of the city where flooding was normal. Their house flooded at least five times during their years in Tainan. They learned early that when the typhoon season came, they must be prepared at any given moment to get their appliances on bricks, furniture on benches and bricks, and make their way to the attic. Most of the time the rains would stop in a day or two. The men in the neighborhood would remove the debris and open the sewer pipes on the street in front of the house, and the family would clean up the house and arrange the furniture and life would go on until the next typhoon – sometimes a week or sometimes six months. They learned early in their missionary career the meaning of what Dr. Baker James Cauthen said to them at their appointment service, "Take things to the mission field in your hands and not in your heart."

One of the most painful experiences was the murder of their missionary colleague, Gladys Hopewell, by her deranged cook. It was a very stressful time, as Bob and Nell worked with other missionary colleagues who were in the city to assist with the various tasks – dealing with the police, entertaining guests, preparing for the funeral, arranging for the body to be sent to the U.S., counseling the grieving students, helping their daughters deal with their fears, and coping with their own grief and loss. They found in each experience that God's grace was sufficient as He promised.

Becky and Bobbie graduated from high school and returned to the U.S. to attend college. The military and international community became smaller and smaller. Trinity Church had grown and was a stable church. It was time to call a Chinese pastor who could minister to a larger Chinese membership and the remaining foreigners.

Bob had come to feel their ministry in Tainan was finished and they were again open to God's direction. Morrison

Academy had recently opened a newly built school, grades K-8 in the large port city of Kaohsiung, to the south. Bob was asked to become principal of the school and to teach some of the junior high grades. Nell was invited to serve as librarian and teach junior high literature. Nell and Betsy were also in agreement with the move to Kaohsiung. So in the summer of 1978, the Beard family joined a small missionary community – five missionaries in Kaohsiung.

They again found the world had come to them. The children came from Holland, Finland, Sweden, Denmark, France, England, South Africa, Hong Kong, Philippines, Korea, and the United States. Some of the children were from missionary families but most of them came from business families. Religion-wise, there were atheists, Buddhists, Taoists; Muslim, Jewish and Christian; and the Christian denominations were from Seventh Day Adventist to Southern Baptists. The Beards did not feel the students just happened to attend MAK, but they were rather sent to the school. They were there not only to receive quality education, but to receive the Gospel, perhaps the only Christian influence some of them would ever have.

Furlough is always a shocking experience for the missionary family. This was true with the Beards. Reunion is one of the priceless gifts of the human experience. Furlough is a time to be reunited with family, church family, country and culture. After such a long absence, there is a kind of "re-entry" experience that confronts the returning missionary. There is not only the jet lag to contend with, there is also the "knowledge and experience" lag with regard to country, friends, and family. There are many changes that have taken place while one is away from one's homeland.

During one such furlough, the Beards lived on the beautiful, quiet campus of Judson College, owned and operated by Alabama Baptists. One of the many unexpected "pluses" of living on the Judson College campus was that Nell had the opportunity and privilege to complete a BA degree in English. The highlight was that Nell and Becky graduated from Judson together! Bob served as chaplain for the college. As campus chaplain, he made himself available to students on a formal and informal basis, and shared with them about missions and the needs to take the Gospel of Jesus Christ to the nations.

The year was 1982. Back in Taiwan, Bob and Nell experienced what most missionaries do: they sent their youngest child, Betsy, to the U.S. for college. Betsy went to Taiwan when she was three years old and Taiwan was home to her. She found the University of Montevallo a lonely place, and homesickness was a daily experience for her for a short time. Her parents prayed much for her to make friends and put down new roots in her new land. She says, "I did experience homesickness, but the Lord gave great grace quite quickly. Boarding school at Morrison really helped prepare me for leaving Taiwan and living on an American college campus." Bobbie, the second daughter, had graduated from college and was working at the University of Alabama medical center. The oldest daughter, Becky, was married to a young man named Bill Detrick, whom she had met in Tainan, and they lived in Kansas.

Bob and Nell were able to give more and more attention to the needs of Kaohsiung Morrison School. They improved the curriculum to meet the needs of the students, hired local and foreign faculty members, and supervised the construction of new buildings on the Morrison campus.

They found the various nationalities in the student body so rich in culture and traditions that one year, they requested the students dress in their "traditional" national costumes for the Fall Festival and chose "He's Got the Whole World in His Hands" as the theme for the festival. As the program began and the students marched in, beginning with the kindergarteners and ending with the eighth graders, singing the theme song, it gave them goose bumps. They were so aware that they were in the midst of a mission field. It was as if they lived and worked in the United Nations. What an opportunity to share! How open these young hearts were to the Good News. They were so thankful to be where they were.

During Bob and Nell's ministry in Kaohsiung, they had attended both the English services as well as the Mandarin services at the Kaohsiung Mandarin Church. They had offered English classes in their home for the postal workers from the Kaohsiung Post Office, as well as workers from the Kaohsiung Harbor, but Bob wanted to be more involved in Chinese ministries.

They requested permission in 1986 from the Mission to move to Pingtung. Morrison School was located between these two cities. Their desire was to continue to serve as administrator for the school and work more closely with the Pingtung Baptist Church, reaching out to young adults and students.

The Morrison School had a larger enrollment of students, qualified teachers, and adequate facilities, and a new principal had been assigned. Bob and Nell found working in both places very draining on their time and energy. So, December 1987, they notified the Morrison School System that they were resigning from the Morrison position and would be working full-time in Pingtung ministries.

Bob and Nell taught English classes in their apartment and at the church; they taught English classes at the teacher's and engineering colleges, and also taught children's English classes. These classes weren't always enjoyable, but these teaching opportunities were opening doors for the Pingtung Church to visit homes, and Nell and Bob were planting seeds in good soil. They used their dining table filled with Nell's southern biscuits and sausage gravy to counsel and encourage many young adults and young couples. They went on retreats with young adults and bicycled out in the country with young and old, seeking to find ways to share Jesus with them.

Bob preached once a month at the Pingtung Mandarin Church, performed weddings, counseled, and buried the dead. Most of the time, this was done through a translator, but he tried to use more Chinese in these activities. Chinese friends encouraged him as he used more and more Chinese. The day he preached his first sermon in Chinese was a highlight, a dream come true.

It is more blessed to give than to receive. Nell said, "This is a much-quoted verse and true. However, this is sometimes difficult for a missionary to accept." This was especially true with Nell until 1989, when Bob had a heart attack. She said, "After Bob's heart attack, it took God's grace to teach me to receive from others." She thought her ministry to the Chinese was helping them, but she was put in a position where she learned to be the recipient of ever-flowing blessings from her Chinese and missionary families.

They returned to the U.S. March 12, 1989. Nell wrote friends, "Our plans are uncertain, but our desire to return to our work here in Taiwan is not. We hope to be back in time for the fall semester, but we will leave this in the Lord's hands." Bob had double by-pass surgery one week after arriving in the U.S. He did well, and they returned to Pingtung in July, four months after they left Taiwan. God had heard the prayers of many!

They settled into life – worshiping, playing the piano, teaching English, leading marriage enrichment seminars, counseling, preaching, praying, laughing, encouraging, singing, cleaning, riding their bicycles, entertaining guests (Chinese, missionaries and foreign guests), cooking, shopping, studying, sharing their faith, baptizing new converts, visiting newcomers for the church, playing tennis, taking vacation with missionaries and Chinese friends, and writing letters to their daughters and friends in America. They were satisfied. These were rewarding years.

Bob and Nell often mentioned Oswald Chamber's words: "The Spirit of God needs the nature of the believer as a shrine in which to offer His intercession." The circumstances of a saint's life are ordained by God. In the life of a saint, there is no such thing as chance. God brings His children to places among people and under specific conditions in order that the Spirit might work. They saw God work in amazing ways, bringing youth and adults to faith in Jesus Christ and becoming active church members.

One evening, when Nell and Bob were visiting with Chinese friends, someone asked if they were leaving in July. The response was, "Yes." The next question was, "When are you returning?" The simple reply was, "We are not returning. We are retiring. We have children and grandchildren in America and are looking forward to being close to them after so many years of separation."

There was silence, and then a young lady said, "You have children here, too."

Bob and Nell attended the farewell dinners and parties and said their good-byes. They anticipated spending time with children, grandchildren, relatives and friends. How thankful they were for God's blessings through the years, and they prayed as they left Taiwan that one day, they would not only have children, but grandchildren and great-grandchildren in Taiwan.

Bob and Nell were appointed as associates in July 1967, and planned to stay five years, but the five years became 25 years. They departed Taiwan on July 3, 1992, for one-year furlough and then retirement in Anniston, AL. Their return to America was anticipated, but they found it painfully exhausting. America had changed in 25 years – culture, language, friends, even shopping for groceries was stressful.

Bob and Nell enjoyed their children and grandchildren. They were active at Park Memorial Baptist Church in Anniston, AL, and frequently entertained Chinese friends passing through Alabama. They were always ready to encourage young adults who were seeking God's will for their lives. Many left the Beards' home, after an evening of discussing the struggles and victories of missionary service, with a peppering of Bob's humor mixed in, feeling that they, too, could fulfill God's call for their lives in a cross-cultural setting.

Bob was diagnosed with cancer in 1999. He fought bravely, for he so wanted to be there to take care of Nell, the love of his life, as she had been diagnosed with Alzheimer's. Missionary and Chinese friends visited his hospital room and left refreshed, as he had encouraged them in the faith. He went home to be with the Lord October 15, 2004. Nell lives with Betsy and her family in Anniston, AL. Nell is still connected to her books and Betsy finds time to read to her every day. What a tremendous gift of time and love for a daughter to give her mother!

Bamboo is a tall and strong tree. It blows and bends in the strong rains and winds. After a typhoon, debris and damage are before the eye, but frequently one notices the bamboo, standing straight and tall. It is still beautiful, because the roots are deep and strong. Bob and Nell Beard were like bamboo. They might bend in the rain and wind, but their roots of faith and commitment to the Lord Jesus were strong and deep in His faithfulness. Yes, they have children and grandchildren in Taiwan and children and grandchildren in America, and for both they were truly grateful.

Bob Beard, Harry Raley,
Frances Raley and Nell Beard

Herb and Alice Barrett
Called to be a Coolie

The Boy's Childhood

Herbert Barrett grew up on a hilly farm in northern Missouri. Since his only sibling, a sister, was eight years older than he, she finished her schooling, married, and moved away while Herb was still quite young. So in some ways, Herb grew up much like an only child, including the privileges and responsibilities. He learned farming early – milking cows, operating tractors and other machinery, baling hay and calculating the profits of dairy cattle compared to beef cattle. In fact, by age 16, Herb had his own herd of dairy cattle, his own tractor, and his own debt at the bank.

Herb's family attended a tiny country church named Liberty Union. They had Sunday school every week, but had preaching services only twice a month. It was a closely-knit Christian fellowship where everybody knew everybody. (Interestingly, that small church of only five families produced two international missionaries from one generation – Herb, and David Broyles, an agricultural missionary in Togo, Africa.) Herb made a public profession of faith during a revival service. Like others before him, Herb was baptized in Locust Creek because the church didn't have a baptismal pool.

After high school in Milan, MO, Herb enrolled at Northeast Missouri State Teacher's College (now Truman State University) in Kirksville, MO. He enjoyed college life, but he didn't study much, and by the end of his freshman year he'd decided not to return for a second year. Shortly before the term ended, he obliged a friend and agreed to go with him on a double date with two local high school girls. The evening was pretty much a disaster for Herb's friend, but Herb had an interest in the girl he met, and after a few more weeks, decided to return for a second year of college so he could keep seeing her.

The Girl's Childhood

Alice Nicoletti's growing up years centered around family, First Baptist Church, and a strong emphasis on education. Both her parents were teachers, her father a school administrator and later a university professor and business manager. Alice had two older sisters, both of whom became teachers. Alice's father was a first generation Italian, so their house was often filled with the aroma of pasta sauce mixed with her mom's yummy pies and fresh vegetables from the family garden, cooking on the stove.

By the time Alice went on that blind date with Herb, she'd already yielded her life to Christian service and pictured her future in medical missions. In the months that followed, falling in love with Herb forced her to prayerfully search her life plans. One night, she threw her concerns out before the Lord: she felt sure that God planned for Herb to be her husband, but how could she turn away from her commitment and follow him back to the farm? Besides, she didn't think she could ever be a "good farm wife," and would most certainly be an embarrassment to him and his family. During that night of prayer, God reminded Alice that He had called her to be WILLING, not to make the plans. She had peace.

A Wedding

Herb and Alice were married December 26, 1964, while they were both still students at the university. When Herb graduated with a degree in business administration the following spring, God opened the way for him to work as office manager at Windermere, the Missouri Baptist assembly on the Lake of the Ozarks. For more than another calendar year, Alice spent the weekends with Herb at Windermere, but drove 400 miles each week to finish up her BS of Education in Kirksville.

Almost two years after they were married, and only a few weeks after Alice's graduation, and when they had begun serving together on the staff at Windermere, Herb was drafted into the Army. This was during the war in Vietnam, but God's plan was for Herb to serve his country stateside, in several different locations. During Herb's tour of duty at Fort Knox, KY, their first child, Curtis Michael, was born. Just four months later, when Herb was discharged from the military, the Barretts returned to Windermere. Windermere was a great place for the young family – the lake, beautiful woods, many friends and opportunities of service.

God's Plan

During this time, God was using frequent contacts with missionaries to work in Herb's heart. One night during a revival service that Alice had not been able to attend, Herb surrendered to "whatever God wants me to do, and I think it may be foreign missions." Those words spoken to Alice, just as Herb was going to sleep that night, brought Alice wide awake! What a surprise – God did have missions in their future after all!

Preparation for Missionary Service

The Barretts left Windermere to study one year at Midwestern Baptist Theological Seminary in Kansas City,

MO, before the Foreign Mission Board appointed them to Taiwan during an appointment service in Louisville, KY. It had been a long process of paperwork, reference checking, and discovering just where in the world God wanted them to serve. As a layman, not called to preach, but most certain of God's clear leadership to serve, Herb did not have specific leading to a specific country. His giftedness was in business management, and he wanted to be logistical support to those missionaries God did call to preach. At that time, there were requests for a business manager from five different missions in Africa, the Middle East and East Asia. At a candidate conference, the Barretts met Dr. Charles Culpepper, Jr. and his wife, Dona. Over lunch, they visited and answered the questions the Barretts posed. At the end of the day, Dr. Culpepper was called on to lead in prayer, closing the meeting of missionaries and missionary candidates. His prayer was unique, something like this: "Lord, you know the Taiwan mission has been praying for a business manager for years. Lord, I do not know why anyone would want to go half-way around the world to do somebody else's rat killing, but you know there is a business manager in this room looking for a place of service, and so I'm asking you to direct him to Taiwan. Amen." Well, that was the turning point!

September 2, 1971, the Barretts joined others beginning a 16-week missionary orientation program at Callaway Gardens, GA. September 3, 1971, Julie Nicole Barrett was born in Warm Springs, GA! Alice missed out on a good part of the orientation training because she was coping with a new baby the doctor described as "not thriving." The Barretts and the doctor were concerned that it was not in the best interest of the baby to head overseas, but circumstances made a delay complicated. They called on family and friends to pray, and the little one began to grow. By the time they returned to Missouri for Christmas and family farewells, the tickets were waiting and the baby was on her way toward normal development.

Over the Ocean

Late December, 1971, the Barretts and eleven other FMB missionary families sailed aboard the *President Cleveland* for service in Korea, Japan, the Philippines, Vietnam and Taiwan. The voyage was 21 days of constant seasickness for Herb, but Alice and the children enjoyed the new experiences. At one point, as the ship was sailing from Japan to Manila, they could actually see Taiwan in the distance. Herb always said he wondered that day if, despite his weakened physical condition, he shouldn't just jump overboard and swim to Taiwan! The four families going to Taiwan got off the ship in Hong Kong and flew to Taipei, arriving January 30, 1972. It was time to start a new life in a new land.

The Barretts found a warm welcome, weather-wise and from other missionaries. After staying a week with another mission family, the Barretts moved into a house on Nanking East Road, owned by the Overseas Crusade Mission. There were HUGE adjustments to be made – getting settled with items they had shipped, learning where to get basics like food and fuel, driving in traffic that seemed to have no system at all, leaving the children in the care of a Taiwanese helper who spoke no English, and starting classes at Taipei Language Institute.

Language learning was an ordeal! Herb had been so apprehensive about his ability to learn Chinese that he'd almost rejected Taiwan as a place of service. Sitting four hours a day in a tiny classroom with a couple of other beginning learners who seemed to be catching on much faster and easier was a daily struggle. Herb's likable personality won over most of the teachers, but his personal concept of "un-able-ness" was just about his undoing. Somewhere along in the process, Herb had an "ah-ha" moment when he announced, "Hey, I know more Chinese today than I did last week." Although Herb never did feel he was fully able in Mandarin, he began to view the language as a tool for building relationships, rather than a wall to overcome.

Alice's language school battle was more wrestling with the idea she wasn't really "serving," just going to class and taking care of the family. Even in that she felt threatened – she struggled with letting someone else care for her children while she was in class and when she studied. She found it hard to let someone else do the cooking (something she always enjoyed) and at times felt guilty because they had a "maid," such an extravagance in her eyes. It took time and patience on the part of those missionaries with whom she shared her heart, for her attitude to adjust. She did learn to count that helper as a big blessing, and to see the freedom the helper gave as an open door to explore their new world.

The Barretts visited Sung En Church on the third Sunday they were in Taipei. They actually tried to attend the two Sundays before, but working with a map drawn by a map-challenged fellow missionary, they couldn't locate the church. From the first visit, they felt very welcome at Sung En. Pastor Teddy Chang's good English and encouraging spirit were a big boost! Of course, they did not understand the sermon at all, nor the worship instructions in the bulletin. They just stood when everyone else did, bowed heads with others, and listened prayerfully. That first Sunday at Sung En, the weather was very cold! Alice had carefully dressed the family in their "Sunday-go-to-meeting" clothes typical in Missouri, but since there was no heat in the Chinese church building, they were miserably freezing. Suddenly, partway through the sermon, the elderly lady seated beside Alice stood up and took off her heavy wool coat. She grabbed baby Nicole out of Alice's arms, wrapped her up in the warm coat, plopped her back into Alice's arms, and sat down with her own hands stuffed inside her own sleeves. An amazing lesson in love that didn't depend on language! The Barretts knew immediately they had found their new church home. A few days later, the elderly Bible woman from Sung En, who spoke no English, brought a seminary student who spoke very little English with her when she visited the Barretts at home. Alice was so excited about these, their first Taiwanese visitors, that she welcomed them profusely, then indicating with her hand toward chairs said, "Ching dzou," (walk) when she should have said, "Ching dzwo" (sit). Yes, the people of Sung En loved and forgave the new missionaries much over the years, and taught them a lot about faithful service and obedience. Barretts especially enjoyed hosting the vibrant young people from the church. Years later, they would bump into some Baptist leader or layperson who had been a part of the Sung En youth group and give thanks for their shared experiences.

Only 14 months after they arrived in Taipei, the Barretts moved. It was not a smooth move, in that circumstances forced them to be out of the rental house with only a week's notice, no other suitable rental was available, but with generous help they moved into a small mission-owned apartment as a stop-gap measure. Interestingly, they stayed in that compound apartment until the mission assigned them a house on Ho Ping East Road almost two years later. Alice moved into the newly constructed Ho Ping house anticipating they would be there the rest of their missionary career, so it was a shock when only months afterward, the mission requested the Barretts to prepare to move to Lingtou Baptist Assembly! Alice, the natural nester, learned a very important lesson in that experience: NEVER think you are anywhere to stay. There were so many more moves ahead, so many furlough relocations, so many preparations of apartments for other missionaries, part of Herb's job as business manager, that Alice was known to state strongly, "Moving is one thing that does not get better with practice!"

After finishing his two-year required full time langauge study, Herb happily started as business manager in the mission office. He was excited by the challenge, and quickly began building strong relationships with the office staff. From the start, Herb was certain he was doing just what the Lord called him to do – freeing up a field evangelist to return to that ministry, helping missionary families with housing, cars, visas, travel arrangements and freight shipments, managing mission properties, and relating to the Taiwan government on behalf of the mission. Herb is gifted in recognizing gifts and talents in others, so through the years he surrounded himself with capable office personnel who enhanced what God wanted to do through the TBM. Herb found joy in his service, challenge in each day's tasks, and frequent opportunities to touch non-believers in the world of business who would shy away from a preacher-type.

Alice, on the other hand, was again struggling. Although she'd worked at Windermere, the actual management matters had been Herb's. But now she was supposed to be the missionary director of Lingtou, working with the Chinese manager, and she was "hiding" from the assignment. With both children at Bethany Christian School, a branch of Morrison Academy, her chance to serve had arrived, and all she wanted to do was stay in their house "until everything is settled." Reality? She didn't know what to do. She didn't know how to begin. She feared her language limitations, and lacked confidence she was up to the job. It took the less-than-gentle prodding and encouragement from Herb to launch her into the Lingtou ministry that she ended up enjoying thoroughly.

The MK Barretts became a part of the international congregation at Calvary, next door to the campgrounds, and when they reached middle school ages, transferred to Taipei American School. Herb and Alice invested themselves at Jyan Tan Baptist in Shihlin, and for a while, also helped with a struggling chapel up Yangminshan near the Cultural University. Lingtou became a family ministry as both Curtis and Nicole grew up helping with everything from serving meals and making beds, to post-typhoon yard cleanup and snake killing. The Barretts understood how much Lingtou was a part of all the family when Curtis came home from a week-long school outing at another campgrounds, and was running over with ideas he thought they should try at Lingtou. Lingtou was in all their hearts, and during their 10 years of service there, a new vision was cast, the grounds and facilities were upgraded, staff was enlarged, and occupancy was greatly increased.

In 1986, the Barretts went on furlough to Missouri. Curtis enrolled as a freshman at Truman State University and settled into dorm living. Nicole had one year of high school in Kirksville before three Barretts returned to Taiwan. Exiting Lingtou had been emotional for the family. Going back to Taiwan without Curtis and moving into a different living situation created some tension. They moved into a Wan Fu apartment quickly, and Herb was back in the office, picking up his responsibilities within just a few days. Nicole returned to Taipei American School life, classes, sports, and friends.

Alice had yet another new role: language/orientation coordinator for new missionaries. Although she was overwhelmed by her own limited Mandarin, she did have something important to share with the newcomers. She encouraged them that a fulfilling missionary service was far less about speaking "perfect" Chinese than about loving people and letting God's Spirit speak for you. Alice enjoyed working with the language teachers, especially Jean Lu, the head teacher. Alice was always being challenged – improving teaching principles, translation bug-a-boos, textbook preparation and editing issues, class schedules and counseling needs. Each new missionary brought skills and weaknesses to the program, new ministry potential and plans, and new manifestations of culture shock. In fact, Alice says, "I probably learned far more than all the learners who passed through the language program during my tenure."

Before the Barretts '87 return to Taipei, they'd requested special prayer for direction in their church ministry. On the suggestion of Dr. Carl Hunker, Barretts began worshipping with a tiny congregation in Hsichih, Taipei County. The church had almost disbanded, just a small handful of people gathered to worship on Sunday mornings, preached to by a parade of visiting Chinese pastors. Both Herb and Alice had gifts that might be useful at Hsichih. A few months later, the seminary assigned student Lyou Jau Yang to work in that church. Being a part of the building up of that congregation, helping plant a spirit of evangelism and vision for the surrounding community that was growing by leaps and bounds, proved a joy for both Barretts

While a part of the Hsichih Baptist congregation, the Barretts learned about floods. Two different times during those years, the church facilities, along with the rest of the town, were inundated by the Keelung River. Water marks almost six feet high was one of the minor things left behind when the flood receded. Mud and debris, dead animals, sewage, and totally waterlogged Bibles and teaching materials! The piano even floated and filled up with tiny river fish! The smell was atrocious, the clean-up task was backbreaking, the weather was hot, and yet faithful members came to scrub and discard and to help set things right in time for worship services. It was such a miserable experience in so many ways, but the Barretts realized that when it was too dark to continue the task without electricity, the Taiwanese working alongside them would return to flooded homes while they could return to a clean apartment and warm shower. Great was the example of the believers' faithfulness.

Herb was an excellent encourager, and in addition to his business manager role, he became the confidant of several of the pastors in the Keelung area. A highlight for both Barretts was the monthly co-workers fellowship meetings, where they gathered and shared support and encouragement.

So maybe it wasn't as big a leap, as it appeared to some, when following the Barretts' 1989-90 furlough, Nicole enrolled as a freshman at Truman State, Curtis graduated and began working, and two Barretts went back to Taiwan and accepted the invitation of the Hsichih Church to move into a new Hsichih community called Bwo Jywe and help them start a church.

Herb began what he calls the ride-the-train years. The Barretts had no church planting experience, but just moving into an almost-finished apartment in the new community was a start. Herb commuted by train to the mission office each day. Evenings and weekends, he helped with community outreach, with home visitation and service logistics in Bwo Jywe. They crawled over construction debris to visit folks moving into the many new apartment buildings, getting to know people and building relationships. There has almost never been a dog that didn't like Herb, so while people were out exercising their canine pets, Barretts struck up a conversation about the dog. It was a great way to meet new people, and as soon as the conversation was over, they made a quick note so they could transfer the name and apartment number to the neighborhood map at home. Sometimes if neither Herb nor Alice could remember the family name, the notation just said, "Lucky-German shepherd" or "Syau Bai." Alice did hospital visitation, taught Bible studies, and western cooking classes in their home, plus one-on-one Bible studies with women in the neighborhood. As much as the Barretts enjoyed making new friends and worshipping with the few faithful Christians, it was also a time of discouragement. Some people from Hsichih Baptist Church were helping in the new work, and a request had been made to the seminary that they assign a senior student who would, hopefully, be able to become pastor upon graduation. Instead, the seminary assigned a first year student to work at Bwo Jywe.

His first year, Chyan Jye Syi lived with the Barretts on weekends, a wonderful experience that bonded them in ministry and friendship The next year, he and his new wife lived with the Barretts, and the third year, baby Melody joined the family, earning the Barretts their first-time titles of Ye Ye and Nai Nai. There wasn't time or energy for the traditional "empty nest" syndrome. Both Herb and Alice, along with the Chyans and others, cleaned and set up the Bwo Jywe community center library area, used each week as a worship center. Despite weekly services, many community outreach events, much home visitation, Bible studies, and prayer, the community of believers was not growing much, and those few newcomers were Christians moving into the neighborhood. Everyone longed to see people come to faith. Instead, for almost two years there were several funerals, but not one baptism. Much ministry to families dealing with critical health issues, families in trouble, families who were hurting, but no professions of faith. Finally, one believer's elderly mother was baptized, and then the husband of one of the faithful members professed his faith. Hallelujah! The harvest had begun!

During the Bwo Jywe years, totally without Alice being aware of what He was doing, God also opened up an opportunity for Alice to teach English to teachers at a vocational high school in Chidu, Keelung. Working with teachers was something Alice would grow to love, perhaps more than any other ministry. Her teaching degree was finally being put to use. The potential of one Christian teacher touching hundreds of students each school term fueled her passion to win teachers to the Lord!

In 1997, when the Barretts returned after furlough, more big changes were ahead. The work at Bwo Jywe had grown into a thriving congregation named Dzan Mei (Praise) Baptist Church. The Barretts knew they should invest themselves in another area. Sweet relationships with other Keelung area co-workers and pastors stirred in the Barretts a desire to relocate in Keelung instead of Taipei county. They searched Keelung for apartments in neighborhoods that had reasonable access to a train station, and selected the "village" of Nuan Nuan. Both of them were excited and happy about being the only "tall noses" in the community, and curious how God was going to use them there.

Daily there were opportunities. Even the train time gave Herb chances to share with other passengers. His commute actually was so noticeable that a Nuan Nuan community paper did a feature story on the "a-dou-a" (old foreigner) who rode the train in and out of the Ba Du station each day! It seemed every contact had potential – the gatemen, vegetable vendor, bike repairman, restaurant staff, car wash employees, post office lady, neighbors. Whether eating shao mien (noodles) at the Syau Gwan restaurant, riding bikes for exercise, buying a train ticket, or toting out the trash each evening, contacts were made and relationships built.

Quickly, God opened doors for Alice to teach teachers in an additional two Keelung schools. Her heart was broken by the lostness of teachers individually, yet encouraged by the possibilities. Perhaps more than anything else she'd done, leading teachers to the Lord became her passion. She spent hours locating English teaching materials that opened up opportunities of witness. She spent more hours preparing lessons and praying for teachers. It was a really satisfying time in her ministry, a time when she felt like she really "fit."

During the wonderfully pleasing Nuan Nuan years, the Barretts had major issues to deal with, some of them painful.

A second grandchild was born, Curtis' marriage ended, and Alice's aging parents declined. They made a trip home for Alice's father's funeral, and wonderfully were there to be with Nicole when her first daughter was born a few days later. Only ten weeks after they returned to Naun Nuan, they made another quick trip to the U.S. when Alice's mother died. There were many, many changes taking place within the International Mission Board that impacted the way missions was "done." Questions were asked about the wisdom of missionaries working in existing Chinese churches and institutions, and several other method of ministry issues pushed to the forefront. Through it all, though not outspoken on the subjects of concern in mission gatherings, Herb was confident that as business manager, he was serving just as the Lord wanted, sure that Keelung was the place and ministry for the Barretts.

Trusting in Herb's quiet confidence, the Barretts opted not to pack out as they left for a six-month furlough at the end of 2000. Happily, they prepared the apartment with multiple dehumidifiers and arranged a gentleman to check and empty the machines as needed. Their "farewells" at the Keelung churches, with Alice's beloved teacher classes, with neighbors and missionary co-workers, were all based on a return in six months.

But God's Plans were not the Barretts' Plans

Six weeks after the Barretts settled into the Missouri Baptist missionary residence in Jefferson City, their lives changed forever. Admitted to the hospital with what was termed "a small heart attack," Herb experienced a massive brain bleed (hemorrhagic stroke) and was transferred by ambulance 30 miles to University Hospital in Columbia, MO. The doctors told the family that IF he survived the surgery, Herb would probably never be able to comprehend spoken words, and that he would likely never be able to walk again. After surgery to drain the blood from his brain, the neurosurgeon called the family together and said, "Herb will not be deaf, but he most likely will not understand the sounds he hears. To him, it will be like you are speaking Chinese." The family laughed, the surgeon looked stunned. Then the Barretts' son-in-law responded, "You should have said 'German,' because they all speak Chinese!" Was that moment of levity relief a hint of the miracle God had in store for Herb?

Herb did survive! He spent more than three weeks in neurosurgical ICU, Alice sleeping on the floor of the waiting room. Herb was then transferred directly to Rusk Rehabilitation Center, which treats only neuro and spinal cord injury patients. He spent almost four months at Rusk, Alice sleeping on a fold-out chair by his bed. That was followed by extensive outpatient rehabilitation. Herb progressed FAR beyond the predictions, including still being able to understand and speak both English and Chinese, but his physical function was limited. A year after the crisis began, Herb developed seizure disorder, and several years later was diagnosed with Parkinson's disease.

It was a very painful grieving experience for the Barretts to give up returning to Taiwan. Alice and the children had pledged in the ICU waiting room that they would not ask "why?" because there was neither time nor energy for questions that had no answer. Now unable to return to the ministry they loved, there were too many questions to ignore. Plans had to be made, mountains of paperwork had to be filled out, housing had to be located, a car purchased, new routines established. Rehab schedules and frequent ER visits and hospitalizations seemed to dominate life. What now? Where? How? The world had turned upside down! A partnership marriage was now unbalanced, and Alice was called upon to do what had been done by two people in the past.

Through everything, Alice claimed words from Hannah Whithall Smith, "God is enough." A quote from Oswald Chambers became her constant reminder: "You may not know what you are going to do, you only know that God knows what He is going to do."

The IMB provided Alice a trip back to Taiwan to pack out their Nuan Nuan apartment. Alice's sister and brother-in-law traveled with her and gave invaluable help in that process. Chinese friends and missionary co-workers rallied to take care of too much in too short a time. The Barretts' "son-in-love" and daughter invited them to relocate in a small town in Iowa to be nearby for support and help. A handicapped-friendly house was built, and in May 2003, they moved to Prairie City, IA.

They still do not understand why God did not allow them to continue service in Taiwan, why lifetime dreams of long years of post "retirement" service and travel weren't God's plan. But the Barretts do know without a doubt that every hour of the difficult past few years, they were in God's caring hands. They have experienced new joys – watching five grandchildren grow, welcoming a new "daughter-in-love" into the family, learning about prairie living (including horrific winters and amazing winds!). The Barretts have experienced anew the beyond-description bond of love between members of the Taiwan Baptist Mission, and know the deep care and support of Chinese brothers and sisters in the Lord. They have grown to love a new church family at Cornerstone Baptist Church in Ankeny, IA, and have taken up their place "holding the ropes" of prayer for international missions. They have learned each is able to do things they had never dreamed, and have had opportunity to encourage others who struggle with stroke, seizure disorder, and Parkinson's disease. The Barretts have been challenged physically, mentally, emotionally, and spiritually, and still find, *always: God is Enough.*

Herb and Alice Barrett

Sam and Marian Longbottom
On the Other Side of Vietnam

Grandparents are Home
"Your grandparents are coming home from Taiwan,"
my mom had said. Taiwan was a very distant, hazy
place to my eight-year-old mind. I just knew that my grandparents had been missionaries in a foreign country since
before I was born, and now they were coming back. They
were returning to America to stay for good!

As the passengers began filing through the glass doors
into the gate area, I strained my eyes to look for my grandparents. It seemed like everyone had come off the plane but
them. Then I saw them walking through the doorway. My
Grandmother Marian, smiling from ear to ear, wore a large,
conical hat. I was fascinated by it. She gathered me up in a
big hug and said she was so glad to see me. My grandparents were back to stay." It was 1989. What had happened
between 1955 and 1989?

The Arrival
In 1961, a winding road led the Longbottom family from
the airport to the mountain town of Da Lat, South Vietnam.
The twists and turns in the road kept the passengers, crowded
into a small Ford with the Lewis Myers family, swaying
sharply to the right and left. The children, seven-year-old

289

Sammy, five-year-old Jimmy and four-year-old Lynda, pressed their faces against the car windows, eager to see all they could of this fascinating country.

Family and Preparation

Marian looked out the window at the strange land and thought, "Why am I here?" She was an only child, having grown up in a cultural, polished family in Waco, TX, the home of Baylor University. Marian's mother was a social lady who entertained in style and taught her child to do the same. How could she ever entertain on this scale in South Vietnam?

Marian's father worked for Western Union as a telegrapher night manager for the office. Her parents were able to give her all the things little girls wanted in the 1930s, as well as big girls, for that matter. The family's lives were faith and church centered. Marian gave her heart to Jesus at an early age and listened to her mother tell missionary stories to children, and she was willing to go tell children in a faraway land about Jesus. Marian looked and thought, "When I was little, I never dreamed that one day I would be living in a foreign country, thousands of miles away from my parents."

How different this lush, mountainous country was from the tame blocks of houses, schools, and department stores of central Texas. After seeing meat hanging in the open market, Marian thought, "There are definitely some things I'm going to have to get used to here."

Sam chuckled to himself as he dozed off and on, but his heart was thrilled as he watched the rice fields slipping past and glimpsed the thatched roofs of the farmers' huts. He dozed, but listened to the conversation and thought of what brought him to South Vietnam. He grew up in south Florida. He was the oldest and only son of a Florida banker, and his mother was a diligent homemaker. He had one younger sister, Lynn. His sister had polio very young, so this illness made them even closer. Sam's family was musical. He enjoyed singing in choirs and played piano, organ, and trumpet. He also participated in sports – basketball, baseball, football, golf and tennis, but not on school teams.

His parents were devoted believers and active members of a Southern Baptist Church. He had been saved at an early age and had received a call to missionary service in his early teens. He was influenced by his pastor, Sunday school teachers, VBS, missionary speakers, and family.

His parents took the family several times on summer vacations to Ridgecrest for Foreign Missions Week. They also sometimes hosted furloughing missionaries in their home. Sam wanted the best preparation possible as he looked forward to serving His Lord in overseas service.

Baylor University, Waco, TX, was his dream and so in August 1945, he arrived at Baylor University. He had two majors: English and Bible. He was a good student. He participated in extra-curricular activities – sports, concerts, band, missions teams, and filling Sunday pulpits, but his favorite activity was spending time with a charming, talented, mature, dedicated, lovely, fun-loving freshman majoring in elementary education. Marian Cross was focused and Sam was impressed that she was called to missions, and he didn't have to force her to consider serving overseas.

Sam graduated from Baylor in 1949 and married Marian in 1950. She graduated from Baylor in 1951. Sam studied at Southwestern Baptist Theological Seminary for three years. Marian taught first grade in Ft. Worth for two of those years. Their first child, Sammy, was born during the third year.

Their first thoughts were feeling God's leadership to go to South America. However, that door closed, but another opened with the opportunity to serve in Hawaii. They were appointed to the Territory of Hawaii in 1954. Sam served as pastor to various island churches. Marian carried out the duties of a pastor's wife and cared for their growing family.

Waiting

After statehood came, Hawaii was transferred to America's Home Mission Board and the missionaries were asked to transfer to other countries. They were encouraged to transfer to South Vietnam. "Two rice baskets dangling from opposite ends of a carrying pole." Such is the Vietnamese description of Vietnam. The northern and southern areas of the country contain extensive rice fields due to the fertile, well-watered soil. In between these rice plains stretches a narrower piece of land containing the Annam Cordillera range. Vietnam lies on a peninsula south of China. The country's past is dominated by the rule of other countries, especially France and China. Though the French influence is visible in much of the architecture of Vietnam's large cities, China has influenced Vietnamese society in many areas, including the area of religion. Buddhism is the major religion of Vietnam.

The Christian Missionary Alliance had been in the country since 1911, but in the 1950s their efforts were turned toward reaching the tribal people of Vietnam. The people who lived in the villages and the cities also needed someone to tell them about God's way of salvation. Southern Baptists' first missionary couple, Herman and Dottie Hayes, entered South Vietnam in 1958.

Vietnam in 1960 was a turbulent country – just six years earlier, the country had been divided; Communist Ho Chi Minh led North Vietnam while South Vietnam was headed by Catholic president Ngo Dinh Diem. President Diem maintained that his country was in the midst of war, this was no time for missionaries, especially American missionaries to come to his country. Friends and churches prayed for missionary visas for Vietnam and for the country of Vietnam. Thirteen months of waiting passed. Then, in July 1961, things began to happen. Three months later, visas were granted. Sam and Marian Longbottom with their four children were on Vietnamese soil – God had truly blessed them. They were ready for a lifetime in South Vietnam.

Language and Cultural Lessons

Vietnamese, like Chinese, is a tonal language. The pronunciation depends on small markings above or below the vowels. A falling tone in the word "dau" means "head," while a level tone in "dau" means "where." Mr. Hao was employed by the Vietnam Mission to be a language teacher for Marian and Sam. He came to their home five days each week. They gathered around the dining room table, grateful for the fireplace during that first especially cold, dry season. Mr. Hao gave them assignments to go to the market to chatter with vendors, and he encouraged them to bargain for flowers, vegetables, meats, and assorted wares in the stalls. The Vietnamese were friendly and kind, but Marian and Sam often heard them giggle when they heard foreigners speaking Vietnamese. The helpers in the house were also great language teachers, helping Marian and Sam understand the language and the culture. Hymns and sermons at the Vietnamese church provided invaluable knowledge in language and cultural learning. Sam and Marian struggled and worked to become competent in cross-cultural understanding. Why? Sam and Marian were proving how much they valued and appreciated the Vietnamese people. They wanted to earn the right to share God's love with the Vietnamese people.

Daily Life in Da Lat

Da Lat was home to about 80,000 people, and this is the city where the Longbottoms lived. The city had once been a resort town and vacation spot for French colonists. Downtown, there were all types of businesses and stores: tailors, photo studios, hardware stores, grain stores, gas stations, restaurants, small hotels, jewelry shops, and pottery shops. Minority nationalities came into the city to sell their tools, cloth and handiwork. Da Lat was about 5,000 feet above sea level among pine woods, low hills, and mountains. Bikes, motorbikes, gas-powered scooters, small buses, and walking were the main means of transportation. Sam and Marian adjusted to life in Da Lat and the children loved their new home and their new town from the start.

Inside and Outside Church

There was a large Catholic cathedral and other small Catholic churches in the city. When the Longbottoms first settled into life in Da Lat, no Baptist church existed in their area of town. They attended the Vietnamese church in the city. The Longbottoms and other newly arrived missionaries started a Bible study in their home. This Bible study group grew into an organized, active Baptist church. There were other opportunities for sharing their faith besides those in the Bible study. They witnessed to their Vietnamese helpers in the home and members of their families. They made friends with the people in the market, taxi drivers, Post Office workers, gas station attendants, yard man, and the tailor. They were there to be faithful and God would bring the harvest. Praise His Name, He did!!

A Missionary Child in South Vietnam

Sammy and Jimmy, the two oldest children, attended the Da Lat Christian Missionary Alliance School across town each weekday. The three missionary couples who were in language studies took turns transporting the children to and from school. Most of the children there boarded at the school, since their parents were missionaries who served in other Southeast Asian countries.

In May of 1963, just one-and-a-half years after their arrival in Vietnam, Sam and Marian were transferred to Saigon, the capital of South Vietnam. One of the main reasons the

Longbottoms moved to Saigon was so Sam could become the treasurer for the Baptist Mission. Work included organizing the missionaries' financial paperwork, managing and distributing money for their salaries and ministry budgets for Baptist work in Vietnam – new church starts, orphanages, seminary, publication, scores of refugees coming from the north, nursing and social ministries. He also had to handle the visa renewals and other government documents for missionaries and institutions.

Marian maintained a guesthouse for missionaries who lived in other cities and came to Saigon for meetings/business, and also for any foreign guests who came to South Vietnam. She served on the hospitality committee and ministered to refugees who were moving into the city. She also taught Bible studies for outreach and assisted in church activities. There were home responsibilities. She supervised her three children, who attended the International School in Saigon, and took care of Danny at home. Marian also had time, in the summer of 1964, to give birth to their fifth child, Tommy.

War in the Midst of Daily Life

Soldiers hung around on the street corners. The sound of gunfire would sometimes break the calm of an afternoon. Life in Da Lat, though it consisted of daily doings such as housework, shopping, cooking, washing, visiting with neighbors, did bear the marks of war.

By 1962 and 1963, there was more unrest and tension, and they could see God was working not only in the lives of the Longbottom family and their fellow missionaries, but also in the Vietnamese people around them. People were trusting Jesus as Savior, people were being baptized, many others were seeking answers to life questions, and some were beginning to learn the truths found in the Bible – amidst the unrest of a civil war. And, the unrest grew. The children recall one noon in late October 1963. The family was gathered around the table for lunch. They heard the sound of gunfire and rockets in the street near their house. Sam thought it was wise for the family to stay in the kitchen. The children made no trips upstairs that afternoon. There was no playing outside. The entire family spent the long afternoon huddled under the dining room table. In fact, the gunfire continued through the night, and the little family stayed huddled under the dining room table through the long, dark night. They listened to the sounds of battle. They talked. They sang. They prayed. Sam and Marian taught their children to trust in God in all situations, even under dining room tables in the middle of the night.

Life in Saigon

Sometimes you don't know there's a war going on. Then, one day, you see soldiers and military policemen walking through the streets of Saigon near your home, with bayonets drawn, barbed wire barricades around government buildings, children riding to school in an armored bus with bars on the windows and armed soldiers onboard. Roadblocks and checkpoints were throughout the city. And, often there were explosions when Marian was out in the market. One Christmas Eve, when she was shopping in downtown Saigon for a few last-minute food items for their dinner the next day, there was a very large, loud and frightening explosion nearby. Demonstrations, riots and mob violence were frightening and unpredictable. One time, one of the household helpers found the children standing at the front gate looking through the criss-cross bamboo matting at the demonstration. She got them inside quickly. Marian and Sam wanted the children to enjoy life in Vietnam and to love the Vietnamese people. Yet they had to teach a balance of being positive and exercising caution.

Church Life in Saigon

Marian and Sam worked in the Grace Baptist Church in Saigon. More and more Vietnamese were seeking for the truth found in Jesus Christ. Saigon was truly becoming an international city. An English-speaking church was necessary because so many foreigners needed and desired a place to worship. The beginning strategy was for several missionaries to start evening services in their homes. When attendance grew large enough, they shared the building with the Vietnamese congregation, Grace Baptist Church in downtown Saigon.

In 1965, the English Church was officially organized and named Trinity Baptist Church. Sam served as the first pastor as he continued to work as Mission treasurer and minister with the Vietnamese chapels and mission points. Many young American men and women found their way to Trinity Baptist Church, where they found Christian fellowship and faith in Jesus Christ. Some of the young people were called into missionary service while attending Trinity.

The Return to Da Lat

When their first furlough ended, the Longbottoms settled down in Da Lat again. It was a happy day for all the family. They were getting out of the big city. They had gained confidence through the use of the language and experience, and they had many friends in Da Lat. One of their first friends to visit was Miss Nhan, who had helped them so much the first time they lived in Da Lat. Elegant and attractive, she was an unmarried social worker. Miss Nhan had been born in North Vietnam and moved to South Vietnam some 15 years before. She encouraged them, helped with language needs, invited them to special events in the town, and taught them how to be cautious and yet relaxed in the war worn country. Sam and Marian returned to the Baptist church they had helped to start the first time they lived in Da Lat. Sam preached often and assisted in all the activities of the church. Vietnamese were coming to faith amidst the chaos, were being baptized and becoming active church members.

Marian conducted cooking classes for wives, taught a combination of ESL and Bible study classes to young women, and assisted in the beginnings of a WMU ministry. Sam and Marian also taught Bible classes and ESL, conducted special programs and musicals at the military academy and the political warfare college. They showed films in theaters, parks, and churches. Their goal was to tell as many people as possible about Jesus, using as many culturally accepted methods as possible.

There were many attacks on local people. People were wounded and killed. Then these sad circumstances provided an avenue for Sam and Marian and other missionaries to minister to people in the lovely name of Jesus, and the Lord loved many to Himself through the touching hands of the missionaries.

The more Sam and Marian served in Vietnam, the more they felt the need to train Vietnamese Christians to minister to their own people. Due to the war, none of the missionaries knew how long they would be in South Vietnam; this uncertainty gave them a sense of urgency in mentoring future Christian leaders who were dedicated to serving their Lord. Mr. Huy was a businessman whom God had called and prepared. His most difficult days were ahead.

Home Life

The Christian Missionary Alliance School that the children attended was moved to Malaysia because of escalating hostilities. Marian had no other choice than to home school the children. Home schooling was rare in those days. However, the Calvert School curriculum suited the needs of the Longbottom children. A few years later, Sammy and Jimmy went to high school in Bangkok, Thailand. It was

very painful for Sam and Marian to send their children off to
another country.

Furloughs and Moves

The highlight of their second furlough in Texas from
Vietnam was the birth of Terry. He was five months old
when they returned to Vietnam in the summer of 1971.
They moved to a new city to work. Sammy spent his high
school senior year in Bangkok, Thailand. Jimmy transferred
to Morrison Academy in Taichung, Taiwan for two years of
high school. Lynda went there for her freshman year, and
Danny followed three years later. Sammy and Jimmy graduated from high school and went to the U.S. for college. They
were halfway into an empty nest during this term of service.
They found God's grace to be sufficient.

Southwest of Saigon, nestled deep in one of the "rice
bowls" of Vietnam, is the city of Can Tho (Kung-Tuh).
The city lies in a delta, continually watered by the Mekong
River; rice fields are a common sight because of the wet soil.
To reach Can Tho, one has to cross two wide branches of
the Mekong River by ferry. This was what the Longbottom
family did to reach their third home in Vietnam. Life was
hard in this town, but they were there because God had
called them to Vietnam and to share Jesus with their adopted
family. Sam became the pastor of the little Baptist church.
They conducted services in their home and later rented a
small facility. There were few adults in the small church,
but they had a number of young people. These people were
seeking for the truth in their war worn country. Sam also had
the opportunity to preach to soldiers who had been wounded
in the war. On Sunday afternoons, Sam and a believer, Mr.
Lanh, went out to the government rehabilitation center to
preach. Because of the low land, the center would often
flood, sometimes with knee-deep water. This was simply a
way of life for the residents, but wading through muddy river

water to preach was a new experience for Sam. Some church members worked in centers for crippled children. Sam had the opportunity to preach in this center. It was a thatched-roof hut with a dirt floor. Five crippled teenage boys heard the Gospel and believed. Sam baptized them in a nearby river. Sam had the privilege of teaching English language in the local university. They planted seeds of the Gospel, and some believed.

The Closing Months

Marian and Sam returned to Saigon with Tommy and Terry for Sam to again work in the Mission office. They left Can Tho with sad hearts, but they knew the believers were strong and were committed to continue to live out their faith in difficult times and to assist the church ministry.

Saigon had changed since they had lived there a few years earlier. All the ministries had grown since the Longbottom's first stay there. New believers were in the churches and several churches and chapels had been established in the city. God was blessing the work and the witness of His children. The small seminary where Sam had formerly taught was conducting its first official graduation ceremony. Young men and women were trained to go out into Baptist ministries. God was working.

Climax

As the fighting between the Communists and the South Vietnamese increased, daily life grew more complicated. The exchange rate was fluctuating almost daily. Demonstrations, riots and fighting increased. There were nights spent under the bed with the children. In early 1975, missionary families with children were encouraged to leave the country. The decision was made for Marian, Tommy, and Terry to go to Taiwan, where Lynda and Dan were attending Morrison

Academy. The men would stay and work alongside the Vietnamese Christians as long as possible.

So on April 4th, 1975, Marian left her adopted home of almost 14 years with two of her children and several small suitcases, along with three other missionary wives and their small children.

Sam and the other missionary men watched as the situation worsened. Most of Vietnam was under Communist control, and it seemed that Saigon would fall any day. Fear, panic, and chaos were rampant among the people as the country was collapsing. "What will happen to me?" was the question on many peoples' minds. Some tried to leave the country; parents crowded their children, even infants, into planes so they could escape. However, there weren't enough planes and boats for everyone. Most people had to stay in the country. Sam and other missionaries were involved in helping refugees. They tried to assist Vietnamese Christians first. For example, a large boat was rented to be sent to Danang to try to rescue about 500 believers camped at the Hope Baptist Church. It never reached there, as the government took it over and sent it to Nhatrang. They carried rice and other food supplies to churches. That helped, but it wasn't enough, and they often walked away in tears for being able to do so little for a people they loved so much.

In spite of the terror and panic many people felt during the closing days of the war, God was working through those circumstances to bring people closer to Himself. Sam and other missionaries baptized many, many people. One day they were baptizing a group of over 55 believers in a river outside the coastal town of Quang Ngai. They heard gunshots coming from across the river. The war was very close!

Meanwhile, the terror in the city heightened, and Communist victory seemed just days away. The missionary men knew they had to leave. They could no longer help the believers. Sam left on April 10th, 1975. He met a man at the airport who said he had witnessed an execution in Da Lat. When the Communists took over the city, the invading soldiers rounded up about two hundred Vietnamese people of all ages and backgrounds, and shot them in the city square, right in front of the Binh Theater where Christians had conducted worship services a few years before.

Sam arrived in Hong Kong and then rejoined his family in Taiwan one week later. The area director for Southeast Asia, Dr. Keith Parks, was in Taiwan. He was there to encourage and advise the missionaries. Sam was asked to go to the Philippines to work with Vietnamese refugees. He later worked in Guam. Most of the time, he served as interpreter for doctors at a hospital in the refugee camp. Sam's and other missionaries' faith was strengthened as they met some of the Vietnamese Christians whom they had won to Christ and discipled.

In May 1975, Sam returned to Taiwan to attend Lynda's high school graduation. A few days later, the Longbottom family flew back to Texas for their furlough and to decide where the Lord wanted them to go.

The Next Step

Marian and Sam were saddened to leave South Vietnam and their friends there. They also knew God had a plan for Vietnam as well as a new plan, a new place, a new people for the Longbottoms. "I tell you, open your eyes and look at the fields. They are ripe for harvest," said Jesus to his disciples. In 1976, Sam and Marian asked for a transfer to Taiwan where they would serve for the next 13 years.

The first two years, Marian and Sam lived in Taichung, where they studied Mandarin. Dan and Tommy continued their studies at Morrison Academy. Terry began kindergarten at Morrison. Sam and Marian worked in the Taichung churches, visiting, preaching and teaching. Later, the family moved to Kaohsiung, and finally to Taipei. In this beautiful area of the country, Sam worked in the mission office as treasurer and business manager. Marian worked as the missionary counterpart to the Chinese director at Ling Tou Baptist Assembly. They also worked in the churches in the northern area. Sam became Director of Theological Education by Extension at the Taiwan Baptist Seminary, and taught English. Marian was the English language director for the Convention's Baptist Literature Centers and taught English at the Seminary.

They were active in the Taiwan Mission structure, serving on various committees. One missionary said, "Every mission needs a Sam and Marian. They are mature and caring, committed, and faithful servants of our Lord. They are wonderful encouragers and prayer supporters."

In 1989, Sam and Marian returned to the U.S. and retired from active service with the International Mission Board in September 1990. They settled in Waco, TX, but they didn't stop being missionaries! They worked as missionaries-in-residence at Baylor University. Sam worked for seven-and-one-half years as Minister of Missions for Columbus Avenue Baptist Church in Waco, TX. Marian cared for her aging parents and busied herself in women's ministries, children's work, and with Internationals. In 2000, Sam and Marian moved to the countryside of Magnolia, TX, near Houston, to be closer to some of their children and his mother, who was living near his sister's family. When the family gets together, Sam, Marian and their children swap stories of life in other countries. Grandchildren know they are blessed to have such a heritage. They will pass God's stories of love and grace to the next generation and the next one.

In 1998, Marian and Sam returned to Vietnam for the first time since their evacuation. They were part of a Prayer Walk Tour, which included former missionaries to Vietnam. The Longbottoms revisited many of their previous homes, offices, and church buildings. In Saigon, Sam and Marian were able to worship at Grace Baptist Church, which still met in the same building as before and had opportunity to renew their friendship with Pastor Chanh. Along with the other missionaries on the tour, they prayed as they walked through the neighborhoods and street corners, where so much had happened more than two decades ago.

Sam and Marian were blessed by a country named South Vietnam, and they blessed many Vietnamese. Their children's formative years were spent in Vietnam.

Sam and Marian were blessed by a place called Taiwan, and they blessed many Chinese. They and theirs continue to be influenced by what they experienced in Vietnam and Taiwan.

At a Baptist youth retreat in Da Lat in 1969, one young man asked: "What do we live for?" A Vietnamese pastor answered him: "We were born of human parents. We were created by the great God of all creation. We were born to love, serve, and glorify Him." Those of us who know Sam and Marian, who served alongside them, can say this is their story, "To Honor and Glorify their Savior, Lord, and King."

Marian, Sam and Sammy Longbottom

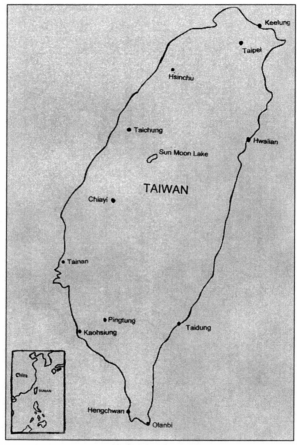

Taiwan, Republic of China
(Major locations where missionaries served.)

LaVergne, TN USA
12 October 2009

160564LV00001B/3/P